In Happy Hollow

COLONEL BANTAM.

IN HAPPY HOLLOW

BY
MAX ADELER
(CHARLES HEBER CLARK)
AUTHOR OF
"OUT OF THE HURLY-BURLY"
"CAPTAIN BLUITT," ETC. ETC.

Illustrated by
CLARE VICTOR DWIGGINS
and HERMAN ROUNTREE

HENRY T. COATES & CO.
PHILADELPHIA   1908

IN HAPPY HOLLOW

By
MAX ADELER
(CHARLES HEBER CLARK)
AUTHOR OF
"OUT OF THE HURLY-BURLY"
"CAPTAIN BLUITT," ETC, ETC.

Illustrated by
CLARE VICTOR DWIGGINS
and HERMAN ROUNTREE

HENRY T. COATES & CO.
PHILADELPHIA   1903

CONTENTS.

3

4 CONTENTS.

CHAPTER XI.

ILLUSTRATIONS.

ILLUSTRATIONS.

IN HAPPY HOLLOW.

never visited the town of Happy Hollow until I went there on a September day to become a teacher in Dr. Bulfinch's Classical and Mathematical Academy.

I did not suspect, as I came into Happy Hollow in a mid-day train, that I should speedily become a figure in a rather queer romance.

The town itself indeed had no strong suggestion of romance. For although the everlasting hills stand round about it upon every side, Happy Hollow itself was forlorn with unpaved streets and shabby houses. But the noble hills, forest-covered, broken here and there by gaps which make them seem undulating and billowy, and with their dusky verdure filling the hori-

9

zon, to north, to south, to east, to west, do make the view from the village beautiful; and then, right through the heart of Happy Hollow, sent down from the hills, runs between grassy banks, under arching trees and beneath three pretty bridges, a swift stream coursing toward the wide, shallow river three miles below.

Along the stream for a little way within the town-borders lay a small park, with trees and grass and shrubs, and here and there a rustic seat for the uses of the wayfaring man and the loiterer.

There were large possibilities of beauty in Happy Hollow, and as I write they have been employed, and the dear old town is beautiful.

On that day in the early autumn when I left the railroad train at the station half a mile or more away from the town I was carried into Happy Hollow in an ancient and battered omnibus owned by the Metropolitan Hotel.

When, from the window of the omnibus, I saw the Metropolitan Hotel, built of wood, with its two stories topped by a French roof and its portico frilled by odd and ugly wooden scroll-work, it did not seem alluring as a permanent resting-place, and when I went into the office to put my name upon the register as an applicant for dinner, the lingering suggestions in the atmosphere of beverages long since consumed by convivial persons impelled me to thankfulness that I had arranged to make my home with Mrs. Joseph Bantam.

One other visitor to Happy Hollow partook with me of the dinner prepared that day in the kitchen of the Metropolitan Hotel, and as both of us were young and courageous we did not flinch until we came to coffee. Then my companion, who had dared that dinner-table before, warned me to stop unless I cared to carry away a medicinal flavor upon my palate.

My companion was Thomas Driggs, who had been in my class at college. Tom was the last man I should have expected to encounter in that little town, away off among the hills; but then it is one of the queer things about this queer life of ours that the man who is most unlikely to appear usually does appear.

Tom Driggs was not a very bright scholar, and I have never been able to understand how he contrived to pass his examinations at college. But he did pass them, and then, wisely refusing to respond to his mother's earnest plea that he should enter the ministry, he found employment as travelling salesman for a shoe-house.

I like Tom Driggs, and I should be sorry to say anything unkind of him, but I have always believed that if he had actually thrust himself into the pulpit, persons who have intellectual requirements with respect to religion would have had an impulse to fall away from the true faith.

After dinner Tom and I sat in the chairs upon the front porch of the Metropolitan Hotel, and Tom, with one foot lifted to the level of his chin and planted firmly against a wooden pillar that upheld the roof, entertained himself by presenting explanatory observations about shoes. He could not have been more comprehensive and eloquent if I had been a possible customer. I tried to appear to be interested in his talk, but this was not an easy thing to do, for, while I permit myself to have enthusiasms, I think I could never succeed in kindling a lively flame over such a subject.

While Tom Driggs talked, I looked at and read a glaring poster upon a bill-board fixed to a tree by the curbstone, ten or fifteen feet away from us. It contained this announcement:

GRAND OPERA HOUSE.

One Night Only.

A. J. PELICAN'S STUPENDOUS STAR COMBINATION.

In the Highly Emotional Dramatization of

UNCLE TOM'S CABIN.

Enormous Aggregation of Talent. Affecting, Thrilling, Exciting. Phenomenal Cast, including ·

Miss Julie Mortimer as *Eliza, the Slave-Mother.*
Miss Ruby Bonner as *Little Eva*

Marvellous Scenic Effects—Realistic Stage-Settings.

Two Real Bloodhounds!

Wonderful Escape of the Slave-Mother on the Ice!

Ran for four hundred nights, and not a dry eye in the House.

Storms of Applause.

Startling Reminiscences of the Days before the Civil War.

When Tom Driggs had said the last word about shoes that he could just then think of, he pointed to the poster and said to me:

"Jack, that's a good thing; you ought to see it."

I have always thought it a misfortune that my last name is Sprat. No matter if my first name is Henry, it was inevitable that the boys at school and college should call me Jack, that absurd nursery rhyme about the Sprats being known wherever English is spoken. However, I found long ago that protest avails nothing, so I answered:

"I don't care for performances of that kind."

"I know," said Driggs, "money wouldn't bribe me to go to see ordinary Tommers; but this is different. I saw the performance down at Aristotle last spring. The company is poor, but Julie and Ruby are wonderful. You will miss it if you don't see them. How old Pelican ever found such treasures I can't imagine. They have genius. I know Ruby, personally."

"'Not a dry eye in the house,'" I said, repeating the announcement on the poster.

"Yes, sir! that's a fact!" said Driggs, with eagerness, and withdrawing his foot from its elevated position that he might turn and look at me. "I cried myself when I saw Julie in the first act. If you go to see her, you will find that it is not as funny as it sounds."

"Perhaps I will."

"I would go if I didn't have to meet a man in Purgatory Springs to-morrow."

While Tom Driggs was speaking almost as warmly of Julie Mortimer as he had spoken of shoes, a man passed the hotel porch and bowed to us.

He was about sixty years old, five feet ten inches high, and with gray hair and gray moustache and imperial. He wore a military hat with a cord about it; he walked with a slight limp, and he carried a silver-headed cane as if it were a sword. He gave to us, indeed, a military salute as he went by us. His appearance and bearing plainly indicated that he was a veteran of the Civil War. His gait encouraged the belief that he still carried a bullet in his leg.

"That's Colonel Bantam, Mayor of the town," said Driggs. "The hotel-keeper told me so. He's related somehow or other to Ruby Bonner. Fine-looking man, isn't he?"

"I am going to board with him," I said. "I must hunt him up and introduce myself to him after a while."

Colonel Bantam passes by.

Tom Driggs then began to betray a tendency to return to the discussion of shoes, so I bade him good-bye and left him sitting there, waiting for the omnibus to take him to the train.

I went into the barber-shop in the hotel to be shaved before I presented myself to Colonel and Mrs. Bantam. It was the shop of Felix Acorn and he was there alone when I entered. He was a small, mournful-looking man, with dark eyes and brown complexion, and with black curly hair glistening with

pomatum. There was about Felix Acorn the suggestion of a vulgar Hamlet and an atmosphere of gloom
that impelled me to think of the graveyard scene in
the play.

Felix Acorn greeted me sadly, as a man might do
who had had a recent great bereavement, and he spoke
not a word while he prepared the towel and the cup.

The silence becoming at last too depressing, I asked
him, as he stirred the brush in the lather:

"Do you know where Colonel Bantam lives?"

"I know where Joe Bantam lives. Some people
calls him Colonel; but he ain't no colonel."

"He is an old soldier, I should think, from his
appearance; and he walks as if he had been wounded."

"Walks! Yes!" responded Felix Acorn scornfully,
but with gloom in the very tones of his voice "And
when there was fightin' he walked and walked, a good
deal faster, too; walked right towards home or anywheres out of danger."

"Wasn't he in the war?"

"He was a clerk in the Quartermaster's department, and he always had a call to go and buy mules
up in Pike County when things was hot and the balls
a flyin'! You can't impose on me. I know it, for I
seen the record."

"These people around yer," continued Felix Acorn,
as he began seriously to apply himself to the duties of
his profession and drew the razor to and fro upon the
strap, "say I'm skeptical, and so I am I used to be
imposed on when I was a boy, but I got to know
about things, and the more I knowed the less I believed. There's mighty few things that people thinks
is so that really is so."

Felix Acorn was by no means exhilarating, but he had succeeded in exciting in my mind some small interest and curiosity.

"What are some of the things that you refer to?" I asked.

"They say we descended from monkeys and shed our tails because they wa'n't of no use. Now I put it to you: would you do that if you had one? No Acorn never was such a fool. A tail that 'd grip things! Why, it 'd be as good as a third hand. Right now I could fan you while I shave you. No, sir! The lies that people tells is awful! Do you believe ostriches hides their heads in the sand when you skeer 'em? Well, I don't! I've watched 'em by the hour and skeered 'em too, and they never put their heads nowheres. It's all humbug; and the same way with snakes in Ireland. I was imposed on when I was a boy with the idea that there wa'n't no snakes in Ireland, but I know an Irishman who's seen 'em and killed 'em there."

"Maybe he didn't tell the truth."

"I'd trust him for anything. It's the books and newspapers you can't trust. There's General Washington; he never cut no cherry-tree with no hatchet; and Benjamin Franklin never flew no kite; and there's no Uncle Sam like you see the picture of in the papers; 'All men are liars,' David said, and he was right, if he really did say it, for I'm not sure he did or that there ever was a David; for if there was a David why didn't he have a last name? That's mighty suspicious, just by itself."

"Are you sure about anything?" I asked.

"Sure enough about some things," he answered with

a tone indicating that he might at any moment fall into a fit of weeping. "Sure there is no Equator like the geographies says there is, and no Tropic of Cancer. Them lines round the world is all lies. No man ever seen 'em or will see 'em. And the North Pole! Do you know the North Pole ain't anywheres near the North Pole? Do you know that?"

"I've heard so."

"Exactly! there ain't no such place. It's a wonder to me how people that goes to church and pretends to be pious can have the face to try to deceive us that way about the Equator and things."

"But still," I said, as Felix Acorn completed the operation upon which he was engaged, "Bantam is a real man who lives in a real house, and you haven't yet told me where the house is."

Felix Acorn shook the towel, and while he folded it I thought he was searching his mind to find some argument to prove the unsubstantiality of Bantam and the deceptive nature of the Colonel's residence. Failing in this effort he turned to me and said:

"Go straight up this street to the right for two blocks and turn to your left, and it is the third house on the west side, with a granite cornice, only the cornice ain't granite. It's sheet-iron painted and sanded to deceive. You can't miss it."

As he spoke Colonel Bantam passed the shop-door.

"There goes Bantam now," said Felix Acorn "He'll show you the way if you ask him."

I called "Colonel!" and the Colonel stopped while I went out and introduced myself to him.

Colonel Bantam drew himself up, placed his feet together, and brought his uplifted cane in front of his face, saluting as if on dress-parade. Then he grasped my hand, and shaking it vigorously, he said:

"Professor, I give you official welcome to Happy Hollow, and a personal welcome to the hallowed precincts of my home. I will have much pleasure in leading you thither. Take my arm."

I put my hand upon Colonel Bantam's arm and we began to walk up the street. It seemed to me that the Colonel limped in a manner indicating lameness of greater degree than I had thought.

"You must pardon me, Professor," he said, "for going slowly. The recent civil strife has left its mark upon me. I still suffer for my country. I do not mind the pain, but I am bitter sometimes when I see the nation rioting in luxury, while the men whose blood quenched the fires of rebellion find the wolf at the door."

"You were in the army?"

"It is my proudest recollection, sir, that I bared my bosom to the foe, and stood with uplifted head amid the flaming terrors of the battle-line."

"You were in many engagements?"

"Engagements, sir! I never speak of it but to friends, and I refer to it now reluctantly, almost shame-facedly, but my companions-in-arms, against my continued protest, would insist upon calling me Fighting Joe; my first name, you know, is Joseph. I plead with you to refrain from employing the phrase in alluding to me."

"I am glad," I said, "to make my home with a brave veteran."

"Not with me," he answered, touching my arm with his right hand, in which he held his cane. "Mrs.

Bantam is goddess of that shrine of the affections. She insists upon taking a few cultured friends as boarders from yearnings for an enlarged domesticity; incidentally, perhaps, for pin-money. Sir, you know how it is with the lovelier sex; always wanting to spend for knick-knacks and trinkets! I permit her to have her way while I attend to my official duties. I am Mayor of the town. I have been called by my

" I permit Mrs. Bantam to have her way."

fellow-citizens to direct the destinies of Happy Hollow, and I do it. The emoluments of the chief magistracy are inconsiderable, but I am ambitious, and it is much to me, excluded by peaceful conditions from manœuvring battalions upon the field of war, to wield the power of the municipality."

As he spoke, we came near to a very large and fat policeman with a red face and huge double-chin. The policeman assumed a military attitude, and as we passed he saluted the Colonel, who returned the salute handsomely.

"Officer," demanded the Colonel, " have you anything to report ?"

" No, your honor !"

"That," said the Colonel, as we walked onward, " is my police force. Faithful, efficient, under rigid discipline. His name is Elias Guff; a valuable man "

" He is the whole force; just one man ?"

" One, and he is a host in himself with me to direct him. We shall have two next spring when the tax assessments are put up."

"We now," said the Colonel, "approach our home. I will open the door for you and usher you into the drawing-room, but you must consent to overlook it if I do not present you personally to Mrs Bantam. We have had a trifling difference. . You know how it is. There are jars. The sweetest bells are sometimes jangled and out of tune. She is a lovely woman, lovely—but, well, no doubt the discord will dissolve itself in harmony very soon; in fact, the storm will blow over. But Mrs. Bantam has insisted that I shall wear a dress-coat to dinner and shall refrain from taking soup more than once, and I have been recalcitrant. A man who has been used to commanding legions does not readily surrender all authority."

"Here we are! I ring for the servant. Helen, say to your mistress that Professor Sprat is here. Dear boy! farewell for a time. I will wait for you near by."

With these words, Colonel Bantam walked around the corner of the house to the garden and sought a bench in the shade of a tree. His lameness seemed really less grievous than it had been when I first met him.

Chapter II. Mrs. Bantam

Mrs. Bantam was quite a plump and pretty gray-haired woman, and when she came into the room with her hand extended in greeting, her manner seemed to me to resemble her husband's.

"How charming to have you with us, Mr. Sprat, and how delightful your profession of opening the budding mind and refreshing it with the dews of learning! I remember my own dear teachers with undiminished affection, for you must know that in my childhood I lived amid all the refinements of luxury and had the most gifted tutors. In my ancestral home the horn of plenty poured forth its bounteous store. But I willingly make any sacrifice for the Colonel. By the way, where is he? Did he come with you?"

"He had an engagement," I answered, "and excused himself for a moment."

"You will like him," she said warmly. "You will like him with all his faults. My revered father always said to me, 'Edith, in seeking for a prize in the lottery of matrimony prefer Intellect to Dross,' and this judicious counsel

"How charming to have you with us, Mr. Sprat."

controlled my decision when Colonel Bantam urged his suit."

"He impressed me favorably," I said, for I could not be disagreeable to the good woman.

"How beautiful!" exclaimed Mrs. Bantam. "The Colonel always does that. What the Colonel needs is scope—a wider scope, an enlarged horizon. Happy Hollow is a dear little paradise, but the vistas are not extended, and Colonel Bantam's intellect is cramped even in the chief magistracy."

When I had expressed sorrow because of these untoward circumstances, Mrs. Bantam, with whom I had arranged by letter the terms upon which I should dwell in her house, called the servant and I went to my room, to which also my baggage was brought.

It was a comfortable apartment, and I was contented. In a little while I came down stairs, and when Mrs. Bantam had said to me "Dinner at six, Mr. Sprat," I walked out into the garden. Colonel Bantam was expecting me.

"My dear boy," he said, as with both hands he drew me to the seat beneath the wide-spreading horse-chestnut tree, "you thought her a lovely woman?"

"Yes, indeed!"

"I knew it!" he said with a smile. "She is more than lovely, she is grand, a grand woman! But then, Professor," and the Colonel's countenance fell, "there is always a fly in the ointment; always a flaw in the diamond! Frailty, thy name is woman!"

"What is the matter?"

"Sir, forgive me for making the disclosure; I do it only in the sacred confidence of friendship. Her weakness is emotionalism, it really amounts to a weakness; a feminine weakness, but still a weakness. You are young; take an old man's advice. Cultivate reserve of feeling. Hold yourself in. Play the stoic, if I may use the phrase."

"And now, Professor, may I trespass in a small way upon your better nature? The wolf is literally at the door. I have had a recent very severe strain upon my financial resources, and the exigencies of the moment imperatively require five dollars. It is repugnant to every instinct of my nature to ask it, but could you without subjecting yourself to inconvenience give me that sum on account of your future indebtedness to my household?"

As I handed him the money, Colonel Bantam arose and said:

"As soon as I can realize on my assets, the loan shall be repaid with usury. And now, forgive the apparent discourtesy, but my official duties summon me. Make yourself perfectly at home here. Act as if you were in your own house."

The Colonel saluted me with his cane and walked away with a more dreadful limp than I had yet observed. He seemed to have varying degrees of lameness.

I believed it to be my duty now, in the time before Mrs. Bantam's evening meal, to visit Dr. Bulfinch that he might know of my arrival and of my readiness for work whenever he should require my services.

While Colonel Bantam hobbled down the street, happy that the wolf and the door were no longer, as he would have said, in juxtaposition, I turned the corner, crossed the north bridge over Aramink Creek and walked out to the school.

Dr. Bulfinch's Classical and Mathematical Academy stood upon the outer edge of the town, in an enclosure in which were several large and handsome trees, but no other vegetation of any kind. The ground was bare and hard, showing indications that the scholars used it vigorously for their sports. The Academy building was made of pale pink bricks which looked as if they had once been crimson and had faded in the sunlight. The woodwork was much in need of paint and of repair; but the structure was large, well-arranged, and I found afterward fully equal to the needs of a prosperous school.

I met a troop of boys coming from the main doorway as I approached it, and when I asked one of them where I could find Dr. Bulfinch, he pointed me to the Doctor's study upon the second floor, and this boy and a crowd of other boys laughed, as if they believed my introduction to the Doctor might have some humorous aspects.

Ascending the worn and dusty staircase, I went along the corridor until I came near to the door of the Doctor's room. As I paused before it I heard a sound which might have been mistaken by an inexperienced person as indicating that some one in the room was beating the dust from a carpet. I made a better guess, and as I opened the door I saw a tall, angular man, with a pale face, cleanly shaven and with a stern smile upon it, holding a boy with his left hand while he applied a switch to the boy's back with his right hand.

Sitting on a bench by the wall were four other boys with mingled grief and mischievousness written upon their countenances. They smiled grimly as I came in, and I thought I discerned in their eyes gleams of hope that the visitor might divert the Doctor from the purpose, plainly entertained by him, to flog them.

But hope died out when the Doctor, continuing the

exercise in which he was engaged without noticing me, at last released his victim, and turning to me with rather more brightness in his smile, said:

"Good afternoon, sir; will you sit here until I complete my task, or will you wait for me in the corridor?"

The boys upon the bench looked as if life for them had surrendered its last drop of joy. I answered that I would wait for him in the corridor.

As I turned to go away, Dr. Bulfinch raising his rod, to begin again his exercise, said to me:

"*Qui parcit virgae vitiat filium.*"

I went out and walked up and down, looking through the windows and upon the playground, while the sounds of castigation came from the study until four boys at intervals emerged from the chamber of discipline and shot down the stairway as if they had engagements of most pressing nature.

Then the Doctor called me in, and as he grasped my hand he smiled still more brightly and drew his thin lips together and said:

"This is the most painful part of the task of educating the young, Mr. Sprat" (the Doctor really did not look as if he found it painful), "but I adhere to the old theories, as you see. You know the old proverb: 'Spare the rod,' and so forth. I want no spoiled boys in this school. I've used the rod for forty years, and I am sure there are pupils of mine in heaven to-day because I flogged them."

"An odd way, too," I ventured to say, "of preparing the young spirit for celestial bless."

"It seems so," responded the Doctor, good-naturedly, "but severe discipline of the body has always been recognized as an important agency in spiritual growth. I have written a pamphlet upon the subject 'The Right Way to Bring Up Boys,' and in that publication I show that love is the most potent of all the forces in training youth. But love, I remark, from its very nature, involves sacrifice, and sacrifice is but another name for suffering, and flogging and suffering are, as it were, synonymous. From this I deduce the fact that the rod is love's most effective instrument."

I was much interested in the Doctor's exposition of his theories, but there were other matters to talk of. I turned from the subject, and when the conference was ended arrangement had been made that I should begin my work at the school as assistant teacher on the following Monday morning. I reached Happy Hollow on Friday.

When I returned to my lodging-place I walked in without knocking, and was abashed to find Colonel Bantam standing in the parlor, while Mrs. Bantam, with her arms about his neck, reclined her head upon his breast and wept.

"Come in, Professor!" exclaimed the Colonel, as I made a movement to pass on. "Come in! You witness here an affecting drama of conjugal reconciliation I find it impossible upon any provocation to sunder the ties that bind me to the beloved partner of my youth. There has been a compromise. I have consented to abandon the practice of requiring soup more than once, and this amiable woman agrees no longer to insist upon the dress-coat for dinner. You are without experience in matrimony. Let it be impressed upon your memory that the secret of happiness is compromise. Mutual concession is the basis of love, and love means peace.

Once more the Angel of Peace spreads his white wings over this sanctuary of the affections."

Lifting her head, and drying her eyes, Mrs. Bantam turned to me, and with joy written upon her face, said:

"Have you ever loved, Mr. Sprat?"

I was compelled to admit that the experience was unknown to me.

"Ah!" exclaimed Mrs. Bantam, "only those who have loved can know the perfect bliss that comes from such reconciliations as this. I would willingly give my life for my best and bravest. The Colonel has spoken of compromise. Call it that if you will, but no considerations of apparel, however imperious may be the requirements of social usage, shall tear me from the bosom of my beloved."

Having expressed, I fear with some awkwardness, my pleasure that these two hearts beat once again in unison, I turned to go, but Mrs. Bantam stopped me.

"Dinner is waiting," she said. "Give me your arm."

It was a very nice dining-room, looking out over a side porch to the pretty garden, and the meal was much better than that of which I had partaken in company with Tom Driggs at the Metropolitan Hotel

There were two other persons present besides Colonel and Mrs. Bantam, and both were agreeable. When the Colonel had said grace in words of four syllables, and with the manner of a man who prides himself upon his skill in elocution, he introduced me to the other boarders, Mr. Emerson Spiker, editor of the *National Defender* of Happy Hollow, and Miss Elmira Bantam, the Colonel's daughter, who was a member of the Blair County bar.

Miss Bantam was fair to look upon, and she had an

intellectual face; but, while she was pleasant, her manner inclined to reserve, as if she felt that the fluency of her father and her mother needed to be checked by the influence of example.

Mr. Spiker talked much and well, and before dinner was ended he had asked Miss Elmira and me and the Colonel and Mrs. Bantam to go with him that very evening to see the performance of Uncle Tom's Cabin at the Grand Opera House. Believing that he saw in my countenance a purpose to decline this invitation, he whispered to me :

"It is complimentary, you know   I am on the free list for everything."

Under these circumstances I consented to go.

"You must go, Mr. Sprat," said Mrs. Bantam. Our darling niece, Ruby Bonner, is to appear in the piece."

I had some curiosity to see Ruby Bonner.

Chapter III — The Tommers

AFTER dinner Colonel Bantam said he must return to his office to hear the police report for the day, and he asked me if I would have the goodness to escort Mrs. Bantam to the play. He promised to meet us there. Mr. Spiker was compelled to go around to his place of business to read some final proofs and to send his paper to the press, and Miss Bantam had a consultation with a client at her office at seven o'clock. Both the editor and Miss Bantam agreed to be with us before the performance began.

Mrs. Bantam was really an agreeable companion, and, as we walked slowly toward the Grand Opera House, she gave me some interesting information. It seems that Ruby Bonner, the little Eva who was to appear in the play, was the daughter of Mrs. Bantam's brother, Amos Bonner. Amos had been badly treated. Years ago his wife left him, taking the child Ruby with her; and Amos, unable to find mother or child, had gone to Australia disgusted with life. He had never written to any member of his family, but rumors had come around the world that he was successful in some unknown occupation, and so Mrs. Bantam talked with interest and affection of "my brother Amos." "The house in which we live," she added, "was his home, and it still belongs to him."

The matter that most strongly engaged my attention was that Amos Bonner's wife had fled with the brother of Dr. Bulfinch, named Simon Bulfinch, and Simon had left behind him a wife and boy who were then living in Happy Hollow, fondly cared for by Dr. Bulfinch, who, it appeared (and the fact imparted pathos to the situation), had been rejected by the poor woman before she married his rascally brother.

"But why," I asked, "do you permit Ruby to remain upon the stage among so many temptations?"

"Her mother put her there," said Mrs. Bantam, "when the girl was very young, and she played child-parts successfully. Now that she is older Miss Mortimer has half adopted her, and the child is unwilling to come with us because—well, you know that the Colonel has not yet succeeded in bringing to what I may call a triumphant culmination the plans which we both feel sure will yet give us riches beyond the dreams of avarice."

There was no difficulty to comprehend the situation, and the curiosity I had already felt to look at Ruby was considerably increased.

The Grand Opera House was a shabby old barrack, with the auditorium upon the level of the street, and with uncleanliness and discomfort as its most striking features.

When I went in with Mrs. Bantam the doorkeeper informed us that the company had just arrived at the theatre, the train upon which it had come to the town having been somewhat delayed. About a dozen persons were present as we took our seats, but in a few moments the Colonel came and Miss Bantam and Mr. Spiker; and by eight o'clock there may have been seventy-five or a hundred people in the house.

" Paper, most of it," said Mr. Spiker, rising and looking around. " There are not fifty dollars in the place."

Then the orchestra of four pieces came out from the mysterious aperture below the stage, and, after preliminary twanging of strings and trilling of the flute, began to play a negro melody. This ended, another and still another air suggestive of life upon the plantation were produced.

The music brought reminiscences to Colonel Bantam's mind. Turning to me, he said :

" Frightful thing, sir, that institution of slavery ! When President Lincoln asked my advice about issuing the Emancipation Proclamation, I said to him : ' Fling it to the world, Mr. President ! Exterminate the unnatural institution,' and afterward he sent me the first rough draft of the document and asked me to run my eye over it. I suggested several emendations, which you can find in the official copy."

Still the curtain did not rise, and the orchestra played " My Old Kentucky Home " for the fifth time.

When the concluding strain had been reached Colonel Bantam leaned over to the editor and asked:

" Anything from Wall Street, to-day ?"

"Not that I know of. I don't follow such matters closely," responded Mr. Spiker.

"Ah!" exclaimed Colonel Bantam, leaning back again in his seat, "I keep in close touch with the street and my interests there. My last advices indicated a feverish condition of the market."

While the Colonel spoke there were sounds of an altercation behind the curtain.

"A. J. is having trouble, I guess," said the editor.

The orchestra returned to "Way Down Upon the Suwanee River," and played *fortissimo* with a manifest purpose to disguise the fact that A. J. was having trouble. The audience showed as much impatience as if it had been a cash audience and not a paper audience.

At last the curtain rose, revealing the interior of Uncle Tom's cabin, with the black people engaged in a prayer-meeting. They sang the hymn as joyously as if no wave of trouble had ever rolled across A. J.'s peaceful breast.

The first thrill was given to the spectators when Julie Mortimer, as Eliza, dashed into the room with her babe in her arms, and flying to the embrace of George, her husband, declared that death alone should part her from him.

Colonel Bantam wept copiously and ostentatiously. I feared for a time that the vehemence of emotion would compel him to withdraw to the lobby; but his wife, who was fairly blinded by tears, contrived to induce him to restrain himself.

In fact, everybody cried—that is, everybody but Miss Bantam, who manifested no feeling of any kind, unless the slight smile that played upon her lips might

3

be interpreted as indicating scornfulness; and Felix Acorn, who sat in the very front row of the parquet circle, actually appeared to be making an effort to look as if he felt happy.

When the curtain fell there was much applause, and it was deserved, for Miss Mortimer surely had manifested no little dramatic power.

The leader of the orchestra brought out some fresh music and whispered to the first violin; but he appeared to change his mind, for " Our Old Kentucky Home " was heard again.

When, after much waiting, the curtain went up again, the players were all upon the stage ready for their parts, but nobody moved or spoke. Then Uncle Tom came forward, hat in hand, and said to the audience:

" Ladies and gentlemen, Pelican owes us for four weeks' salaries, and we will cut the play off right here unless he pays us at once."

As Uncle Tom retreated, a short and quite stout man, wearing a wig, came out from the wings, plainly in a state of much agitation. It was A. J. Pelican.

When he began to speak he appeared to forget that he did not have his hat with him, for he took off his wig and fanned himself with it. The laughter of the audience directed his attention to the mistake and he replaced the wig on his head, backward. Then, as the laughter continued, in a kind of desperation he removed the wig again and began to fan himself vigorously with it, while he said:

" Ladies and gentlemen and friends: the performance is ended. I am very sorry, but I've had hard luck all through this trip. There's not money enough in the house to-night to pay the rent. I am sorry for these poor people here, sorry for you, and sorry for myself, for I'm a ruined man."

Mr. Pelican explains.

Then A. J. Pelican, with his wig in his hand, walked

off of the stage, followed by Uncle Tom and Eliza and all the company; and the curtain fell.

Mr. Spiker showed more feeling than any other person in the audience. It would be hard to express in language the disgust written upon his face when, turning to me, he said:

"It's a nice mess for me, Mr. Sprat! I've got a criticism of the thing in type, speaking in terms of warm praise of the pathos of the fourth act, and remarking of Eva's apotheosis in the last act that it surpassed in effectiveness anything ever before attempted in Happy Hollow. Pretty hard luck, isn't it?"

"Well you can cancel it, can't you?"

"Cancel it! Why, man, it's on my inside, and my inside went to press at eight o'clock."

I said it was too bad.

"Yes," he answered gloomily, "bad enough, and that's not the worst of it. I printed all these programmes, and Pelican owes me for them and for thirty lines agate-measure for ten days for his ad. I'll never get a cent. The *Defender* 'll go into bankruptcy if this kind of thing continues."

We walked slowly up the aisle toward the door and everybody felt sorry for Pelican. Colonel Bantam said he would head a subscription paper to help him out of his trouble, and I believe he would have done so, in large, bold letters, for a large sum, if pen and paper had been at hand. The Colonel's generous impulses were always out of correspondence with his financial condition.

While we spoke softly and sadly of the collapse of A. J. Pelican's Stupendous Star Combination, Felix Acorn brushed by me, and, looking once more downcast, he said:

" There never was no such nigger as Uncle Tom. The whole thing is an imposition on the public."

Colonel and Mrs. Bantam asked me to go with them to the green room, where they should greet Ruby and take her to their home.

" It is," said the Colonel, as we walked around the lobby toward the stage-door, "not only a sacred obligation, but a high privilege, to provide a refuge from the storm for that shorn lamb."

As we entered the green room we saw Julie Mortimer dressed for the street,

Ruby and Julie.

and sitting upon a sofa by the window, holding the hand of Ruby, who sat beside her. On the floor lay the two blood-hounds with tongues out and panting, while with heads raised they looked from one member of the company to another, as if they wondered why the stage-call for them did not come.

A. J. Pelican stood over in the corner looking very unhappy, while Uncle Tom and Legree and other personages of the drama talked with him.

No sooner did Ruby perceive Mrs. Bantam than she rose and flew into the good woman's arms, and putting her pretty head upon her aunt's bosom, fell to sobbing.

The Colonel held out his arms toward Julie Mortimer, and seemed surprised and grieved that that lovely woman did not fly to his embrace and put her head upon his breast and weep. But Miss Mortimer did not move until A. J. Pelican, pushing through the crowd about him, came forward and greeted the Colonel. Then, when Colonel Bantam had grasped the manager's hand and had whispered words of sympathy, the Colonel said:

"And now, Mr. Pelican, introduce me to the lovely sufferer over there."

Turning to Miss Mortimer, A. J. Pelican said:

"Julie, this is Colonel Bantam, Mayor of the town, and Ruby's uncle."

Miss Mortimer rose and greeted the Colonel graciously, while he, seizing her hand, raised it to his lips and said:

"Madame, deign to receive the homage of one who is always a worshipper at the shrine of beauty!"

Miss Mortimer smiled as the Colonel released her hand, and, raising his body, put himself into the position of "parade-rest."

"You are more than kind," she said.

"No, no! Not kind, hardly just," replied the

Colonel. "It would be completely impossible, Miss Julia, to exaggerate the nobility of your impersonation."

"Not 'Julia,'" interposed A. J. Pelican, laying his hand gently upon the Colonel's arm. "Her name is Julie, pronounced z-z-joolie, with a slight buzzing sound on the J."

"I am your debtor, sir, for the correction," said the Colonel, bowing to him. "I thank you. My mastery of the French methods of pronunciation is by no means so nearly complete as I could wish. But Miss Julie will not care for so trifling a circumstance as indifferent accuracy in the matter of pronouncing her name, when I tell her that her histrionic genius stirred the deepest recesses of my nature."

"Not quite that, I think," said Miss Mortimer, laughing.

"Quite that! Much more than that!" said the Colonel, reaching for his handkerchief and wiping from his eyes the tears that flowed from the impulse supplied by the memory of Julie's performance. "I must speak of the surpassing splendor of your impersonation. You swept the strings of feeling with the fingers of inspiration. Mrs. Siddons in the day of her glory couldn't have surpassed you."

Before Miss Mortimer could reply, Mrs. Bantam, with her arm about Ruby, turned to the Colonel, who embraced the young girl and kissed her, and said:

"No more tears, my child! After the storm, the sunshine. The clouds are dissipated. We take you into the fold. Uncle and aunty clasp you to their loving hearts. Come with us to that haven of peace which bears the hallowed name of home. Come!"

"And Julie, too," said Mrs. Bantam.

"Of course, certainly," said the Colonel, turning quickly toward Miss Mortimer, and extending his arms again, as if he hoped she might have an affectionate and better second thought, and conclude to pillow her head upon his bosom   "Julie understands, of course, that our home is hers."

Miss Mortimer began to explain that she thought it better to remain at the hotel.

"No!" exclaimed the Colonel, vehemently. "Never! Never! I will never consent to it. What! the adopted mother of this darling child doomed to the loneliness of a house of public entertainment! My whole nature revolts at the thought."

"We could not bear it," said Mrs. Bantam, warmly.

"I welcome you," said the Colonel, "to the shelter of my humble roof-tree. My house is yours; take it, empty it! The wolf may howl at the door, but no child of genius shall fall a victim to his ravening fury while the hand of Joseph Bantam is on the knob! Come!"

So, then, the Colonel placed Miss Mortimer's arm in his, while Mrs. Bantam and I walked with Ruby, to whom Mrs. Bantam introduced me.

We bade good-bye to A. J. Pelican and to the actors, and going through the stage-door to the street, walked slowly toward the Colonel's house.

Ruby Bonner seemed much pleased to be with her aunt, and as we went homeward she talked freely of all the misadventures of A. J. Pelican's Stupendous Star Combination, and told us how the season had been a failure. Then she said:

"Poor Mr. Pelican! It has been very hard for all

the members of the company, but nobody blames him."

When we reached the house the Colonel released himself from Miss Mortimer's arm, and dashing ahead of the party, opened the front door. Drawing himself up like a sentry on duty, he saluted each of us with a wave of his cane as we passed through the portal to the hall. Then, closing the door, he followed the company into the parlor, where, once more standing stiffly erect and making a gesture of welcome, he said:

"The hearthstone of valor, if I may be permitted to employ the expression, is honored by the foot-steps of genius! Julie! Ruby! Your wanderings are over! It is the proud privilege of Joseph Bantam to say to you: Weary pilgrims, rest."

While Mrs. Bantam led Ruby and Miss Mortimer upstairs the Colonel and I sat by the fireside awaiting their return. It was not yet late, and the Colonel was glowing with the happiness that always follows the performance of an act of benevolence.

I sat and looked at the sword which Mrs. Bantam had hung above the mantel and draped with the American flag, to which was pinned a placard bearing the inscription "The Sword of Gettysburg," and the Colonel talked of Julie Mortimer.

"Did you ever see her equal, Professor? Her intellect shines like a star. We shall simply bask in the radiance of her marvellous genius, shall we not? And Ruby, dear babe! she will fill this humble dwelling with reminiscences of the little one who was snatched away from us by the grim reaper."

Then the Colonel drew out his handkerchief and

touched his eyes with it. I arose to look more closely at the sword.

"You are attracted by that implement of war?" said the Colonel. "Inspect it closely. It is worthy of your consideration. With that very sword I held back Pickett's charge at Gettysburg. It is stained with

Bantam at Gettysburg.

blood and consecrated by hallowed memories. I do not like to speak of it excepting to those I love, but General Grant said he would rather be the owner of Colonel Bantam's sword than be President of the United States."

"You knew Grant?" I asked.

"Knew him! The word 'knew' is inadequate. You recall David and Jonathan? Our souls blended. But the fact is;—no matter;— I had thought to say;— however, perhaps I need not hesitate to speak it in the confidence of my own home. I had an impulse to remark that I consider Grant's fame much beyond his real merit."

"What is your theory about it?"

"Why, just this: I told President Lincoln early in the war that if I could have a perfectly free hand I would suppress the rebellion in eight weeks. Grant took years to do it.

" You had a plan?"

" A perfectly simple one, sir. I should have stretched the armies in a line from the Potomac to the Ohio, and simply driven the entire Confederate force step by step into the Gulf of Mexico. Mr. Lincoln was with me, but he was overruled by his cabinet. Oceans of blood were shed uselessly because the President was not permitted to accept my system.

At this juncture Mrs. Bantam and Julie and Ruby entered the parlor, and Mr. Spiker, coming into the house and placing his hat upon the rack in the hallway, entered the room with them. He looked downcast, but he expressed pity for Pelican, whom he had arranged to meet at his office in the morning. Just as he had finished speaking, Elmira Bantam joined us, and greeted the newcomers affectionately

The Bantams talked with Julie and Ruby about the catastrophe that had befallen the company of players, and then about the future of the woman and the girl who had been compelled by A. J. Pelican's failure to abandon the means by which they had been used to earn money. Miss Mortimer had no regrets for herself.

" I am tired of it," she said. ".Tired of strolling about and of associating with rough people and of facing audiences. I should have given it up long ago but for Ruby, and I am not sorry she has been compelled to quit the stage. It is not a good business for her, but she seemed to have no other way of maintaining herself."

" We shall care for her now," said Mrs. Bantam.

" She may repose securely," added the Colonel, " upon the strong arm of Uncle Bantam."

"I should go to school, uncle," said Ruby.

"And you shall," replied the Colonel, extending his hand to pat her golden hair. "You shall drink deep of the springs of learning, and no doubt our friend the Professor will help to press rich draughts of knowledge to those lovely lips. Won't you, Professor?"

"I will do what I can," I said, not displeased to think that I might have so charming a pupil.

And so it was arranged that Ruby Bonner should stay with us and should try to complete her education, while Julie also should remain and endeavor to maintain herself by literary work.

"I have written much, and nearly always with success," said Miss Mortimer. "Really, I have made and saved money by writing, and I am sure I shall find profitable employment."

"What, may I ask," inquired the Colonel, turning to her and bowing, "is the special department of literature in which you have achieved these triumphs?"

"I write stories," said Miss Mortimer, modestly, "usually short stories. I find it rather easy work to write them, and I get good prices for them. I have three or four in my satchel now."

"Here?" demanded Colonel Bantam, leaping to his feet and manifesting some excitement. "With you? In this house?"

"Yes."

"Grand!" exclaimed the Colonel. "We must hear one of them. May I beg, as a personal favor to one whom you have already thrilled with the manifestation of your genius, that you will this very night read one of your stories to this assembled company?"

Miss Mortimer was diffident and reluctant, but she

could not be ungracious when Mrs. Bantam and
Ruby, and Mr. Spiker and I, and even Elmira, warmly
seconded the Colonel's appeal.   She went to her room
and returned with the
manuscript.

It was a pretty story,
and she read it with
singular grace, and
when she reached the
scene where the de-
serted mo-
ther held her
dying child
in her arms
and mourned
over it, all
of us wept.

Mrs. Ban-
tam put both elbows
upon the centre-table
and bedewed with her
tears the great clasped
family Bible, while her
back hair began to
come down. It was
really odd, and I do not
at all under-
stand it, but
Mrs. Ban-
tam's hair
always gave
way whenever she cried.

Ruby's eyes glistened, though she dried her tears

again and again. Spiker pretended to be asleep, but the drops oozed from his closed lids, while I did not try to hide my feelings. The Colonel, as usual, was most deeply moved. His sobs were actually convulsive ; the movements of his frame, as he yielded to the storm of passion, shook the chandelier. Mrs. Bantam was at last compelled to turn away from the centretable and to try to calm him by putting her arm about him and softly saying, " Joseph !"

Elmira alone seemed unmoved. She sat by the card-table over by the fireplace and glared at Mr. Spiker. I really think she was trying to maintain strong restraint upon her feelings, and while she glared and looked hard and stern, she drummed upon the table with the fingers of her right hand.

When the tale was ended, and there was a movement all around the little circle to return the handkerchiefs to the pockets, Elmira said:

" Women need to free themselves from these tearpractices Let the men do the crying, if there must be crying. Dry up the tear-ducts, I say !"

" Elmira," said the Colonel sternly, removing the traces of tears from his temple with his forefinger, " have you no heart ? Didn't you see the men crying too ? These are not tears of weakness. They are the tribute of sensibility to the eloquence of genius. Julie has unsurpassed effectiveness in unsealing the fountains of emotion. I thank you my child," he said, turning to Julie. " Hard is the heart that can remain untouched when you strike it with the wand of your pathetic eloquence."

But Elmira Bantam was still grim and resolute.

" I find no fault," she said, " with the literary art or

the elocution; both are admirable. They do credit to American womanhood. But we all need to look at life coldly. Eliminate emotion. Life is frigid fact, and woman particularly should learn that lesson. Emotion may be employed with juries. Juries are men. Make them cry if you can, and you want a verdict not warranted by the evidence; but women should cry only when there is something to cry for, and not much even then."

" I am shocked to hear such unwomanly sentiments," said the Colonel, " from the lips of my own offspring "

" And then," continued Elmira, without noticing her father's observation, " while there is much grace and no little ingenuity in the construction of the tale to which we have listened, you will find it, when you look into it with the cold light of reason, defective in important particulars."

" How *can* you say so, Elmira," said Mrs. Bantam sorrowfully.

" It is most distressing," added the Colonel.

" For example," continued Elmira, " you say plainly that the wife had no power to compel the husband to return home. Now Judge Stokes, in a Maryland court, has decided, and in my opinion justly, that in such a case the wife may seize the wretch by the collar and drag him home, if moral suasion will not suffice."

" Elmira," said the Colonel warmly, " it is little short of outrageous to attempt to apply these stupid legal principles to a tender little drama of sentiment "

" The character to whom you have given the name of Ezra is plunged into a dungeon upon clearly fabricated evidence and chained there. Think of it! Where did you say was the scene of the tale?"

"In a town in Pennsylvania," said Miss Mortimer.

"Exactly," rejoined Elmira. "In the first place, no magistrate who wished to avoid impeachment would commit a man upon such evidence; and if the man were committed he would not be chained, and I would have him out upon a writ of *habeas corpus* in about fifteen minutes, instead of shedding useless tears over him."

"There is force," said Mr. Spiker, "in Miss Bantam's view."

"Do not, sir, if you please," said the Colonel sternly, "aid and abet her in this repulsive vivisection of a creation of the imagination."

"It is just horrid in you, Elmira," said Mrs. Bantam.

"I need hardly speak of your reference to the removal of the living child from the custody of the mother while she weeps over the child that dies. The Supreme Court long ago, in a dozen cases, decided that the mother's right of possession under the conditions referred to is absolutely indisputable. Show me a case of that kind, and I'll give the child to the mother, and have the father locked up if he doesn't behave himself."

Colonel Bantam rose and left the room, unable to listen any longer with patience.

"You understand, Miss Mortimer," said Elmira, rising and putting her hand upon Julie's shoulder, "that I admire your work very much, even if I criticise it. We women need to stand by each other and I want to stand by you in your brave fight against the world that refuses to give us fair play."

Julie rose and kissed her, and Elmira looked as if she wanted to urge the view that women should release themselves also from kissing practices, but she did not. She pressed Julie's hand and smiled, and after some desultory conversation we went to our rooms.

On the stairs Spiker invited me to come to his office in the morning, the last week-day morning I should have before my duties began at Dr. Bulfinch's school.

4

Chapter IV.
A. J. Pelican Bottles An Account
The Office

of the *National Defender* was in a frame building two
stories high and next door to the post-office on the
main street. Ascending a narrow staircase, without
balusters, which ran between whitewashed walls
covered with the grime of printers' ink, and laced over
by the lead-pencil scribbling of idle travellers up and
down the stairs, I reached a landing with a door at
the right. Pushing open the unpainted door, also
darkened by ink, and shut by a weight affixed to a
rope running over a pulley, I came into the room where
the compositors worked. Threading my way among
the cases, I came to the editor's room in the front of
the building.

Mr. Spiker sat in an armless chair at a desk littered
with papers and dotted with ink-stains. He had his

pen in his mouth as I entered the room, and was engaged in clipping from a newspaper some material for his next day's edition.

The editor was a small man with a small mouth shaded by a scanty moustache; with sharp gray eyes, lean jaws, a pointed chin, and a head of good shape with reddish hair, just now in much disorder. He was about thirty-five years old. I judged from his appearance and the appearance of his establishment that the *National Defender* was not in large measure a prosperous journal.

Mr. Spiker put his pen upon his desk and laid down his scissors as I came in, and, after greeting me warmly, he pushed the paste-pot over by a pile of exchanges, placed his feet upon a corner of the desk, and asked me to sit down and be comfortable. As I gazed about me, Mr. Spiker said:

"Not much of a place to look at, is it? But there is power in here that is felt all over the country. You wouldn't give much for that desk, would you?" (and the editor pounded it with his fist) "and yet on that desk, mean as it is, public opinion is formed. That is my business: to manufacture public opinion; political scoundrels tremble when that pen runs backward and forward over that old desk."

"No doubt," I answered, "and it must be a fine thing to sit here and feel that the written word has such tremendous force."

"Fine enough in one way, from the editorial side; but from the business side most exasperating. It is too bad that a man cannot be permitted to wield the pen that moves the world without being harassed and bothered by the basest and most sordid money troubles! My mind and hand ought to be free, but they are shackled—yes, that's the word, shackled—by these petty and ridiculous dollar considerations."

" You have to manage the commercial end of the thing, do you ?"

" Yes, of course, I own the whole paper."

" But it pays ?"

" In a way it pays. It doesn't pay in the right way, though."

" I don't understand you."

" Why, I'll tell you. There is advertising enough in the *Defender*, but the trouble is most of it is paid for in trade."

" How do you mean ?"

" Nearly everybody wants me to take pay for advertising in goods instead of in cash. It's the worst system! This suit I have on cost me fifteen hundred lines on my third page. My shoes stand for a reading notice under the Dead and Married ads. That hat represents thirty-four lines of nonpareil type e. o. d. t. f. (every other day till forbid, you know), and the man owes me sixteen more hats, and is likely to owe me sixty. I haven't got a thing on me that isn't running in the *Defender* either in the shape of an agate reading notice or a display ad. Why, hang it, man, even Felix Acorn shaves me for one inch four times a month in the department of Home and Neighborhood. I'm sick of the system."

" Yet you get what you want for your comfort ?"

" I get things I want and some things I don't want. I don't complain so much about hats and shoes and clothing, but what would you do if you had dozens of washboards and coal-scuttles and slate mantel-pieces."

"I hardly know."

"Very well! I have 'em down in the back cellar behind the press-room, and three sets of harness, although I can't afford a horse. And chemical fire-extinguishers: I have eight of them in the cellar. It's not the right way to run a business, Mr. Sprat, but I can't help it. The advertisers won't advertise if they have to pay cash. It worries me a good deal sometimes to know how to make the thing work out even. Do you want any tombstones or fire-proof safes?"

"I think not; not just now at any rate."

"Well, if you happen to meet a man who does, won't you let me know? That's a good fellow. I have a running account with Martin, the marble-yard man, and with a safe concern in the city, and I can't sell a safe or a headstone. I should judge that Martin must owe me six or seven good-sized monuments, and it simply makes me ill when I think of the safes that are due to me. I wish you were married and going to keep house. I could fit you right out with tinware and groceries, and at reduced rates, too."

"I'm sorry I'm not. But you must get some money?"

"Oh, yes, some of course; I get some. But half

the time the cash ads. are not paid for. There's that theatrical concern of Pelican's, I thought there was money in that, for sure, but you see how it has turned out, besides making the *Defender* ridiculous by breaking down after the notice was printed. I do seem to have the worst luck."

Just at that moment A. J. Pelican came into the room, after rapping timidly upon the door. Mr. Spiker greeted him politely and asked him to take a chair. Pelican looked sad and uncomfortable as he sat there, with his face to the window, twirling his hat in his hand and trying to frame his first sentence.

The editor was not unkindly.

"Pelican, old man," he said, "you have my sympathy and I ought to have yours; but I believe you are a square man, and as I know what bad luck is, I'm not going to make your bad luck any harder by scolding you."

"Thank you," said Mr. Pelican, manifestly much relieved.

"At the same time, A. J.," continued Spiker, "if you could really manage to scrape together a few dollars, so that I could have something on account, I would—"

"Can't do it," said Pelican, making with his hand a gesture of despair. "I had to pawn my watch to get my railroad fare."

"Oh, well," said the editor, "let that pass. You are going away at once?"

"This afternoon."

"You wouldn't care to do a little work to earn something for a few days?"

"What kind of work?"

"You might call it canvassing."

" For what ?"

" I was just saying to Sprat, here, that I have a lot of stuff on hand, taken in trade—safes, tombstones, harness, and washboards—and I thought maybe you might pick up a dollar here and there for yourself and me by endeavoring to dispose of—" •

" Impossible," said A. J. Pelican, " I must hurry back to town to-day. I have bigger things in my mind than peddling washboards. The fact is, I came around to make you a proposition for settlement of your claim against me."

" What kind of a proposition ?" asked the editor, with a look of suspicion in his eyes.

" Are you fond of dogs ?" inquired Mr. Pelican.

" Not so very fond of them."

" The thought occurred to me," said the manager, " that maybe you'd be willing to take the two bloodhounds for your bill and call the thing square."

Mr. Spiker removed his feet from his desk and laughed. It was not a laugh of joyousness, but rather such a laugh as might come from a man in a semi-hysterical condition. The editor rose from his chair, thrust his hands deep into his trowser-pockets, and walked to the window, where he looked into the street. Wheeling about suddenly, he said:

" Bloodhounds, hey ! And that's what it has come to ! Bloodhounds ! Well, I never expected that. Imagine, Sprat, what the effect would be if the report should get abroad that the advertising in the *Defender* is paid for with bloodhounds ! A. J., old man, do you think I can pay my compositors in bloodhounds ?"

" One of them might want a good dog," said Pelican, modestly.

"Can I buy ink and type and machinery with bloodhounds, do you think, Pelican? Will the paper-mill take bloodhounds and give me a receipt in full? A. J., you are carrying the thing too far. I have hesi-

"Bloodhounds, hey !"

tated about taking gravestones and mantel-pieces, but bloodhounds!" and Mr. Spiker laughed again in a strange, unnatural manner.

"Your bill," said Pelican, "is only $37.48, and a single one of those dogs is worth at least $75.00. I refused $160.00 for the two not four weeks ago. They are the most affectionate dogs you ever saw."

"It's a bad precedent, A. J.," answered Spiker. "I take bloodhounds from you; the next thing you know a menagerie will come to Happy Hollow and fail, and the time won't be long before I'll have a whole zoological garden on my hands. Pelican, I want to oblige you, but I can't do it."

"You could take them right up home to the Colonel's," said A. J. Pelican, in a soothing voice, "and they love Julie and Ruby, and would make splendid watch-dogs. I'll give you a pointer (not another dog, but a business idea), Mr. Spiker, if you will close the bargain with me."

"What is it?"

"You know Julie?"

"Yes."

"Well, sir, she's a very remarkable woman. I never saw her equal for drawing tears. Her forte is emotion. I've often stood in the flies when she was on the stage and said 'Now the sobs are due,' and, sure enough, the whole house was weeping. Drew tears every time! Women used to come to the show just to see her so's they could have a good cry. Men, too, and particularly editors. I've seen a whole row of critics in the front seats with their eyes streaming. I'll let you into a secret. Do you know that lovely woman has had proposals for marriage from no less than eight editors, with a combined circulation of over twenty-one thousand?"

"Refused them, did she?"

"Refused them! Refused them all. But, I was going to say, it will surprise you to learn that she writes as well as she acts. She has written stories that no right kind of man can read without crying."

"I heard one of them last night," said Mr. Spiker.

"You did? Well, then, you know. Now," continued A. J. Pelican persuasively, "you engage her to write for your paper and she'll double your circulation in three months,"

"Not a bad idea, A. J.," said Mr. Spiker, resuming

his seat and gently tapping his desk with the point of his scissors. " Not bad. I'll think it over."

" And the more you think the better you'll like it."

" Do you s'pose she'd be willing to take part of her pay in bonnets and cotton hosiery ?" asked Mr. Spiker, thoughtfully.

" I don't know, I'm sure. You might ask her."

" I know she wouldn't care for fire-extinguishers, of course."

" Now," asked A. J. Pelican, " will you take the bloodhounds and give me a receipt in full?"

Mr. Spiker accepted the offer, and when A. J. Pelican had gone away to arrange to deliver the dogs into Colonel Bantam's back yard, I rose to bid the editor good-bye.

" Sprat," he said, as he shook my hand, " that was a good suggestion of Pelican's, but it was better than he thought. Do you know what I'll do with Julie's stories ?"

" What ?"

" Put 'em in the *Defender*, of course, but I'll also make them into plate-matter and sell 'em to a syndicate of other papers ; sell 'em for cash too !"

On the evening of the day of my visit to the editor, I sat in Mrs. Bantam's parlor with Julie and Ruby and our good hostess, while Julie entertained us with stories of her experiences upon the stage. She was a woman of brilliant beauty. I never saw eyes so black and so handsome, and her thick and splendid black hair surmounted a face that was not less lovely because her skin was that of a true brunette. She was a good talker, and despite her tear-compelling power, she was more fond of a bit of fun than any woman I ever met.

As she sat by Ruby, and sometimes held the girl's hand, stroking it affectionately, the contrast between the two was remarkable. For Ruby had true golden hair and a fair white skin, with the bluest of blue eyes, which were filled with tenderness as she turned them upon the woman whom she loved so much.

As we talked together, and as I looked at Ruby with admiration which I might have known was perilous, we were startled to hear a yell of terror at the back of the house. In a moment a door was violently slammed, and then another. There was a sound of rushing feet, and Colonel Bantam fairly flew from the dining-room, through the hallway to the parlor. His face was white and drawn with fear. As he came into the room he fell upon the sofa, and it seemed to me that he swooned for a moment.

We sprang up in alarm and hastened to him, Mrs. Bantam falling upon her knees by his side and taking his hand.

" What is it, dear ?" she asked in great alarm. What is the matter?"

For a moment there was no response. Then the color slowly came upon the Colonel's cheeks, and half raising himself upon one elbow, while his breath came short and quick, he gasped :

" The wo—wo—the wol—wolf—the wolf."

" The wolf!" we exclaimed. "What wolf? What do you mean?"

The Colonel breathed quickly for a moment or two, until he could obtain better control of his utterance

"Out there!" he panted. "The wo—wolf! I've often said he was—at the—do—door, and now he is— two of 'em."

"Joseph," said Mrs. Bantam, tenderly, "compose yourself, your mind is wandering. There is no wolf at the door or anywhere else."

"I tell you there is," said the Colonel indignantly, getting himself into a sitting posture, and beginning to look somewhat as if he were ashamed. "My mind's not wandering—not wandering a particle. They chased me. I barely escaped with my life."

"They were only the bloodhounds, I guess," said Julie calmly and with a smile. "They were just in play. They won't hurt anyone"

"Bloodhounds!" shouted the Colonel, "what bloodhounds? What do you mean?"

"Why you know, love," said Mrs. Bantam, taking a seat beside the Colonel upon the sofa," that Mr. Pelican sent the two bloodhounds here in Mr. Spiker's care, just for a few days."

"Hypothecated them to Spiker," I added, "for security for his advertising bill."

"Hah!" exclaimed the Colonel, scowling, as I got up and walked to the mantel, so that I might hide my feelings under pretense of examining the sword of Gettysburg. "Spiker sent them here, did he? It surpasses the most ordinary requirements of decency to set wild beasts prowling about a man's premises without asking his permission. It is an outrage! Spiker shall answer to me for it," continued the Colonel angrily. "I will not remain in the dwelling where such a scoundrel is domiciled."

Thereupon Colonel Bantam rose, walked with dignity to the hallway, took his hat and his cane, and placed his hand upon the knob of the front door. As he did so, the thought seemed to strike him that the dogs might be at large in the front yard; so, after a moment's hesitation, he released the knob, limped to the hat-rack, replaced his hat and cane, and hobbled upstairs.

We sat silent, not knowing what to say, and fearing to laugh, for Mrs. Bantam looked sad and troubled. Finally she said:

"Brave men so often have strange idiosyncrasies. Do you remember how Napoleon hated cats, and how Ajax was afraid of the lightning?"

It would have been ungenerous under the circumstances to attempt to readjust her reminiscence of Ajax, and so, when Julie very sweetly had said:

"Nobody could help dreading those huge strange dogs," we began to talk about the stage.

When we met at breakfast next morning Colonel Bantam seemed to have forgotten all about the unpleasant experience of the preceding evening, but we knew that it troubled him, because he related at much length an episode of the Civil War in which he charged a Confederate battery, and, without support, captured it, cutting down the gunners with his own hand.

Ruby and Mrs. Bantam were going to church, and they asked me to go with them. Spiker and Julie agreed to stroll by the brook beneath the trees, and the Colonel insisted that his duties at the Mayor's office would detain him from the house of devotion. After breakfast he drew me aside and whispered to me:

"My dear boy, you oblige me by escorting Mrs. Bantam to church. I stay away from principle. In strict confidence I tell you, for Mrs. Bantam doesn't know it, I am a Fire Worshiper."

It was delightful to walk along the street on the

bright autumn morning with the lovely girl by my side. She talked in the most charming manner to me and to her aunt, who also appeared to find pleasure in listening to her pretty chatter. I was grateful, as I heard her and looked at her, for the kindly fate that had made me an inmate of the home to which she had so strangely come.

As we reached the door of the Episcopal Church a handsome carriage came up at a rapid pace and stopped, while the glossy bay horses champed their bits and rattled their silver-plated chains. The door of the carriage was opened by a footman and a portly woman of forty-five years descended. Holding a prayer-book in her hand, her black silk dress trailing upon the pavement and her head held high, she walked into the church and up the aisle as if she owned the premises and knew that everybody was looking at her and envying her.

"It is Mrs. Purvis-Hyde," said Mrs. Bantam. "She is very rich, a widow. She gives tone to everything—really everything. There would be no tone in Happy Hollow if Mrs. Purvis-Hyde should leave us. None in this church either. She runs it all."

That was plainly the impression Mrs. Purvis-Hyde made upon the observer. We sat two pews behind her, and while she was most precise and particular in assuming all the attitudes required by the service, the manner in which she flirted her fan, and moved her head, and toyed with her handkerchief, plainly indicated that her feeling about herself was not largely infused with humility.

The service was what Mrs. Bantam called "ornate," and nobody could doubt when looking at Mrs. Purvis-

Hyde that any service not ornate would have failed to satisfy the cravings of her nature.

The minister was Rev. Dr. Malachi Fury, and I regretted to discover that he had not yet learned how to read the English language properly, and that, while his vestments were rich and correct, his sermon, when we could discover what he said, was almost supernaturally dull.

I am sorry to say Ruby went to sleep, and I am also sorry to say I was unjust in forming during the sermon a prejudice against Mrs. Purvis-Hyde. I thought her proud and haughty and selfish. But when the congregation was dismissed and we had come into the church-porch, I was surprised that she should push toward Mrs. Bantam and say :

"My dear Mrs. Bantam, welcome, most welcome to the church! How much better to come with us than to endeavor to worship with the denominations that are around us! And this sweet girl," she said, turning to Ruby and taking her hand, while Mrs. Bantam formally introduced Ruby to her; "this dear girl is your niece. How charming! I shall love you, my dear!" she added, and then, when I was presented to her, she said:

"I hope you will like Happy Hollow, Professor, I must have you to my conversazione. It is the home of intellect."

Then 'she stepped into her carriage, and the bays rattled their silver chains as she swept away from us.

In fact, I liked Mrs. Purvis-Hyde; liked her for her graciousness to me and because she liked Ruby Bonner.

Chapter V

THE SCHOOL

ON Monday morning when I left
the house to go to the school where I was to begin
my career as a teacher, Ruby Bonner walked with me
over the bridge to the street upon which was the
school in which she was to become a pupil. This was
Madame Bertolet's Academy for Young Ladies, which
had been established in Happy Hollow through the
efforts of Mrs. Purvis-Hyde, and was directly under
her patronage. The irrepressible yearning of Mrs.
Purvis-Hyde was for culture, and this school had
been provided for the purpose of supplying to the
girls of Happy Hollow and the neighboring regions
an opportunity to acquire under strictly church influences what Mrs. Purvis-Hyde called the higher
education.

It was not Ruby's intention, nor mine, when we
prepared for our movement toward the schools, that

we should walk together, but we happened to leave the house at the same moment, and so we began on that day a practice of companionship which could have nothing but charm for me.

"I wish," she said, as we left the garden-gate of Colonel Bantam's house, "that I were going to your school."

I inclined at first to regard this expression as conveying something like a compliment to me, but in fact she had no thought of that kind.

"I don't like girls' schools," continued Ruby, "and I don't care for girls. I wish I were a boy."

"Then you would care for girls, maybe," I said.

"I suppose I should," answered Ruby, "but that isn't the reason why I want to be a boy."

"What is the reason?"

"Oh, a boy has none of the horrid restraints that are put upon girls. He doesn't always have to be prim and proper, or to sit in some particular way; and he can have so much fun. He can play ball, and run and shout, and go swimming and camping and hunting; and then he needn't have some old lady tagging after him to see that he behaves himself when he goes anywhere; and he can do anything nice he wants to do without shocking people. It's just horrid to be a girl, I think."

It was really difficult for me to frame an argument on the other side of the case. I couldn't imagine myself wanting to be a girl, and in fact, I never knew a man or boy who felt dissatisfied with his sex. So instead of attempting to show Ruby that women have great advantages, or to impress upon her young mind the wisdom of accepting unchangeable conditions with cheerful resignation, I talked to her about her studies. She made it plainly apparent in a few minutes that before she attempted any extended flights under Madame Bertolet's system of higher education, accompanied by church influences, there was great need that she should wrestle with some of the problems of lower education.

"I never could remember," she said, "how much nine nines make—eighty-one, isn't it? and I don't see why they do, anyhow; and that horrid cube root! what does anybody want with one? I never needed one. I shouldn't know what on earth to do with it if I had it."

It seemed not a favorable opportunity to impart information to Ruby's mind, and so when we came to the point where I must leave her, I comforted her with the assurance that, as we were to live in the same house, I should be glad to fulfil my promise to help her to master the arithmetical and other difficulties that were likely to obstruct her onward march toward the goal set by Mrs. Purvis-Hyde and Madame Bertolet.

"Oh, will you really help me, though?" said Ruby. "That will be so kind, and it will make everything so easy. Thank you, thank you, very much!"

I bade her good-bye, and went on until I came to Dr. Bulfinch's Classical and Mathematical Academy. The yard swarmed with boys, who looked at me curiously as I said good-morning to them; and then I entered the building and found Dr. Bulfinch moving about the great school-room, preparing for the morning session.

It was a large room, filled with desks, excepting

Going to school.

that at the very front there was a row of low benches
on which the boys sat while they recited their lessons.

These benches faced a platform, ten inches high, on
which the Doctor had his chair by the side of a desk.
Over the Doctor's desk, upon the wall where every
boy could see it and read it, were the words :

"LOVE IS THE FULFILLING OF THE LAW."

Adjoining the great school-room were three other
rooms in which the assistant teachers conducted their
operations, hearing and teaching lessons. One of
these smaller rooms was allotted to me.

"I hope, Mr. Sprat," said Dr. Bulfinch, as he
grasped my hand and greeted me, "that our asso-
ciation with each other will be both pleasant and profitable."

The strenuous life.

When I had re-
sponded to this kindly sentiment,
and had spoken with him about the books
and the plan of work, he said to me :

"Mr. Sprat, I have had large experience with boys,
as you may imagine ; very large ; and you may depend
upon it that in dealing with them you must start upon
a basis of the total depravity of each boy ; that is, if
he is well. I mean boys in rude physical health. The
boy is lost, to begin with ; and the duty of his elders
—your duty and mine—is to try to save him."

Dr. Bulfinch looked like a man who could not have
entertained any more hopeful and cheerful theory. He

was tall, and so thin that he appeared taller than he really was. His face was white, almost fleshless, and he had narrow jaws, the bones showing plainly through the skin, and his firm, closely-set lips conveyed an impression of severity which was heightened by a strong, protruding, squarely-cut chin. His bushy gray-brown hair was usually in disorder.

He always wore a very long black frock-coat, cleanly brushed, but inclined to glossiness about the elbows, and he had a low turned-down coller, tied with a black silk cravat. I have often wondered how Dr. Bulfinch would have looked in a short sack-coat of colored cloth and a standing collar with a gay neck-tie. But it is hard to conceive of such a figure The clothing that he wore really seemed as if it alone could have been possible upon the person of such a man.

The Doctor had silver spectacles, worn often upon the tip of his nose, and his habit was to depress his chin and to look over the spectacles when he surveyed the boys in front of him, while, when he wished to examine the book he held in his hand, elevation of his chin to a horizontal position was necessary that he might look through his spectacles.

Always during school-hours Dr. Bulfinch carried a stout switch in his right hand. His practice was to strike his desk with it, as a kind of emphasis, when he spoke at large to the school, and often he would walk up and down before the class that was reciting and gently switch the legs of each boy as he came to him, as an indication that the turn of that particular boy to answer questions had arrived.

Before I had been with the Doctor many months I discovered that he had peculiar theories about education—theories which he did not venture wholly to apply in practice. He believed that the Latin Grammar and the Shorter Catechism contained nearly all the knowledge that a boy really needed in this world.

"The Grammar," he said to me one day, "opens the past to the young mind, the Catechism reveals the future."

He conceded something to the simple mathematics; a little to history; not much to literature, which he regarded as a weakness upon the part of parents, and nothing at all to science.

I am bound to say that he was a learned man in the departments of learning which he thought important, and he was a careful teacher. There was a touch of sarcasm in his method, and my own experience has taught me that sarcasm, used sparingly and without great unkindness, is a most effective instrument with boys. Much is to be said for love, but sarcasm puts love into the second place.

When the boys at the summons of the bell began to troop into the room and to take their places behind the desks, Dr. Bulfinch, standing by his platform, smiled grimly as he watched them; but all the sternness faded from his face when one of the boys came up and shook hands with him. The Doctor put his arm around the boy's shoulders, and the light of affection came into his gray eyes as he presented the youth to me, saying:

"Mr. Sprat, this is Charley, my nephew; Charley Bulfinch. He will be with you a good deal, and you must be stern with him."

Charley was a rosy, hearty, handsome boy, with a

Doctor Bulfinch.

look of intellectual alertness which seemed to have no promise that he would be a dull scholar.

When I had shaken hands with him, and the Doctor had patted his shoulder again, Charley went back among the other boys, and I am much mistaken if I did not see him make a gesture, while his back was turned toward me, indicative to the other boys of Charley's belief that he had arranged things comfortably for himself at headquarters.

Dr. Bulfinch's practice was to open each session of the school with a few verses of Scripture. When he finished the reading and offered a brief prayer on this morning, he took up his switch and proceeded to greet the scholars. As he spoke to them he struck the desk from time to time. The act seemed to help him to find utterance.

"Boys," he said, "it is well for me to say, as we begin our work together here, that the law of kindness is the law of this school. The hill of learning is not easy to climb. Upon your part strenuous effort is required; upon mine, that the influences of affection shall be applied to keep you from straying from the right path, and to impel you upward. These influences may sometimes take the form of gentle remonstrance, or the sterner shape of flagellation of the person; but the rod, you must learn, is the symbol of the strenuous life, as it is the very flower of love in its richest aspects; and so," said the Doctor, giving a final and vigorous blow to his desk, "it will be liberally used, if need be, to stimulate your aspirations for higher things."

I thought the boys looked promising. The restraint of novelty was upon them, and I could perceive that they were unconsciously trying to take the Doctor's measure and mine; but really they seemed to me to be a fine lot of boys, with whom we should have little trouble.

"They were remarkably orderly," I said to the Doctor, when the first recess came and the room was empty. "I am very hopeful of them."

Dr. Bulfinch looked at me as if he felt I had much to learn, and said:

"Wait. The evil is there. It is latent. It will develop."

Before the week was out I saw the ceiling of the room fairly covered, during the few minutes occupied by the Doctor's prayer, with paper dolls dangling from wads of chewed paper, and from the corner of my eye I discovered Charley Bulfinch discharging one of these wads toward the ceiling just as the Doctor was saying "Amen."

·As in all schools, I suppose, there were dull boys and bright boys, and, as usual, the smartest boys were the most mischievous. I never observed any marked misconduct upon the part of Hosea Blinn, who defined the word "hypothecate" as relating to "apothecaries," nor was there ever any need that Dr. Bulfinch's rod should be applied to the back of George Grass, who supplied the class one afternoon with the surprising information that "'Javelin' is the name usually given to the inhabitants of Java," but Charley Bulfinch, who rarely missed a lesson, and Thomas Hopkins, known to all the boys as "Polly Hopkins," after the name of the heroine of a famous song, and always near to the head of his class, went up to the Doctor's private room for discipline with the rod three days out of five.

My class in etymology usually supplied food for

amusement as well as subjects for corporal punishment. I remember well in what manner, at the time
of my first lesson with them, they dealt with the word
"indigenous." The first boy who made a dash at it,
without having examined the subject at all during the
study hour, said that it might be defined as "the practice of being constantly indignant." The next boy
differed wholly from this view. His theory was that
indigenous means "referring to Indians." The third
scholar held that it meant "partaking of the nature of
indigo," and the conclusion reached by the next mind
to which I appealed was that indigenous had its source
in a Latin word which he represented to be *Indigeno*,
and which was a verb of the first conjugation, with the
parts *Indigeno, indigenare, indigenavi, indigenatum,*
meaning, in plain English, "to dig into." These varying views resulted in the detention of the ingenious
authors for half an hour after school, so that they might
have leisure in which to acquire more nearly accurate
opinions. With the scholars thus detained was one
dexterous boy who gave the correct answer so
promptly that my suspicion was excited, and I examined the book he had before him, opened apparently
at the last page, upon which he seemed to be scribbling. I found that he had torn the book from the
cover, turned it over so that the page of the lesson
would seem to be the final page, and was reading the
answer from the book while he pretended to be scribbling upon it.

I have long known that to many children lessons
are simply tasks without meaning. The lessons are
learned because older people who are accustomed to
command require them to be learned, and the poor

little students do the work as a part of the general and mysterious hardships of life, but without any notion what it is all for. There are Sunday-school scholars to whom the affecting story of Joseph and the amusing tale of Cinderella are precisely alike in the particular that both are presumed to be creations of the imagination. All boys, however, appear to accept American history as representative of fact, although few of them ever succeed in separating the Revolutionary War from the Civil War, or in realizing the period of time that lay between the two struggles.

Ancient history to most boys is simply romance, and dull romance, excepting when there is lively narrative of combat. No boy ever fails to regard with intense interest the story of a fight.

I am sure I tried to infuse into my lessons upon Roman history some elements of vitality, and if the boys had really heeded what the teacher said they might have grasped the fact that Julius Cæsar was once a living person, and not an imaginary being like Jack the Giant Killer. But in truth, many boys do not heed. They have made up their minds, unconsciously, that the whole thing is fiction, and so the earnest and repeated declaration of the teacher that history is fact makes really no impression upon their minds.

One day, in talking about Vercingetorix and his captivity in Rome, I mentioned that I had seen and entered the dungeon in which that warrior had been cruelly confined. I happened at the moment of speaking to look at George Grass, and I saw spreading over his rather dull countenance an expression of mingled scorn and incredulity.

"What is the matter, George?" I asked.

"Nothing, sir," he answered.

"Speak your mind freely," I said. "Have you some doubts about my visit to the dungeon or about Vercingetorix?"

"There never was no such man, sir, now was there really?" asked George.

"You think, do you, that all this story of Cæsar and his wars is false, then?"

"It's just made up, sir, isn't it?" asked George, and while the other boys in the class laughed, all of them looked as if they were ready to take George's opinion without hesitation.

Dr. Bulfinch had passed the period when he cared to make nice observation of the attitude of the young mind toward such matters. He knew of the infidelity, of course, but he disregarded it, and riding right over it, compelled the boys to take the facts, no matter whether they were regarded as facts or fiction.

One morning about three weeks after the school opened, Dr. Bulfinch began the session by reading from the Scripture about "the ornament of a meek and quiet spirit," and after pausing for a moment to explain to the school why such a spirit is ornamental, he tried to clench the lesson by asking in his brief prayer that all of us might learn to be "quiet and peaceable."

Half an hour later, while in the adjoining class-room I strove to have the minds of the boys grasp the reasons why the square of the hypothenuse of a right-angled triangle is equal to the sum of the squares of the other two sides, noise of a great uproar came through the door opening into the room in which the Doctor sat. I stopped my work and listened for a moment, and then as the noise increased I went to the door and into the Doctor's room, followed, of course, by my whole class.

I was astonished to find Dr. Bulfinch grappling with Polly Hopkins, and rolling over

Polly Hopkins and the Doctor.

and over him upon the floor. It seemed that the Doctor had called Hopkins to him and ordered Hopkins to hold out his hand that he might switch it. At the third or fourth blow Hopkins withdrew his hand and the Doctor hit his own leg in a painful manner. Hopkins was unwise enough to laugh, whereupon the Doctor leaped upon him, and Hopkins, who prided himself upon his ability as a wrestler, locked himself around the Doctor's neck and legs.

When I entered the combatants were upon the floor, in vigorous motion, rolling from one side to the other, overturning the recitation benches, and giving really a rather humorous suggestion of a large black cat and a small gray cat engaged in a fight. Every boy in the room was on the top of his desk in a condition of wild excitement, and some of them actually ventured to give cheering advice to Polly Hopkins. It was plain enough that the sympathy of the spectators was with the smaller warrior. That he knew it, and was resolved to win laurels for himself on that great day, was indicated by the tenacity with which he held his antagonist, and strove to retain his place on top whenever the fortunes of war, or intervention of an overturned bench, placed him in that position.

The spectators dropped into their seats when I appeared, but the combat upon the floor raged until as I came to the place Dr. Bulfinch succeeded in turning Hopkins face-downward and sitting triumphantly upon him.

The vanquished boy struggled no more, and Dr. Bulfinch arose, and looking at me with mortification written upon his face, ordered Hopkins to take his seat and to report to the Doctor in his study at quarter past three.

The Doctor then, after partially brushing the dust from his coat with his hand, resumed his seat and his lesson with flushed countenance, but with a strong effort to appear tranquil.

I laughed to myself a little bit when I returned to my room, for I recalled the Doctor's morning reference to the ornament of a meek and quiet spirit; but I did not then know Dr. Bulfinch.

He asked me to come to his study when school was over, and while I sat there with him Hopkins came in What was the attitude of the spirit of Hopkins must remain unknown, but his physical aspect conveyed an impression of humility. A boy always surrenders when he has been fairly beaten; and no doubt the thing in Hopkins which answered to the name of conscience told him that he richly deserved the flogging he came to Dr. Bulfinch's study expecting to get. He was ready for it.

"Sit down, Thomas," said the Doctor, as the boy entered the room and closed the door.

There was an unfamiliar tone of gentleness in the stern man's voice that surprised the boy, and he looked at his teacher sharply.

"Thomas," said the Doctor, retaining his seat in his great arm-chair, "I am very sorry I attacked you this morning, very, very sorry. You had done wrong, but I should not have forgotten myself so far as to do another wrong by losing my temper. Thomas, I ask your forgiveness," and the Doctor went over and tried to take Polly Hopkins's hand. But Polly had both hands to his eyes, and then dropping his hands and head upon the table by his side he began to sob.

Tears came into the Doctor's eyes as he put his hand upon the boy's shoulder, and patted it and said in a gentle voice:

"Never mind, my son, never mind, we were both wrong. We will forgive and forget, and we will both try to do better in the future."

Then he clasped Polly's hand and led him to the door and sent him away. I rose to go, and the Doctor held the door open for me.

" I wanted you to hear my confession, Mr. Sprat," he said. " God forgive me for my reckless wicked anger."

But, somehow or other, I liked Dr. Bulfinch that day far better than I had ever done, and I think Polly Hopkins liked him better too.

In truth, as time rolled by I liked both the Doctor and the school better and better, and I found in the boys, with their pranks and follies, only such evidences of depravity as I discovered in myself when I remembered my school days, not far distant in the past.

But the most delightful work that came to me as a teacher was performed in the dining-room of Mrs. Bantam's house, where Ruby in the evening studied her lessons, and whither I was summoned very frequently when the tasks seemed to her too hard.

_She was passionately fond of literature, particularly of poetry, but for the ordinary dull learning of the school-books she had no taste, and her mathematical faculty was almost no faculty at all.

" I simply *can't* understand," she said, "why you turn fractions over before multiplying them. It seems just funny to make a fraction turn a somersault and to stand it on its head before you can use it."

The reason why fifty added to one hundred makes an increase of 50 per cent., but makes a decrease of only $33\frac{1}{2}$ per cent. when it is taken off, was always hidden from that lovely woman.

" It seems just unreasonable," she insisted ; "and I am sure I shall never know what holds up the moon or why we are not upside down when the world goes round. We must be upside down now, mustn't we ?"

" It is so awfully tiresome," she pleaded, "to have to know where Borneo is. I shall never want to go to Borneo, shall I? and I never expect to know any Borneoers, if that's the name of them And don't you think it was simply outrageous for the Latin people to call a woman *mulier?* I don't think women are any mulier than men; and it really seems foolish, now doesn't it, for people to have said *amo*, when to say 'I love' is so much easier?"

"Was it Plutarch," she asked, "or Plato or Pluto that was god of the lower regions? I never can remember, and I always get them mixed, and do you know, Mr. Sprat, I can't get it out of my mind that Bacchus was the god of tobacco; but he wasn't, now was he?"

But, somehow, these things, which would have seemed stupidities if I had heard them from George Grass or Hosea Blinn, had an aspect of charm when they came from the pretty lips of Ruby Bonner Tom Driggs would have thought himself lucky to have heard them, and to have the privilege now given to me of revealing to this lovely girl some of the mysteries of knowledge.

Tom wrote to me, a few days after school began, that he had given up the shoe business, and now, travelling for a soap-house, he had concentrated upon soap all the intense enthusiasm with which once he had regarded shoes. In a postscript to his letter he said:

"I hear you have Ruby Bonner with you. I shall be glad if, as a friend of mine, you will praise me to her and try to endear me to her"

In reply, I asked him if he remembered the case of Miles Standish, and he answered:

"I don't remember the Standish you refer to. Was he in our class at the University?"

6

Chapter VI

Dr. Bulfinch's Brother

When school was done one Friday afternoon, two months after my arrival in Happy Hollow, and when Dr. Bulfinch had faithfully applied to the backs of the culprit boys the symbol of the strenuous life, the Doctor invited me to stroll with him by the side of the brook that intersected the village. He wished to talk of matters appertaining to the school.

We walked and talked and sat for a while beneath the trees along the banks of the stream, and then we came to a pretty house of wood, near to the end of one of the streets, half covered with the broad green leaves of the ampelopsis vine. It stood beyond a fence of pointed palings in a small garden, wherein upon this October day some of the shrubs still were flowering, and the grass was green with the loveliness of the spent summertime.

The Doctor stopped and put his hand upon the

latch of the gate, and was about to say farewell, when his thought changed and he said to me :

"You do not know my sister, Charley's mother. Come in with me for a moment that you may meet her."

He knew that if I stayed in Happy Hollow I must learn sooner or later the story of the tragedy that lay in that house and in his heart, and I suppose he thought it better that he should face the matter boldly and that I should know the worst of it from him.

Mrs Bulfinch, who lived there, was the wife of his brother, who had long ago begun an evil life and deserted her, and I knew afterward that the Doctor had loved this woman with a love from which she turned to find misery in the affection she preferred, poor soul, to lavish upon a man who never loved her. I found also from Mrs Bantam that the father of the woman had favored the Doctor's suit and hated the brother; and with clear vision and sound judgment had made Dr. Bulfinch the sole trustee of the small fortune he had left to his daughter

Mrs. Bulfinch opened the door in response to the Doctor's summons, and greeted us I thought with coldness as she ushered us into her little parlor.

She was a woman of thirty-five or forty years, who might once have been handsome, but now sorrow had marred her face, which was white and pinched as if physical suffering had come to her to supplement and make more bitter the pain that filled her soul with bitterness. She was clad in black, with a muslin collar about her neck, and her hair was drawn simply from her forehead as if she were indifferent to her appearance.

There was an odd constraint in her manner, and a look upon her face of nervous apprehension, as if she

were afraid of some impending catastrophe. But I am
sure Dr. Bulfinch did not observe this. He was near-
sighted, and it was never his practice to discern anything of an unusual nature about a person's demeanor
unless his attention were called to it. I doubt if Dr.
Bulfinch ever in his life read the countenances of the
boys in school, whose faces often had so much to tell
to a man of quick vision.

When I had been presented to Mrs. Bulfinch and
had greeted Charley, who came into the room about as
we entered it, we sat down, and the Doctor began to
talk pleasantly of the school and of me and of Charley
and of the weather. But I could see that Mrs. Bulfinch listened indifferently, if not indeed with manifest feelings of impatience ; and while she responded
courteously, and even exerted herself to appear pleasant to me, I could not help perceiving that she wished
us to be gone.

I felt quite uncomfortable, and I made up my mind
after a few moments to take my leave without waiting
for the Doctor ; but, just as I was about to rise from
my chair, a door at the back of the room opened, and
in walked a man who looked as much like Dr. Bulfinch
as one man can possibly look like another.

He had the same figure, the same face, the same
bushy brown hair, even the same voice ; but he was
dressed in half-shabby clothing of material and shape
that would have been fitting in a much younger man,
and not only was his face marked by dissipation, but
he had a sinister look in his eyes which would have
excited distrust at once, I should think, in anybody
who met him for the first time.

I do not know precisely what the old Scriptural

phrase the "evil eye" means, but if it means that the wickedness of the soul may sometimes flash out from the windows which open the way to the soul, then Simon Bulfinch had the evil eye.

I saw a shiver pass through Mrs. Bulfinch's frame as he came in, and her white cheeks seemed to turn whiter as she first clenched her hands and then thrust them down into her lap as if to control herself, and then, rising, said:

"My husband, Mr. Sprat"

Simon Bulfinch did not extend his hand to me. With a smile upon his face he said:

"Glad to know you, sir."

But not a word did he say to the Doctor, who sat upon his chair looking surprised and shocked, but bravely maintaining his composure. Simon knew that he had startled his brother, and I think he felt a kind of savage joy that he could give him pain. The husband put his hand upon the wife's shoulder, and made as if he would caress her, and then as he sat down he drew Charley to him and flung his arm about the boy; and whether he touched the wife or the boy, he perceived, and so did I, that it was as if a knife were driven into the flesh of the schoolmaster.

Before a minute had passed or another word had been spoken, Mrs. Bulfinch rose, and excusing herself, withdrew from the room. Then the Doctor, in kindly tones, asked Charley to leave. His father ordered him to stay, but the boy without hesitating followed his mother. A flash of anger swept over Simon's face at this, but instantly the mocking smile returned. Thrusting his hands deep into his pockets, and stretching out his legs wide apart, he said to the Doctor:

"Well, my jolly old pedagogue, aren't you glad to see me? You are not married yet? Ah, what a mistake. How much loss for some fine woman! And this," he said, nodding his head at me, "is your assistant paddler of the little boys."

I rose to leave   There could be no reason, I thought, why I should quietly endure insolence.

"Will you stay with me, Mr. Sprat?" said the Doctor earnestly, "I shall think it a high favor."

"You had better stay, my young friend," said Simon, "and take some lessons in brotherly love. Maybe you will hear something that will interest you. Suppose, dominie, I should tell your lieutenant here something nice about your past life? Perhaps he might think you need whipping more than the little boys do."

"Will you never cease to do evil, Simon?" asked the Doctor calmly.

"Shall I become a schoolmaster," replied Simon, "and wear a black coat, and plaster my wall with Scripture texts, and snivel prayers, and look solemn, and go to church? That pays sometimes, if you can have trust funds in your hands. Sprat, how do you like living under the reign of love according to the Shorter Catechism?"

I did not answer.

"I thought and hoped," said the Doctor, "that we had seen the last of you, and that you would persecute this poor woman no more."

"I must come back," said Simon, laughing, "to watch you. You know you don't pay my wife her full income."

"I need give no account of that to you," replied the Doctor, "but your statement is, of course, untrue."

" I believe you have stolen part of the principal,"
said Simon savagely, but still smiling grimly   " I will
compel you to give an account of it."

" You will compel me !" exclaimed the Doctor scornfully.   " Your day of doom will have come when you
go into a court against me."

Simon's appearance of mocking gaiety began to
vanish.   He grew white about the nostrils.

" My wife needs a thousand dollars of her own
money now," said Simon, " and unless you give it to
her I will—"   He hesitated.   " This community and
the parents of the little boys will be interested to learn
what I know about you."

" I do not fear you," said Dr. Bulfinch, quietly.

Simon went to the door and called Mrs. Bulfinch.
She came into the room and sat over by her husband.
She looked like a woman half distracted.   Simon put
his arm upon the back of her chair as if to appear to
indicate a caress.

" My dear," he said, " I have told this schoolmaster
that you badly need some money for your own use.
That is so, isn't it ?"

" Yes," said Mrs. Bulfinch, timidly.

" But, sister—" began the Doctor.

" Sister !" said Simon, scornfully.   " Don't insult her !"

" You know," continued the Doctor, " exactly what
your income is, and that you have it all.   There is no
more."

" You want a part of the principal, don't you ?"
asked Simon.   " We are going away from here, Helen,
to start life again together."

Mrs. Bulfinch did not say yes, but she looked an
affirmative answer.

"It is impossible, sister," said the Doctor. "I cannot believe that you would trust this man again. He wants your money, not for you, but for his companion in crime."

Mrs Bulfinch shivered, and did not answer. It was clear enough she believed what the Doctor said, and yet was trying to believe that her husband had come to her again to be faithful to her.

"You lying rascal!" said Simon, savagely, all traces of mockery having disappeared from his manner.

Mrs. Bulfinch put her hand upon her husband's arm, as if to implore him not to speak in such a manner.

"I must withdraw you and Charley from this man's evil influence," he said. He thought that threat, which he might perhaps have executed, would fill the Doctor's soul with terror. "You will come with .me, won't you, Helen?"

Again she refused to speak, but seemed as if she would have found it hard to refuse to obey her husband's summons.

"The income stops when you leave here, sister," said the Doctor. "I am instructed to retain it all until Charley is of age if Simon touches it."

"I will kill you, you scoundrel," said Simon, in a rage, half rising and shaking his fist at the Doctor. "Will you give her her money or not?"

"Not a dollar while you are within reach," answered the Doctor, quietly.

Simon saw that he had lost the game. It is hard to believe he could ever have really hoped to win it in such a fashion. He dropped his eyes for a moment as if he were reflecting, and then, resuming his old manner, he said to me:

" When you know the schoolmaster, Sprat, you will understand the kind of man who can persecute and bully a woman all through her life because he was so repulsive that she shrank with disgust from marrying him."

That thrust plainly went home.   Dr. Bulfinch's face indicated horror and dismay.   Mrs. Bulfinch put her

" Will you give her her money
or not?"

hand again upon Simon's arm and tried to stop him. He pushed her away as if she too were disgusting, and as she shrank aside, looking as if he had stabbed her, he rose and said :

" Sprat, I say to you, for I won't defile my speech by addressing your friend, that the schoolmaster's day of grace is past.   He wants war to the knife, and now he will get it. I will break up his school and drive him from the town."

Then Simon Bulfinch strode to the door, opened it and went out, while his wife, watching his retreat as she stood by the window, began to cry bitterly.

I had seen and heard more than enough, and so I also withdrew, and left Dr. Bulfinch with the woman who cared not for him, though he alone was her stay, her protector, and her friend.

The day was not yet ended as I strolled by the side of the brook on my homeward journey, and as the air was warm and the sky bright, I thought to linger by the stream, while my mind was filled with thoughts of the scene I had just witnessed So I sat upon one of the rustic benches looking out over the water; and as I looked I wondered if Simon Bulfinch did indeed know of any action in the brother's life that would hurt him if it were revealed, or if Simon's talk were merely the foolish, angry vaporing of a bad man. And then I was selfish enough to try to conjecture what my position would be if the school should be broken up. My thought even went so far as to consider the possibility that I might take the school if the Doctor should be driven out. But that notion seemed upon reflection to be almost shameful.

While I turned over these matters in my mind, I saw approaching me 'Lias Guff, Colonel Bantam's big policeman. He had in leash two large dogs, evidently Mr. Pelican's bloodhounds, and it was plain enough that the policeman regarded the dogs with much respect, perhaps even with apprehension. When they hurried he hurried, and when they were disposed to linger he good-naturedly stopped, and his address to them was always framed in soothing language and expressed in tones of tenderness.

Perceiving me, he halted, and finding the shade of the trees and the comfortable bench inviting, he tied the dogs to a nearby tree, and sitting beside me, he removed his helmet and wiped his very red forehead with a very red and very large handkerchief.

'Lias Guff.

"What dogs are those?" I asked.

"Them's Spiker's bloodhounds," answered the policeman. "His honor the Mayor didn't like 'em around the house, and so I'm a-taking them up to the station-house to use them to ketch criminals. I don't really care much about them myself," and 'Lias Guff turned his eyes toward the dogs, which were lying quietly under the tree, with their tongues out, panting.

'Lias Guff's voice was deep and husky. Once, no doubt, it had been a bass voice, but now it conveyed the idea that the vocal cords had either lost their tension or become rusty. There was not a clear vibration in it, and it seemed to come from some point in his body far below his lungs.

'Lias Guff, looking away from the dogs, glanced upward at the trees, and then said:

"Let's see, this is Friday, ain't it?"

"Yes."

"And you don't see no jaybirds around yer, do you?"

"I haven't looked for any."

"No, and no matter how hard you look, you won't see none, not *this* day."

"Why not?"

"Because all the jaybirds goes to purgatory every Friday."

"What for?"

"I dunno. All I know is that they goes; and they

all come back prompt on a Saturday. You'll see 'em yer in the morning, swarms of 'em."

"It is curious, isn't it?" I ventured to suggest.

"Yes, and there's lots of other curious things in this yer life; not that I care for

life," said 'Lias with a vast sigh, "for to me life is holler, empty, and woid. I never got no fair start in it; for, ef the truth were known, I'm a changeling."

"You are?"

"Yes, sir," said 'Lias Guff, with strong emphasis,

"changed by the fairies in my cradle.   I am really the
son of a great lord, and I was born rich; born in a
higher spear.   You know Felix Acorn, the barber?
Well, he's the seventh son of a seventh son, barring
one daughter that slipped in betwixt and between the
fourth and fifth boy   He has second sight, and he
told me I was a changeling, and I think I have second
sight myself, for I've seen my doppelganger many's the
time."

"Where?"

"Right yer in this Happy Hollow, on this yer
street; seen it a walking ahead of me, uniform and
buttons and all   Some people don't believe in sech
things, and maybe I don't believe in 'em, because I
know 'em, and knowin' is better than believin'.   Do
you wear an eel-skin on your left leg when you go in
swimmin'?   No?   Well, I do.   It's a sure thing agin'
cramps, and a hoss chestnut in your pocket is a sure
thing agin' warts, and I never have no luck when I
leave my rabbit's-foot at home.   And there's some people don't have no faith in dreams; but I never knowed
them to miss once when you have the right kind of a
dream-book.   Did you ever see a mermaid?"

I told him I never had.

"You know, Mr. —, Mr. —, what did you say your
name was, sir?   Sprat, and a mighty good name Sprat
is, too, sir.   I knowed a man in Barbadoes named
Sprat.   Well, Mr. Sprat, this Felix Acorn, who in
spite of his natural gifts ain't got wery good sense, he
says to me there is no sech bein' as a mermaid; and I
says to him, 'Yes there is, because I seen one; seen
one and knowed one, and had conwersation with
one.'"

" Where ?"

" Why, sir, I followed the sea man and boy twenty years, and I seen many's the strange sight. Would you believe me if I was to tell you that on my voyage in the bark *Wm. I. Heffelfinger* we sailed through miles of wines that was a-floatin' on the sea, and that the wines sprung up on the riggin' of the bark, and growed there and growed there till it seemed that the bark *Wm. I. Heffelfinger* was just a sailin' bower of beauty ? No, you wouldn't believe it, but that werry thing happened to me, sir, jest as it happened to me that I seen and conwersed with a mermaid.

" It was whilst we were anchored in a bay in the island of Samoa out in the Pacific Ocean. You must know, sir, there's two kinds of 'em, one with scales and one without, like a catfish, and the scale kind is the most intelligent and agreeable ; only to talk honest, I don't keer so much for any of 'em.

· " Well, sir, I met this one when I was a-fishin' one evenin'. She came up to the boat and seemed to want to be kinder sociable, takin' hold of the gunn'le with her hands and h'istin' herself half out of the water. Her name, I think, was Lulu, but I'm not quite certain ; something like that, anyhow, and I hardly knowed what to say that would interest her, but kinder keerless-like, without thinkin', I asked her if bait had any attraction for her, and it made her so mad I thought she'd upset the boat. Howsomedever, I made it up with her and gave her some candy, and then she ups and tells me that the longin' of her life was to learn to play on the pianner, and she would a-done it only she could never manage to set on the stool.

" Candy seemed to warm her heart   She said she

was awful tired of sea-food, and she asked me if I had
any chewin' gum about me, but of course I hadn't;
pore thing! Mr. Sprat, I'd a-married Lulu could I
a-lived under water, exceptin' that it would a-gone
hard with me to give up smokin' terbacker, which of
course I'd a had to do in them circumstances.

"So then when I spoke of marryin' she said if she
could live on land she was willin'. She said she wanted
to leave her home anyway, because she was mad with
her ma."

"What was the difficulty?"

"Her ma wouldn't let her wear ribbon on her dorsal
fin, and that seemed to wex Lulu so much that she
said she wouldn't care a cent if she never seen her ma
agin"

'Lias Guff sighed once more, as he thought of the
lovely vision that had appeared to him, then he rose
and pulled down his jacket and put on his helmet, and
said:

"But I must be a-goin', I know my duty, and his
honor'll tell you I tries to do it. His honor often says
Duty ought to be my motter, and I always say to him,
'Add Wigilance to it, and I'm your man.' Them's
words, sir, for a p'liceman: Wigilance, Wirtue, Wigor,
and Wictory."

And 'Lias Guff began to untie the bloodhounds.
While he was doing so, Colonel Bantam came up,
whereupon 'Lias straightened himself, drew his feet
together and saluted the Mayor, who returned the
salute with his cane. He seemed surprised to find his
police force lingering here.

"Why, officer, how is this? Loitering upon duty?"

"Obeyin' orders, sir," said 'Lias. "I was a leadin'

the dogs to the station, and I tied 'em yer to let 'em get their wind."

The dogs moved nearer to the Colonel and appeared to wish to be sociable with him; but he came round to my side of the bench and said, sharply:

"Officer, remove the hounds at once. Make them secure in the rear yard and report to me at eight o'clock."

As 'Lias Guff led the dogs away, the Colonel and I began to stroll homeward. Linking his arm in mine, and limping more heavily than usual, he began to tell me that he was descended from the Plantagenets. He showed me how the name Bantam was really a corruption of the name Plantagenet I forget exactly how the change gradually was made, but I remember he insisted that the syllable "ant" in the two names was "a root syllable," which, taken from Plantagenet, had produced Bantam.

He said further that all the evidence indicated Henry the Eighth as his ancestor, and that he made this confession to me in the confidence of friendship because he was by no means proud of such a forefather.

A later member of the family, he said, had become weary of affairs of state, and had retired to his castle at Cnwyddl, in Wales; where the clan had remained for several generations, until his own great-great-grandfather, to escape persecution, fled from the country, and reached the hospitable shores of this continent in severely reduced circumstances.

"In truth, Professor," continued Colonel Bantam, "that primitive and original condition of reduced circumstances has remained with all his descendants down to the present time. It is distasteful to me to dwell upon matters of the kind, and particularly with a friend, but I know I can count upon your affectionate solicitude when I mention to you that an unforseen combination of events has produced a momentary lull in my finances, and if you *could* let me have five dollars on account, strictly on account, without subjecting yourself to embarrassment, you would impart a new aspect of sacredness to the bonds of our friendship."

I handed him the money.

"Sir," he said, as he thrust it into his vest pocket, "this represents a debt of honor. I make you a preferred creditor."

Dinner was ready when we reached home, and at the table I mentioned that I had called

"I make you a preferred creditor."

with the Doctor at the house of Mrs. Bulfinch; but I did not tell what occurred there.

The Colonel, however, in affecting language, deplored the lonely situation of Mrs. Bulfinch, and said:

"Sir, the sorrow of it is that every woman, like a feeble vine, needs a sturdy oak of a husband to cling

7

to and to reach out to with her tendrils; and to think that that unfortunate woman can cling to nothing, absolutely nothing!" and Colonel Bantam touched his eyes with his napkin.

But Miss Bantam openly scoffed at the theory.

"I have heard you and other people talk in that way before, paw, and to my mind it is perfectly absurd. Clinging vine! Imagine me a clinging vine, indeed! I see myself clinging to a man! Tendrils! Humph! If I ever have a husband I expect to keep him in pocket-money, and have him run about and play and do errands while I attend to the stern duties of my profession."

"Elmira, I am ashamed of you!" said Mrs. Bantam.

"Miss Mortimer wants nobody to fasten her tendrils on, I think, do you, Miss Mortimer? She is fully able to take care of herself."

Miss Mortimer colored, and I thought Mr. Spiker looked warm and uncomfortable.

"We want no trellis to hold us up," continued Miss Bantam. "If it were not for women society would go to pieces. They are usually more honest and have more sense than men. The men are all afraid of us anyhow," and Elmira helped herself a second time to dessert, wielding the spoon as if it were an implement of war.

"I never could have imagined," said the Colonel, as we left the table, "that I should have such pernicious and revolutionary sentiments expressed within the sacred precincts of my home by my own offspring. It is simply shocking! Frail indeed would be Mrs. Bantam's hold upon existence if she could not sustain herself by clinging fondly to me."

Miss Bantam went to her office after dinner, and while I remained in the parlor with the rest of the family, and was talking with Ruby and Miss Mortimer, Colonel and Mrs. Bantam, on the other side of the room, engaged in conversation in an undertone; but at last Mrs. Bantam burst into tears, and as her hair, as usual, began to disengage itself from the knot in which it was tied, she exclaimed.

" It will kill me, Joseph."

The Colonel seemed worried and angry. Turning toward us, he said :

" These conjugal disagreements must be unpleasant for my friends, as they are mortifying to me, but I cannot yield a fraction of an inch where important principles are involved."

" Not principles, Joseph," exclaimed Mrs. Bantam, with streaming eyes.

" Yes, principles. I will explain, Professor. It falls to my lot, in my capacity of chief magistrate of the city, sometimes to join affectionate couples in the sacred bonds of matrimony. My charges are moderate, and I perform the function in an impressive and solemn manner. Now Mrs. Bantam is so inconsiderate as to insist that I shall not kiss the bride."

" I cannot bear it, Joseph," moaned Mrs. Bantam, bursting afresh into tears. " It pierces my very soul."

" The operation, Professor," explained the Colonel, " is a pure formality. It is the mere official seal of approval to a solemn ceremony. It is perfunctory. It was done in the most ancient times, as far back as Babylon, and I have always been unwilling to break away from the past, from tradition."

But Mrs. Bantam refused to be comforted, and as

the Colonel's heart was hardened to her, he left her, weeping and trying to put up her hair, and walked out with me as I started for the post-office.

When we were upon the street I ventured to remonstrate with him. I said that Mrs. Bantam was an angelic woman, and that something should be conceded to her feelings in such a matter.

"Hardly angelic, Professor," said the Colonel, tapping my arm with the knob of his cane. "The classification is lacking in precision. Not an angel. Let us say a peri. The peri place is just about her level. Ultimately, perhaps, angelic, but not now; possibly after a period of probation."

I came home early and was summoned to the library, where Ruby Bonner wished for help with her lessons. I spent at least an hour with Ruby, showing her how the mysteries of arithmetic and geometry might be solved. She had been carrying with her thus far in life the conviction that a hypothenuse has some relation to a musical instrument. This belief seems to have been formed upon the basis of the fact that a hypothenuse is part of a triangle, and, not unnaturally perhaps, Ruby's experience with Mr. Pelican's orchestra had warped her mind away from the idea of a geometrical triangle. We were just completing our readjustment of the facts relating to the hypothenuse when we heard Colonel and Mrs. Bantam coming through the hallway. They stood at the door of the library hand-in-hand and smiling, and Mrs. Bantam inquired:

"Can we come in?"

"It is only fair, Professor," said Colonel Bantam, as he and Mrs. Bantam entered the room, "that as you were present when the recent unhappy breach of friendly relations occurred between Mrs. Bantam and myself, you should now become a witness to the fact that there has been a complete and affecting reconciliation. The wound has been healed"

I expressed satisfaction.

"You were right, Professor," continued the Colonel, passing his arm about Mrs. Bantam's waist "She is an angel; a perfect angel. It stabs me to the heart to think that my unfeeling conduct brought tears to those lovely eyes. May this sad experience teach you, when you are married, to practice unselfishness. This seraphic woman has agreed to forgive the past and to continue to enshroud me with her affection if I will consent hereafter merely to kiss the bride upon the forehead, and I have consented. Believe me, compromise is the secret of conjugal happiness."

"The forehead," said Mrs. Bantam, looking fondly at the Colonel, "is the seat of the intellect; the lips are the abode of the affections. I could not bear that Joseph should even tinge with the appearance of affection the magisterial act which he is summoned to perform. I could not survive it. That he should have consented to restrict osculation to the forehead is characteristic of that nobility of soul that has always endeared him to me."

Colonel and Mrs. Bantam having received my congratulations, they withdrew to the parlor, and Ruby and I, turning from the school of the affections, resumed our examination of the science of geometry.

the breakfast table in the morning Mr. Spiker supplied the surprising but agreeable information that A. J. Pelican had recovered himself financially, and was about to return to Happy Hollow to pay his debts, and to begin an enterprise concerning which Mr. Spiker would say nothing of a definite character. The mystery was unquestionably stimulative. Mr. Spiker also said that he should have a call from Pelican that very day at the office of the *National Defender*, and as Saturday was my day of leisure, he invited me to call with Miss Mortimer, with whom, indeed, he had an important engagement.

When Mr. Spiker and the Colonel had left the house after breakfast, I sat for a while in the library reading the *National Defender* and smoking. I was alone in the room, but after a time Mrs. Bantam entered. Closing the door, and seating herself near to me, she said:

"Dear Mr. Sprat, I have ever found you a sympathetic friend and a judicious counsellor, and I come to you now to ask if I may in the strictest confidence give free expression to the feelings that agitate my mind and fill it with deepest concern. Will you with your accustomed generosity help me if you can?"

I was more than indisposed to have the burden of Mrs. Bantam's troubles pressed upon me, but I could not be unkind, so I asked her what service I could perform for her. She answered:

"It may seem very strange to you, dear Mr. Sprat, very, very strange, but I state the case in absolutely unaffected language when I say that I am most un-happy."

I said I was distressed to hear this, and I asked her the cause of her suffering.

"It is Joseph's love. I cannot explain it. I know you will laugh at me and think me silly, and perhaps censure me; but you do not know a woman's heart, Mr. Sprat. I am so happy in possession of Joseph's affection that it makes me perfectly, perfectly miserable."

I hardly knew how to offer any comfort to a sufferer under such circumstances, and so I said I thought the information surprising.

"It *is* surprising, Mr. Sprat, perhaps, to you, but all love is mysterious, and I cannot hope to excite a sym-pathetic throb in the soul of one who has himself never loved; but, surprising or not surprising, the appall-ing truth is that Joseph's love for me fills me with both joy and anguish."

I said that I was indeed sorry to hear this, but my sorrow could not overcome the curiosity I experienced to know just how the suffering in question was pro-duced.

"In this way," said Mrs. Bantam, drying her eyes tenderly with her handkerchief. "His love first makes me perfectly happy. Then I begin to realize that if he should ever cease to love me I should be filled with wild despair, actual despair. Then I think of the many things that might naturally happen to diminish the ardor of his feelings, such as giving the official salutation to brides, and similar things; and this reflection simply fills my soul with darkness—black darkness."

Very heartily I wished that Mrs. Bantam would carry away her load of misery and permit me to finish reading Spiker's impressive article on The Impending Crisis; but it seemed clearly my duty to suggest some method by which the poor woman's suffering could be alleviated, and so at last, at a venture, I said:

"Well, Mrs. Bantam, really I am a poor counsellor about such things, but it occurs to me that if the Colonel's love makes you so unhappy, you might possibly find happiness by inducing him not to love you."

"Oh, not that, Mr. Sprat; not that!" and Mrs. Bantam wept and put her hand to the back of her head to restrain the dishevelling impulses of her hair.

"Because," I continued, "if when he loves you you are miserable at the thought that he may stop loving you sometime or other, mere untrained reason would suggest that if he didn't love you, you might be happy in the thought that perhaps some day or other he might begin to love you. Just turn the thing, so to speak, around the other way."

By this time Mrs. Bantam's utterance was completely choked by tears, and the knot at the rear of her head was gone, and so I resumed examination of The Impending Crisis until the storm should blow over and her tresses could be rewound. At length Mrs. Bantam acquired control enough of herself to say:

" How little you know the soul of woman ! Yes, Joseph's love and the apprehension of losing it makes me wretched, but far, far more wretched would I be in the contingency suggested by you."

" Then, Mrs. Bantam," I said almost desperately, " I give the thing up. If love makes you wretched and absence of love also makes you wretched, I really don't see what is to be done about it. There is no possible condition in which a woman can be both un-loved and loved, no middle ground; now is there? Look at the thing calmly."

Despair appeared to settle down upon Mrs. Ban-tam's soul, as she clasped her hands upon her lap and permitted her mind to consider the situation; and Mrs. Bantam would not have been herself if tears had not glistened in her eyes.

" There is no solution," she said at last, " no solu-tion ; none, excepting that I might perhaps persuade Joseph to bind himself again by a solemn obligation taken upon our dear family Bible that he will never cease to love me."

This did seem to be some sort of a way out of the perplexities of the situation, and upon Mrs. Bantam's earnest and tearful request I reluctantly promised to bring the matter to Colonel Bantam's attention at an early moment.

I joined Julie Mortimer at the front door, and to-gether we walked to the office of the *National Defender* She was bright and happy and full of good talk, and I was glad to hear that two or three of her short stories had found acceptance from the magazines and weekly papers at really high prices. This bright and beautiful woman would be fully able to take care of herself.

Spiker was fond of consulting with her upon literary subjects and concerning his paper, and there were very plain indications that his feeling for her was beginning to go much beyond mere admiration.   It seemed to all of us not unlikely that she might become Mrs. Spiker, and while the entire household observed with interest the movement of the little drama of sentiment, Mrs. Bantam felt enthusiasm kindle in her bosom as she contemplated it.

Mr. Spiker's office had been prepared for this visit from Miss Mortimer.   There were no exchange papers upon the floor; the desk had less dust in the unused corners; the editor's paste-pot was more cleanly, and

The Woman's Department.

his feet were upon the floor rather than upon the corner of the desk, where he most frequently held them.

"I asked you to come around, Miss Julie," he said, "to have you consider starting a new department in the *Defender*. Almost all the great dailies now have what they call a Woman's Department, devoted, you know, to distinctively feminine matters. We need such a thing in this paper, and the thought occurred to me that maybe you would consent to manage it."

Miss Mortimer expressed willingness to think of the matter.

"You see," continued Mr. Spiker, taking up one of the city dailies, and folding it over so that he could examine the woman's page, "there are certain kinds of things that women-readers seem to want. Here, for example, is an article entitled 'How to Make Home Happy,' and another, 'How to Remove Freckles,' and still another explains 'How to Do Up Lace Curtains,' and so on."

"But I don't know how," said Miss Mortimer, smiling.

"And here's one telling 'How to Be Beautiful' You needn't pretend you know nothing about that," said the editor, gallantly. "I get inquiries of such a kind all the time, and hardly know what to do with them. A letter came yesterday from a woman living out in the country somewhere asking how to wear side-combs; and of course, as you may believe, I just had to make a rough guess at the right answer."

"I could have answered that," said Miss Julie, laughing.

"That is what I say: a woman really ought to run the department," continued Mr. Spiker. "And here's an inquiry how to clean paint and varnish, and how to wash cut-glass, and a whole lot of such things"

"Well, but Mr. Spiker, as I say, I don't know how."

"Oh, that makes no difference. Nobody really knows how, not more than half the time at any rate. You don't have to know how. What you want to do is just to make interesting reading. That side-comb woman, for instance, will find when she reads my advice that she can't wear side-combs in that way, and

so she'll write to us again, and don't you see, that
keeps up the interest. You can get all the actually
useful information you want from the cook-books and
the exchanges."

"I am quite willing to try my hand," said Julie.

"Every now and then, too," said Mr. Spiker, "you
can put in some sentimental things. That little poem
of yours on 'Vistas' (and, by the way, how perfectly
lovely that is!) would fit right in for a filler. But—
but—I hate to speak of it, Miss Mortimer, but would
it be entirely agreeable to you to accept part of your
compensation—only a part, of course, in bonnets and
overshoes?"

Miss Mortimer seemed to think this might be arranged to suit the editor's convenience.

"The fact is," continued Mr. Spiker thoughtfully,
"I'm half snowed in with some of those things. How
would it do, do you think, to try to work off some of
them through the Woman's Department? You might
have puzzles and enigmas and offer prizes for their solu-
tion; shoes and gimp and the like. I suppose mantel-
pieces would be almost too bulky, wouldn't they? It's
funny kind of luck for a single man, but do you know,
Miss Julie, there's a man who won't advertise with me
unless I'll take it out in women's dress goods, and I
declare I haven't the least idea what to do with them.
And breastpins; I judge that I must have a hatful of
breastpins due to me."

Miss Mortimer thought the case not so very bad.

"It's a queer business," said the editor reflectively,
"forming public opinion upon a basis of mantel-pieces
and overshoes; and then what an outrage it is that
etiquette won't permit doctors to advertise? Worse

yet, you daren't reveal your sentiments half the time
for fear of offending your advertisers. I believe in
vegetarianism, but if I say so in the paper, I not only
alienate the butchers who advertise, but all the grocers
who sell ham."

When Mr. Spiker had concluded his arrangement
with Miss Mortimer about the Woman's Department,
she withdrew, and she had hardly left the room when
A. J. Pelican walked in. His outward appearance had
been transformed. He was handsomely dressed, but
there was an intensity of newness about his clothing
that I never noticed before in any clothing. Everything about him was new, even his
wig, which had a new color as well
as a new curliness, and the splendor
of the glitter of his shoes would have
been actually impressive but
for the surpassing glossiness
of his silk hat. As he held
the hat in his hand it was
almost dazzling.

When last I saw Mr. Peli-
can his mood was sombre;
but now he was in
high spirits. He
greeted us both with
much heartiness and
joyousness, and very
plainly showed by
his manner that his
newly - found pros-

"I've come to make things hum."

perity had not uplifted his mind to the vanity of haughtiness. When he had withdrawn his rather gay and friv-

olous leather gloves and dropped them into his hat, and
had shaken hands with us, and pressed upon us better
cigars than I had ever smoked before, he sat down and
began to joke about having paid Spiker with the bloodhounds.

"And now, old man," he said, "what was the amount
of that bill, anyway?" and Pelican pulled out a swollen
pocketbook and withdrew from it a bunch of bank-
notes.

Spiker knew the amount to a cent without referring
to his books, but he said, with affected reluctance:

"That bill is settled though, Pelican. We called it
square on the dogs."

"But you didn't want 'em," answered Pelican, as he
counted out the money upon the editor's desk, "and
I'm not the man to go back on a friend who has ac-
commodated me. There's the money; never mind the
receipt. There's plenty more where that came from,
and more for you, too."

A. J. Pelican did not reveal the source of his prosperity, but, when he had asked about Julie and Ruby,
he said that fortune had given him command of almost
unlimited money, and he had come back to boom
Happy Hollow.

"I always did like the town," he said, "and when I
was here last I saw big possibilities in the place, and
I made up my mind I'd develop 'em. Well, here I
am, and you can make up your minds that Happy
Hollow has a future I've come to make things hum."

And, indeed, as A. J. Pelican unfolded to us only a
part of his plans there could be no doubt at all of the
splendor of the future of Happy Hollow if Pelican
should succeed. To begin with, he had already ap-

plied for a charter for the Happy Hollow Improvement Company, which should be the instrument
wielded by the enchanter who was to produce all
these astonishing transformations. And when Pelican
had explained that the company would have two
million dollars capital, and that the money was in
sight, and that Spiker and Colonel Bantam, and even
I, should go in upon the ground-floor almost without
cost to any of us, Spiker's eyes glistened, and I could
not help feeling that my salary at Dr. Bulfinch's was a
poor, little, insignificant thing after all.

"I'm going to stand right by you, Spiker," said A.
J. Pelican, warmly, "because you did the fair thing by
me when I was in trouble, and I'm going to give
Colonel Bantam a chance because he was kind to Julie
and to Ruby when they were homeless; and as for the
Professor, we'll take him in because he is our friend
and a mighty good fellow besides."

Thus the outlook for Happy Hollow and for all the
folks who were to go in upon the ground-floor seemed
most alluring and delightful I felt rich as I listened
to Pelican's talk, and as I began to cast about in my
mind what I should do with the wealth that would
come tumbling in upon me, I found Ruby included in
all the plans I could think of.

When we had talked over all the projects that A J.
Pelican had presented to us, and had arranged for a
great mass-meeting in the Opera House at which Pelican should speak so as to enlist popular interest and
excite enthusiasm, Spiker, after reflecting for a moment,
said:

"You hadn't arranged to start a new cemetery, had
you?"

"Why, no," said Pelican, who seemed to think the question queer. "I hadn't thought of that. But it might be well to put that into the general plan. Cemeteries always pay. Does the town want one, do you think?"

"I'm not so sure it does," responded Spiker, "but it occurred to me that perhaps a new cemetery might open a market for some of the tombstones I've had to take in trade."

A. J. Pelican laughed, and rising and patting the editor's shoulder, he said:

"Don't you bother about things of that kind any longer, Spiker. Let the *Defender* back me through thick and thin, and you can afford to snub your tombstone advertisers; and your bloodhound advertisers too, for that matter," and then Pelican laughed heartily again.

I went away leaving A. J. Pelican and the editor busy preparing a poster which should announce that the mass-meeting would be held on the following Monday night. The poster was to be put upon the streets, and also to occupy the whole of the last page of the *National Defender* on Monday morning.

"It is a cash ad., Spiker," said Pelican, in comforting tones.

Before I tell of the mass-meeting and of the particulars of the plans with which Pelican astonished the people of Happy Hollow and spread the fame of the little town far and wide over the land, I must relate the fulfilment of my promise to Mrs. Bantam that I would persuade the Colonel to renew his vow of devotion to her.

The Colonel at first was inclined to be vexed and

angry when I opened the matter to him, but as he reflected that Mrs. Bantam's anxiety not only indicated
passionateness of devotion upon her part, but conveyed
plain intimation that she perceived the Colonel to be a
certain winner of hearts whenever he should begin
such a game, his feelings softened. He affected to regard Mrs. Bantam's apprehension with good-natured
levity, as a tribute from the weaker to the stronger sex,
and finally he agreed to perform the ceremony of re-
plighting his troth to her.

Julie and Ruby and Mrs. Bantam and I were in the
parlor after dinner when the Colonel came in to play
his part.

Putting his arm about Mrs. Bantam, and kissing her
tenderly, he said :

"It was hardly worth while, dear friends, that I
should be called upon to give fresh pledges of devotion
to my heart's idol, but to demonstrate to her and to
you that the sacred flame burns still with undiminished
brightness, I am ready to make most solemn affirma-
tion of the fact. You wish me, dearest, to say so upon
our domestic copy of the sacred Scriptures; I now
do it."

And the Colonel put his left hand upon the great
family Bible, which weighed, I should think, twenty
pounds, and lifted his right hand at arm's length
toward the ceiling. He was about to speak, when
Mrs. Bantam, rising hastily and moving toward him,
said :

"Not in that way, my love. Open the book and
place your hand upon the record of our marriage."

The Colonel dropped his uplifted hand, looking as
if the interruption, offered at the very moment of his

8

most dramatic action, had been irritating. Then he stooped to try to unlock the great brazen clasp which held together the heavy lids of the book. The clasp presented difficulties; but the Colonel pulled and pulled and twisted and twisted, growing redder in the face from exertion and vexation, until I came forward to help him. The clasp refusing to yield to our united efforts, the Colonel at last jumped up and sat on the book to force the lids together while I strove to undo the clasp. I tried my best, for I saw there would be an unpleasing demonstration of some kind if the Colonel's temper should continue to gain heat; but I could not move the clasp, and I said so to the Colonel.

Leaping from the table with an angry expletive upon his lips, Colonel Bantam went to the fire-place, seized the poker,

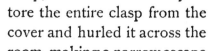

The family Bible.

inserted it behind the clasp, and with a fierce jerk tore the entire clasp from the cover and hurled it across the room, making a narrow escape from breaking a window-pane. Then, flinging down the poker, he opened the book hurriedly, found the place, put his hand upon it, said over almost hysterically the vow in the Episcopalian marriage service, slammed the covers together, and limped out of the room.

Mrs. Bantam at once burst into tears; and while Julie and Ruby strove to comfort her and to help her put up her hair, the Colonel's voice was heard calling me to come into the hallway. He seized my arm, and together we walked out into the front garden, in the darkness. He was much excited.

"Professor," he said, "you are not married. Stay single! Take my advice; be warned in time! Remain a bachelor. Women are—" he seemed to be feeling for a word which would give full expression to his anger. "Women are—are—sir! you said 'angel,' I said 'peri'; but I conceded too much, far too much. I put it now at demon, and you may let it stay there so far as I am concerned."

But all traces of anger had disappeared by the morning, and the Colonel greeted Mrs. Bantam at breakfast with a manner that indicated her complete restoration to his favor.

The Academy of Music was crowded on Monday night, and A. J. Pelican had round after round of applause when, dressed in a brand-new suit of evening clothes, he appeared upon the stage and unfolded to the audience a part of his plan for the development and general exaltation of Happy Hollow. In response to his request, the chairman named a committee of influential citizens which should co-operate with Pelican and put the Happy Hollow Improvement Company upon its feet and into immediate operation.

When the committee had been chosen and the band had played an inspiriting air, Colonel Bantam came forward, in conformity with a design he had prepared, and in a flowery but impressive speech presented A. J. Pelican with the freedom of Happy Hollow, which freedom was signified by a large key (I think it was the Colonel's own front-door key) tied with red, white, and blue ribbon. Mr. Pelican responded in a handsome manner and put the key in his pocket, where it must have made him very uncomfortable, proud as he was of possessing the symbol of the fact that the gates of Happy Hollow for him had swung wide open. I think I saw him, as he went out of the stage-door, pass the key over to 'Lias Guff, who stood at that place all through the evening, the faithful guardian of Happy Hollow's public peace.

A. J. Pelican fulfilled his promises, and he did much more. When the Happy Hollow Improvement Company had been organized, Spiker was a shareholder, and Colonel Bantam had a fairly large block of the stock, and a few dozen shares came to me almost for nothing. Nearly everybody in the town who had influence or money took the stock, and the excitement and enthusiasm created by A. J. Pelican's plans were so great that all the countryside flocked into the company's offices to procure shares. The books were closed within a week. The company could have sold four times as many shares as Pelican was willing to offer to the public.

That was a great time in the history of Happy Hollow. "It is a resurrection!" exclaimed Spiker, as he observed the improvements making headway, and Spiker's strongest words in the columns of the *National Defender* expressed inadequately the condition of popular feeling. The Improvement Company began to cover all the streets with asphalt, under profitable contract with the City Council, which issued a new loan for the purpose. It built a horse-car line which ran from Purgatory Springs right through the town to

Grigsby's Bluff. It dammed the brook a mile outside of Happy Hollow, forming a lovely lake, which was named Lake Aramink, and from the dam it obtained water-power which not only lighted all Happy Hollow, but supplied force to the woollen mill which the Improvement Company took and equipped with machinery. By the side of the lake the company began construction of a summer hotel, The Aramink House, which was to offer two great attractions in the way of lovely scenery and elegant accommodations such as no other resort in the state could hope to rival.

The great field on the far side of the brook at the lower end of the town was bought and thickly planted with trees and shrubs, and named Happy Hollow Public Garden. After awhile fountains would play there, and swans would float, and pretty pleasure boats would swim, in the brook at the edge of the park.

The old Opera House, absurdly named, was torn down, and upon the site a new and resplendent Academy of Music, rich with blue and gold and red and white interior decorations, was constructed. Dozens of rickety frame buildings on the main street were demolished to make way for the Pelican Arcade and Aramink Row, two blocks of brick buildings six stories high, with plate-glass windows, and supplying places of unsurpassed attractions for retail businesses. The Happy Hollow National Bank began business in its new marble building, with A. J. Pelican for President; and the spring upon Farmer Tulliver's farm at the edge of the town, having been found by Pelican's own chemist to contain health-restoring and life-saving ingredients in very surprising quantities, the farm was bought in for cash by the Improvement Company, and a noble building was put up, right by the spring, and named The Happy Hollow Sanitarium.

Plans were drawn for a new Water Works, which should pipe water from the Wallabout Hills, three miles away, and Pelican began for himself a large and beautiful house right across the street from the house of Mrs. Purvis-Hyde, in that part of the town which was called by Mrs. Purvis-Hyde the West End. With the assistance of the Improvement Company he began a movement to have Happy Hollow made the county town. It was intimated that, in the event of the success of the undertaking, Dr. Bulfinch's school building would be purchased for a fabulous price and torn down, to make way for the finest court-house in the state.

Thus it was unquestionable that Pelican had made Happy Hollow hum, and that the humming would be in a sense, continuous appeared to be assured by the fact that to his own energy Pelican had added that of Elmira Bantam. She was chosen the counsel for the Happy Hollow Improvement Company, and plainly manifested ability to direct all its legal affairs.

Everybody was prosperous, happy, and hopeful; everybody but Felix Acorn, the barber. He did not count for much, but from the beginning his want of faith in A. J. Pelican and the Happy Hollow Improvement Company was complete.

"Mind what I tell you," said he to me one day, in his shop, "no water'll ever run through them waterworks pipes, and there's no medicine in old Tulliver's spring, and the sheriff'll have the Opera House. I'm tired of being imposed on It's all wind. They tell you there's a Goddess of Liberty, but there ain't none; and Robinson Crusoe never lived on no desert island; and Mahomet's coffin never was suspended; and, jest so, Pelican ain't no real capitalist. Stand from under, I say, when I see these goin's on in Happy Hollow."

Chapter VIII

Mrs. Purvis-Hyde's Uplifter

ALL through the months of the autumn
and early winter the streets of Happy Hollow, once so
quiet and dull and empty, were filled with the bustle
and lively movement of A. J. Pelican's great operations. The improved pavements with the horse-car
tracks were going down, and with them the pipes for
the new Water Works, and the buildings which were to
make Happy Hollow beautiful were going up. Wagons
filled with stones and brick and lumber went hither
and thither to supply the needs of the swarming workmen, who dug and sawed and hammered and trowelled ;
and among the other vehicles, in and out and around
·the town, dashed Pelican's own handsome team. In
glossiness of coat and jingle of silver-plated chains, it
really surpassed the hitherto unsurpassed team behind
which Mrs. Purvis-Hyde drove on every fine afternoon.

The boom in Happy Hollow seemed to gain in
vigor and intensity. · Everybody in the town was busy
and cheerful, and confident that he would soon be rich.

Colonel Bantam felt already rich and his friends

thought he showed it in his manner. ⹀ Some of the
stock of the Improvement Company had been given to
him ; but he had sub-
scribed for several
thousand dollars'
worth more, writing

Pelican's own handsome
team.

his name upon the list in a large, bold, rounded hand,
which conveyed the impression of confidence upon the
Colonel's part that he could pay for it, and that the
company's operations would be successful.

He always spoke of his shares as "my blocks of
stock," as if the magnitude of the number held by him
was so great that the shares could hardly be handled
or enumerated without extended subdivision into heaps.

In his demeanor, especially when he had contact
with the plainer people, there was a new touch of
something like haughtiness.   There was an unfamiliar
tendency to reserve.   He was still affable with his
friends, and usually voluble ; but we all noticed that he
held himself straighter, and carried his chin a little
higher, while he had an air of loftiness and grandeur in

his salutation of humble citizens which was in almost painful contrast with his old democratic manner.

This change may have been due in part to the circumstance that the town of Happy Hollow was taking on new dignity, and the Colonel believed it to be his duty as chief magistrate to give official representation of the fact. The increased responsibilities of the office seemed to press upon him. He drew up a plan for a paid fire department, which he urged upon the Town Council, and he addressed that body eloquently upon the necessity that the police force should be increased to two persons. He cherished hope that one day he might have three; and sometimes, in moments of intense mental exhilaration caused by the upward tendency of the value of the Improvement Company's stock, he predicted that the time would come when there would be four men on the force. But he did not advise rash action.

"We are," he said to Spiker, "but in the early dawn of a brighter day for Happy Hollow. When the full glorious noontide of prosperity has filled the town with its radiant splendor, we shall have a force worthy of the place."

For Spiker a larger and better day had come, and I was glad of it, for at heart Spiker was really a good fellow. He was brisker in his manner, and there was an atmosphere of cheeriness and hopefulness about him. It was enough to permit him to seem less worried and mournful that he could now more lightly regard the patronage of the tombstone man and of the storekeeper who owed him hats.

The Improvement Company had in the *National Defender* a vast standing advertisement, inviting persons inhabiting less lovely neighborhoods to come to a town which "to a salubrious climate, a picturesque situation, and extraordinary educational advantages, added uplifting social influences and an atmosphere of refinement and culture." Mrs. Purvis-Hyde no doubt read this advertisement every morning, and found comfort in the reflection that to her and her church-school much of the attractiveness thus referred to was attributable, but the announcement brought more solid comfort to Mr. Spiker in the shape of weekly payments in cash.

Thus it was natural that his views of everything, as they were expressed day by day in the *National Defender*, should have a tone of joyousness, and that his readers should even discern a tendency to greater boldness in the use of metaphor. This poetic inclination may have been due in some measure to the frequent presence in the *Defender* office of Miss Mortimer, who now conducted the Woman's Department with surprising grace; but if Miss Mortimer's restraining influence could have been exerted, I am sure she would have induced Mr. Spiker to make some modification of the suggestion offered by him to the Town Council that, in overcoming a certain difficulty, it should "take the bull by the horns and cut the Gordian knot." Miss Mortimer's taste and intelligence would have saved her from the employment of so odd a figure.

Of course Mr. Spiker's enthusiasm for the town improvements exhausted at an early day the adjectives at his command When he had used all the known superlatives until straining had seriously weakened them, he resorted to double leads for his editorials, and if any other method of expressing almost wild intensity of fervor had been within the compass of metal type and the printers' art, Mr. Spiker would have adopted it.

He was positively feverish with enthusiasm; and particularly for A. J. Pelican. He had compared Pelican during the boom months with nearly all the noted philanthropists and leaders of the race, and he had even gone so far as to suggest that the name of the town might well be changed from Happy Hollow to Peliconia.

It was really surprising to me, unfamiliar with the craft of the journalist, to perceive how Spiker could say the same old things over and over, day after day, in new forms, and always with a bright freshness of manner as if the thoughts had just occurred to him for the first time He never cooled off, he never permitted his enthusiasm to fall below one hundred and fifteen in the shade; he never seemed to have the smallest particle of doubt that what he said was true, and truth in its most important, significant, and weighty form. I know I should have grown tired of hurrahing for Happy Hollow with double leads and inflammatory adjectives twenty-seven days in the month for months at a time. But Spiker kept right at it with unflagging vigor, and on the seventy-fifth morning or the one hundred and fifth morning he seemed as fresh and as highly charged with ardor as ever, and the editorial page of the *Defender* fairly rang with the exciting language that depicted the increased and increasing glories of Happy Hollow.

But always there must be the flavor of bitterness in even the highest of our joys, and Mr. Spiker, with Happy Hollow booming all about him, and his cash advertising steadily increasing, still had trouble. To

all of us members of Mrs. Bantam's family it seemed
odd that every three or four weeks Julie Mortimer
should quietly vanish and remain away for a day or
two. She never told anyone when she was going or
where she was going, but, preparing copy in advance
for the Woman's Department, and taking a satchel in
her hand, she would leave us and return without a
word.

Mrs. Bantam's curiosity fairly burned her soul, but
hinting questions to Julie brought no answer. Really
I felt somewhat curious myself, and Spiker was not
only curious, but anxious. It was clear enough to his
friends that he regarded Julie with warmer feelings
than those of mere admiration, and he showed plainly
that he feared these flittings of the lovely woman had
some relation to her affections. He spoke to me about
it in a serious manner once or twice, and once he tried
to learn if A. J. Pelican knew the secret. Evidently
Pelican did know it, but Pelican's manner of dealing
with anxious inquirers gave evidence of the useless-
ness of endeavoring to sound him. He would tell
nothing.

Mrs. Purvis-Hyde at first inclined to look coldly
upon the effort to lift Happy Hollow toward higher
things. She would not participate in the fiscal operations of the Improvement Company, nor would she
admit that any of the great enterprises proposed by
the company were of an admirable character. She
said plainly to her friends that she thought Pelican a
vulgar adventurer, and that it was really too bad to
have such a person with such a shocking name in-
truding himself upon Happy Hollow, and actually
imitating the practices of members of refined society.

But A J. Pelican was not the man to permit a woman of Mrs. Purvis-Hyde's standing and influence to maintain an unfriendly attitude toward him. All the churches coveted Pelican, but not many Sundays passed before he rented the most expensive pew in the Episcopal Church. It was in the middle aisle, directly opposite Mrs. Purvis-Hyde's pew, and the lady's heart at once softened. When he had given to the church a handsome new altar-cloth the victory was won.

"It is much," she said, "that Mr. Pelican should perceive the influence of altar-cloths upon sound religious practice, but even more that he should turn his back upon the denominations that are around us, and seek the blessings offered by the church."

Mrs. Purvis-Hyde nodded graciously to him after the sermon the first Sunday he sat in his pew, and the next day she purchased for a thousand dollars' worth of the stock of the Improvement Company.

My seat in the church was at the rear, among the humble people, but I was almost certain Pelican went to sleep every Sunday as soon as Dr. Fury's sermon began. He always stood up and sat down with the congregation, but I thought he fumbled in an unfamiliar way with the prayer-book. Mrs. Purvis-Hyde seemed to notice this also, for in response to an eloquent gesture from her, another devoted churchwoman in the pew behind Pelican's found the places for him, and exchanged books with him several times during the service on successive Sundays.

I like people who thoroughly believe in their own things, and maybe this is one of the reasons why I inclined to like Mrs. Purvis-Hyde. She was an Episcopalian in every fibre of her being. The human

race, for her, was divided into two classes: Episcopalians and other people. She did not hate the other
people; she regarded them with pity, excepting when
they presumed to claim that they belonged to churches
and not to mere "sects." She prayed, and perhaps
hoped, for their final salvation, but I found upon enlarged acquaintance with her that whatever hope of
that kind she had rested upon a rather vague notion
that there are uncovenated mercies which might somehow be stretched far and wide enough to let such people into an odd corner of that better world toward
which she and all other sound church-people believed
themselves to be moving, with positive assurance of
getting there.

It might, perhaps, be said of Mrs. Purvis-Hyde that
she sometimes carried her Episcopalianism to extremes.
Dr. Fury had a very disagreeable dog that had actually
bitten several persons, and the discovery was made one
day by a vestryman in Dr. Fury's church that every
one of the victims was a member of one of the sects.
Further inquiry and experiment disclosed the somewhat remarkable fact that this unpleasant animal was
not known even to bark at any member of Dr Fury's
congregation. He never bit an Episcopalian. In speaking of this animosity of the beast for dissenters, Mrs.
Purvis-Hyde, with a smile upon her lips, designated it
as "quaint"; which, indeed, I suppose it was, although
I should never have thought of selecting just that
adjective for application to the case; and Mrs. Purvis-
Hyde, with true earnestness, added that the dog's
behavior was "really an extraordinary manifestation
of discriminating intelligence upon the part of a dumb
animal."

Early in the autumn the members of the Bantam household were invited by Mrs. Purvis-Hyde to attend a conversazione at her house. Mrs. Purvis-Hyde had a purpose to maintain a *salon* in Happy Hollow in which people of culture and talent might meet and have intellectual pleasure. Mr. Spiker, with that tendency to ribald speech which I have often found among journalists, always alluded to Mrs. Purvis-Hyde's conversazioni as "uplifters"; but, as this vulgarity had never reached the ears of Mrs. Purvis-Hyde, Spiker remained upon her list, and he went with us upon this occasion. He wore a suit that fitted him so nicely as to indicate that it had been purchased for cash, and not by barter for nonpareil advertisements and special notices.

Mr. A. J. Pelican was there, shining for the first time in the higher society of Happy Hollow; literally shining, for his evening suit was glossy to the very tip of each swallow-tail, and the shirt-bosom framed by the coat was altogether the most radiant shirt-bosom good society had ever seen in Happy Hollow. Mrs. Purvis-Hyde had taken up A. J. Pelican, and when she took a man up socially his position was fixed.

Rev. Dr. Fury was there, of course. The doctor wore a rigidly exact clerical costume, and had his shirt-collar buttoned behind. Mrs. Purvis-Hyde would not have considered a clergyman sound whose collar was fastened or lapped over in front.

I found Dr. Fury a much more pleasant person than I had thought. He was inclined to jocularity, as so many clergymen are, I suppose as a result of reaction from professional solemnity. Dr. Fury, I was surprised to discover, articulated perfectly in his social speech;

in fact, he talked plainly and well, with an agreeable voice, and I wondered—and I wonder now—why when he had the power to speak intelligibly he exercised it only upon unimportant topics in the drawing-room, and persisted upon being almost unintelligible when he read the sacred Word and preached to sinners.

Dr. Bulfinch had been invited in spite of the fact that he was a Presbyterian. The favor to him was a concession made by Mrs. Purvis-Hyde to culture. Dr. Bulfinch, after Dr. Fury, was altogether the most learned man in the county. He came to the "uplifter" dressed precisely as he dressed for the school-room, excepting that his elbows were not rubbed threadbare, and his black neck-tie was folded with nicer precision.

Colonel and Mrs. Bantam were there, with Ruby Bonner and Julie Mortimer: Ruby in a pretty white dress and blue ribbons, and Julie dressed in canary yellow, looking well with her jet hair and the bright color of her cheeks.

" Perfectly lovely, isn't she?" asked Mr. Spiker of me, as we watched Mrs. Purvis-Hyde introducing her to Dr. Fury.

" Isn't Ruby just sweet?" whispered Mrs. Bantam, as Professor Midges led her to the piano to begin the evening with a song.

Professor Midges, a little man with thin sandy hair and large steel spectacles, was the organist of Dr. Fury's church, and besides being positively trustworthy with reference to the Thirty-nine Articles, he was a good musician, whose taste in accompanying the voice, not less than his orthodoxy, justified Mrs. Purvis-Hyde in bringing him into her charmed circle.

Ruby sang a sweet little love-song or two, and to

9

one man who stood there and listened, that was the rapturous experience of the evening.

When, after a time, Julie came to the piano, and with her deep contralto voice gave another song, all of us were moved.   But Miss Mortimer had more eloquence than she could supply through the medium of melody. She stood by the pier-glass at the end of the room and read one of her own poems, entitled " Longings"; and then, when we were all filled with emotion, she began to recite " The Land o' the Leal."

Before the first verse was ended, Colonel Bantam withdrew his handkerchief from his coat-tail pocket, wheeled half around upon the seat, put one arm over the back of his chair, and yielded himself completely to his feelings.   Dr. Fury wiped his gold spectacles twice, and when the recitation was ended he went across the room and shook hands warmly with the charming woman.   I know Mrs. Purvis-Hyde was filled with regret that Julie was not an Episcopalian.

Then Julie read a portion of one of the " Idylls of the King " with perfect expression, and when she had ended, the Colonel stopped clapping his hands to remark to me :

" That knight-errant business, Professor, really has had an exaggerated valuation put upon it.   No brave man would consent to be nickel-plated and riveted-in before engaging in combat; and, sir, when you go about trying to poke men off of a horse with a pole, it is an abuse of language to characterize the performance with the name of war.   To a genuine soldier · King Arthur and his conflicts seem ridiculous.   A man cannot really fight, sir, with a brass kettle upon his head and his body embedded in hardware.   If you want poetry, very well, but don't honor such a man with the name of warrior."

General conversation followed, and Dr. Fury happening to refer to the suffering of a missionary, a friend of his, in one of the Pacific Islands, the subject of cannibalism was touched upon. Colonel Bantam inquired if anyone present knew of the origin of this dreadful practice:

"The true source of anthropophagy," he said, " is the attractive, perhaps I might say succulent, appearance of infants of the colored races. You have observed, no doubt, Dr. Fury, that the babe of the Ethiopian is not only plump and smooth and unctuous, but that it has precisely the color given by the oven, let us say to roast-pig.   In short, it looks well-done ; and we may be sure, sir, that this resemblance to crustiness, and the consequent suggestion

The source of anthropophagy.

of the presence of stuffing, impelled some hungry savage in the past to begin the practice referred to.   Observe that the colored races alone follow it.   Reason: the Caucasian infant looks under-done."

"I always thought negro babies looked like chocolate," said Mrs. Bantam.

"Very well, Edith," responded the Colonel, "and chocolate also is appetizing.   The barbarian, famished, weak of will, and unrestrained by considerations of morality, was doubly tempted, and he fell."

The talk then tended to drift into ecclesiastical and

theological subjects. Dr. Fury, I remember, looked
pained when he overheard Professor Midges say to
Ruby that he thought Santa Claus was the first bishop
of Cappadocia and one of the Black Letter Saints
But the Doctor soon became involved in a controversy
about the book of Deuteronomy, which not only, before long, engrossed the attention of the whole company, but subsequently spread over the .entire town
and caused much bitter feeling among the people.

The discussion had hardly got fairly under way
before A. J. Pelican interrupted it to ask if Deuteronomy was in the Old Testament or in the New
Testament. I thought he wished to put himself into
the right position to comprehend the argument as it
went along ; but this could hardly have been his purpose, for five minutes later he was fast asleep on the
end of the sofa that was hidden by the piano. Mrs.
Purvis-Hyde, who sat by me, filled with admiration for
the skill and learning displayed by her rector, stopped
listening long enough to say to me that she really did
not care so much about the matter.

"If you have the Apostolic succession all right," she
said, "the rest will take care of itself."

Mrs Bantam, I thought, felt very little interest in the
subject. She sat upon the other side of me, and when
Dr. Fury was quoting a particularly interesting pas-
sage from the Fathers, she whispered to me to notice
the lace on Mrs Purvis-Hyde's dress.

"It didn't cost a cent less than ten dollars a yard,"
she said.

Colonel Bantam never could bear any conversation
which neglected him and forced him to be silent, and
so, at the very first interval in the talk between the

two doctors, the Colonel said to Professor Midges that he always regarded Moses as a narrow man.

"As for his generalship, sir," added the Colonel, "it was deficient in the elementary principles of military science."

When the Professor pressed the Colonel for particulars, the Colonel answered:

"Sir! He should have turned Pharaoh's left. If I had been there I would have outflanked Pharaoh and crossed the Red Sea on pontoons higher up."

Mrs. Purvis-Hyde, returning for a moment to her favorite subject, said to me:

"You know, Mr. Sprat, we have conclusive evidence that the Church is the direct successor of the ancient Jewish Church."

"May I ask what is the evidence?"

"Why, the prescribed limit of punishment among the Jews was forty stripes save one, and we have the Thirty-nine Articles, clearly proving historical continuity; don't you think so?"

I evaded an answer. The thought was new to me and surprising. I felt that I should like to consider it before committing myself.

As the discussion of Deuteronomy proceeded, Dr. Fury became warm and Dr. Bulfinch became warmer. The faces of the two doctors were flushed, and although both men maintained perfect courteousness, they were beginning to treat the subject with some intensity of feeling. All other conversation was suspended while the company hearkened to the doctors, excepting that Professor Midges asked a question which plainly showed that he had never divested himself of the notion, conceived in his youth, that the Pentateuch was one of the five books of Moses.

Mrs. Purvis-Hyde began to look worried as the argument acquired heat, and at last, with no little grace, she interposed and asked the two theologians to suspend it while Ruby sang another pretty song. Then the refreshments were served, and after a while the company parted. Dr. Bulfinch shook hands with Dr. Fury as they went away, but both looked serious, and I felt sure we should hear more of the differences about Deuteronomy.

Spiker walked home with Julie and I took Ruby in my company, quite willing to walk slowly with her and to praise her for the singing she had given us. She was very grateful, and not at all inclined to be vain about her performances.

Chapter IX

The Face at the Window

RUBY BONNER and I had got to be good friends, and my most delightful occupation was to guide her with her studies. She had a good mind and learned rapidly, excepting when she had mathematics. With languages, dead and living, she succeeded fairly well, and although she did one day translate *Virginibus Puerisque* into " And the boys of Virginia," she managed her Latin lessons with some dexterity.

We got along very well together, and she seemed really grateful that I helped her to stow knowledge in her poor little head; but the fear grew upon me that she regarded me as a much older person than I was; and then I thought that the pupil does not often give her warmer feelings to the schoolmaster. One day she said something that showed to me that she had been corresponding with Tom Driggs.

I had never mentioned him to her, because his notion about her future and my notion were violently antagonistic. When I found that Tom Driggs had begun the campaign without waiting for an ally I was startled. Instantly I had a mean curiosity to know how far he had gone, and to know with what sentiments she regarded him. To tell the truth, I could not help feeling bitterly jealous, and not only jealous, but much afraid lest the absent lover, in the intervals of his operations with soap, might indeed succeed in impressing this fairy of a girl with an exaggerated idea of his value.

Perhaps it was not wise or right for me to venture to remonstrate with Ruby about her correspondence with Thomas, but I did so, upon the ground that a young girl in her position must needs be very careful in matters of such a kind.

But at this she took fire, and, looking at me with her cheeks hot, informed me that she did not need a counsellor in that business; that she was well able to take care of herself, and that to Tom Driggs, one of her oldest friends, she should write very, very often, and she hoped he would answer every one of her letters.

I was much abashed, and, indeed, stricken at the heart, by the repulse she had given me; and I suppose my face showed the dejection of my mind; for a moment later, falling into her chair and burying her face in her hands, which rested upon her lesson-book on the table, she began to sob and say:

"Oh, why am I left alone? How terrible it is to be all alone!"

Poor child! I had the heartache for her at once. And so I tried to comfort her. I asked her to forgive me for speaking to her as I had done. That I meant well. That I thought she might need and care to have a word of counsel. That I was her friend, and would do anything that she might be happy. And so then she lifted her head and dried her eyes, and gave me her hand while she said:

"And you are my kind friend! You have done so much for me! Forget that I spoke so unkindly to you, and believe me I am not ungrateful for all your goodness."

Then, withdrawing her hand, she went away, and I sat there in that study-room a long, long time, thinking of her, and looking at the book she had left there, and feeling hunger for her, and I fear hatred for Tom Driggs.

One of the strangest things in life, surely, is what is called coincidence; but I am not clear it is just by chance that events so often come, as it were, in groups. More than likely there is some mysterious faculty in the human mind which permits one will to operate upon another, so that the unspoken thought may exert influence that impels another person to action.

It was very odd indeed that the incident of which I am about to tell should have presented itself upon the very next night after Ruby alluded to the fact that she had been deserted by her parents. Did that utterance of hers, I wonder, obtain its impulse from the mind of one whom she did not see and who was not near to her?

Her outburst of anger, followed by grief, occurred upon Saturday night. On Sunday afternoon we all went up to Dr. Fury's Sunday-school, where A. J. Pelican, upon the earnest entreaty of the Doctor and Mrs. Purvis-Hyde, was to address the children. A. J. Pelican's handsome equipage, with a liveried driver, dashed up to the front of the church at half-past two, and for fifteen or twenty minutes Mr. Pelican spoke in

quite an agreeable manner. His argument was intended to impress the infant mind with a sense of the
utter worthlessness of riches, and no doubt it convinced every one of tender years. Spiker and Colonel
Bantam would hardly have cared for it; and Mrs.
Purvis-Hyde probably accepted the theory only in a
loose general way, without caring to have it applied
personally and pressed home too closely. Little Sunday-school folks must sometimes be puzzled as they
find one kind of doctrine coming to their ears while
another kind is plainly presented to their eyes.

That night, after tea, Mrs. Bantam and Elmira and
Julie and Ruby and I were sitting in Mrs. Bantam's
front parlor, reading and chatting. The four women
were gathered about the table whereon the lighted
lamp stood beside the huge and somewhat rusty family
Bible. I sat alone upon the sofa at the back of the
room, and, happening to look at the front window,
which had the outside shutters open and the curtain
raised, I saw a human face almost pressed against the
pane.

The sight startled me; but I said nothing and did
not move. The face was withdrawn, but at once it
reappeared, and it seemed to me to be the face of a
woman. I waited until it vanished again, and then
quietly withdrew from the room.

Picking up a heavy cane in the hallway, I entered
the dining-room, softly opened the door to the side
porch and went out.

It was a black night; there were no stars; the wind
blew cold and damp, rustling the dead leaves upon the
grass and whistling through the bare limbs of the trees
with a doleful sound. I am not a coward, but the

gloom and the soughing of the wind, and the grim, silent loneliness of the garden filled me with a kind of shivering dread.

Who could the person be that would come prowling about our house in such a night? And a woman, too! For it was a woman. As I reached the corner of the house I saw her plainly by the light of the lamp in the room. She could not see into the window without holding the sill and lifting herself upon her tip-toes; and, after looking for a minute at a time, the effort tired her, and she would release her hold and rest.

I turned the corner and said to her in a low voice, for I feared to alarm the people in the parlor:

" What are you doing there?"

She turned a frightened face to me for an instant, and then started rapidly toward the gate.

I followed her and took hold of her arm Then she stopped, and speaking quietly, for she too was unwilling to be heard in the house, she said:

" Oh, please let me go, sir! Please do not hurt me. I meant no harm "

I was not satisfied. She must have had a purpose in coming there. How could I tell that she was not the companion of criminals, for whom she was examining the premises.

" No," I said. " I will not let you go until you tell me plainly what you are doing here?"

She began to cry and to tremble violently.

" I must not stand here," she said; " they will see me. Do not let anyone see me. Oh, will you not let me go?" and she fairly pulled me over toward the side porch, where the beam of light from the window could not reach her.

I said to her that I wished her no harm, but her conduct was suspicious and alarming, and she must either explain it in a satisfactory manner or be given into custody. She hesitated, and then asked me:

"Do you live here, sir?   And what is your name?"

I gave her my name and told her who I was.

She sat down upon the

edge of the porch, and as I released her arm she cried bitterly, and said:

"I am Ruby Bonner's mother."

That was enough; she need have said no more. I understood the matter perfectly; and I pitied the poor creature as she sat there in the darkness sobbing. I should have been far from sorry if she had risen and gone away without speaking again. She knew that I had heard of her, and that she need not tell her story; but she had hunger in her heart which she would satisfy, and now she was not sorry I had come to her.

This was once her home, she said; a happy home. She came to it as a bride with a beloved husband; and it was she who had made all this garden and planted some of these trees; and the time was when she sat in that parlor and laughed and sang, and went from room to room and out upon this very porch and along the garden-walks, full of joy in life and in her love and in her little children

But now the door was shut upon her for ever. The heart of the man she had sinned against was hard against her. One child was in the other world; the other must think of her with scorn and hate. All the old happiness was dead, and life was torment; the memory of the past was full of the horror of remorse; the future, of desolation. But sometimes, when remorse became too fierce and bitter, and life seemed intolerable, she fled from the city and came back here in the night to look at the places where love used to be; to walk the old paths, to gaze at the windows which once shut in her happiness, as now they shut it out; to try to filch from the past some atom of peace that could comfort her in her black misery; and then —and then—if she could only chance to see Ruby!

"I did see her," she said, with hysterical exultation. "I saw her. I saw her side-face. May I go again to the window and have one more look? I will do no harm. Please let me see her once again?"

How could such a request be denied? And while she strained her fingers upon the window-sill and I looked at her, I had for the first time in my life a glimpse of the nature of that awful law of retribution. The sin was alluring, and all the peril and the punishment were hidden. But now! How frightful the anguish that racked the sinning soul!

She came back to me. She was glad to have some one to whom she could talk of Ruby.

"Is she a good girl? Does she go to church? Is there anyone to warn her of the wickedness that is in the world? Are her eyes blue, like mine? I could see her sweet hair. It is golden, as mine was—when —when—I was married. Does she ever speak of her mother? Not to you, sir, of course, but to Mrs. Bantam? Oh, I wonder, I wonder if she hates me. She must hate me. I hate myself. If she is a good girl she ought to hate me, oughtn't she?

"But I would give my life for her. I would willingly die now if she would come out and put her arms about me and kiss me. That cannot be, can it? I am too wicked for her to touch. You do not know how vile I am; but once I was good like Ruby. It is bitter to think how, long ago, I sat upon this very porch and—my—husband was here; and Ruby and my other dear little girl played with us and laughed, and we were so happy. I have crept in here in the night sometimes and sat on one of these chairs, and thought of it all until I felt that I would shriek and beat in the door of my home; mine; mine in the old days! And now—!"

She rose and stood with her arms outstretched, and as in the gloom her form was dimly outlined against the white stuccoed wall of the house, there was a startling suggestion of crucifixion.

"I wish God would take my life!" she exclaimed

passionately. "I wish he would strike me dead, here;
right here, now!"

There was a wail of despair in her voice. She made
as though she would rend her garments; she seemed
as if she could hardly restrain herself from screaming.

Then she went down on the floor in a heap and
grovelled there.

"Come here!" she said; and she seized my hand
and kissed it again and again. Then she thrust it
away and said :

"Go and put them on Ruby's cheek, on her head,
on her shoulders—my kisses!"

She rose and came down the steps, and turned to
go along the gravel-path.

"Where are you going?" I asked.

"Where? Back to the city; back to the hell prepared for such as I am," and she started toward the
gate.

I would have stopped her, I felt so great pity for
her, but she fled through the gate and down the street,
and was gone.

I stood there for a few moments, with my hand that
she had kissed fast clenched as though it held something sacred. I hardly knew what to do. I was so
much agitated (was it for Ruby's sake or for her
mother's?) that I actually hesitated to re-enter the
house. But I went in softly, and as I came into the
brilliant light of the parlor, the four women were
laughing heartily at some jest of Julie's They seemed
hardly to notice my incoming; but I went over and
laid my hand on Ruby's head, instantly apologizing
for it as though the thing had been done by accident.

Ruby turned and looked at me.

"What is it, Mr. Sprat?" she asked.

"Oh, nothing! I am weary; that is all." And so then she and her companions turned again to their own matters and I sat upon the sofa; and while I saw the form of the fair girl before me, my mind was filled with the image of the woman, so near to her, who was flying in the darkness to the misery with which she had enshrouded her life.

Chapter X

An Adventure in the Hills.

Through all the duties of the day that followed my adventure in the garden I carried with me sad and troubled thoughts of that poor creature I had met there; and sometimes it seemed to me as if, even in this world, true repentance should win a larger measure of forgiveness.

When school was done, and Dr. Bulfinch went up into his study to perform his daily task of retribution to his young offenders, I sauntered homeward, and when I reached the bridge athwart the brook I crossed so often, I stopped, and, leaning upon the low parapet, gazed downward upon the rushing yellow water. It seemed like a living thing urged by a strong, passionate impulse to hurry toward a destination. And as I looked at it swirling against the stone piers, and eddying and foaming about them, and then plunging onward as if it could not tarry even for a moment, I said to myself, "It is eager to get home again. In the ocean from which it came it will find cleansing and peace."

And so the fancy came to me and pressed strongly upon me that in like circuit, perhaps, the human soul that comes from God, and is perturbed by passions of the earthly life and soiled by its sinfulness, will rush back to its source, and in that bosom have purification and perfect rest. All things come out from him; all things return to him. There is a way, surely, even for the stained soul of that forlorn and broken-hearted mother to reach clear to him whose very nature is love.

While I mused, half-forgetting all else, some one came near with light step, and before I could turn about Ruby's sweet voice greeted me. She, too, came from school, and she stopped beside me, laying her books upon the parapet, and together we looked at the flowing stream.

"It seems so happy," she said, "as if it would fairly dance with joy;" and I did not tell her that it conveyed to me rather the idea of passionate eagerness. The things we see respond to our own feelings, and I would not sadden her if she could perceive joyfulness in that swift rush of the waters.

We began to walk homeward together, and after some idle talk, she looked full away from me and said:

"Why did you lay your hand upon my head last night?"

I pretended that I did not recall the act.

"I know you did not do it by accident, although you would have had me think so. You meant something by it."

I tried to put the question by, but she was persistent.

"You were out of the room, and I thought you went out of the house, and when you came in you looked so dreadfully and put your hand upon my head. Was anyone there? tell me truly," and she turned her face and her blue eyes looked fairly at me.

I could not tell her the truth; I dare not be false; and as I must answer, I said:

"Won't you believe it was an accident?"

"You will not say so, now. You know it was not."

"It was an act of blessing," I said.

"From whom?" she asked.

"From me, if you will. I can say no more."

She was angry at me, and in her eyes shone as much fire as those lovely eyes could command. She made as though she would walk faster than I did, keeping a distance ahead of me. Thus we went through the little park and came to the street, when she diminished her pace until we were together, and she smiled gravely at me and said:

"I should not have asked you such a question. I will believe you wanted me to have a blessing."

"Blessing on blessing," I answered. "May there be nothing else in life for you."

So we came to our home.

As the days of the wintertime went by she seemed with strange suddenness to come to full womanliness. I had never thought of her as a child; but she did have girlish ways when first I knew her, and at the beginning her methods with her studies, as I have said, were much more childish than her years

But all this changed before the year was out, and long before the new year had rolled far around she had acquired dignity of manner and self-confidence with her studies which warned me that her girlhood was past. With this new exaltation of womanhood there

came a reserve of manner which seemed to separate
me from her more than had been the custom, and this
I grieved over, although I knew it to be inevitable and
necessary. But still she was cordial and gracious
with me, and she did not fail to accept my help when
there was difficulty in her lessons.

I could not doubt the nature of my feelings for her,
and I found new grace in her now that both mind and
body had attained to riper loveliness. I fully perceived
the advantages of propinquity. How much that counts
for in such matters! Nearly every Sunday I walked
to church with her, sometimes accompanied also by
Aunty Bantam, whose presence upon these occasions
always vexed me ; and usually I sat by Ruby's side
while Dr. Fury conducted the services and preached.

Often there was but one prayer-book for both of us,
and so she held one corner of it and I the other while
we made the responses or sang the canticles. The
worship at such times had great fervency for me. Professor Midges's choir, like many other choirs, in singing
the *Te Deum* always sang of " anguls and archanguls,"
and of the " sharpnuss of" death, just as in the hymns
it sang of "immortul" life, and " brightnuss," and
" Edun," and " heavun," and of the " evul " that is
" with us day by day." Ruby was not critical, and she
liked to sing and I loved to hear her sing, and so we
both had joyfulness, in spite of the slovenliness of the
choir.

Many, many times during Dr. Fury's drowsy ser-
mons have I looked from the corner of my eye upon
her sweet profile, her chin slightly uplifted as she
watched the preacher, her eyes wide open, as if she
were trying to understand him, and with the tender

bloom upon her cheeks. She had a straight little nose, delicately cut, and the prettiest I have ever seen ; so her profile was almost more beautiful than her full face.

Long ago she went away from me into the mystery-land, and left me to awful silence and blinding tears ; and, strange to say, the one strongest memory of her appearance that stays with me is that of her face as she sat by me in the church.

Later in the winter Mrs. Purvis-Hyde wished to have some private theatricals as a help to the intellectual elevation of her friends, and she persuaded Julie and Ruby to participate in them. Both did so with reluctance, for both desired to have no further relation of any kind with the actors' art; but they were good-natured, and Mrs. Purvis-Hyde, now so urgent, had been kind to them ; and so we had a pretty little play in Mrs. Purvis-Hyde's parlor.

Few but our friends were there, and there were good acting and good fun.

The drama was named "Home Rule"; and Ruby was the heroine, a wife whose husband I represented, while Julie was the wife's mother. It was much to me even to pretend that I was the husband of so sweet a girl ; and willingly I bore with the laughter of the players at my awkwardness and at the ill-grace of my action, so strongly emphasized by the skill of my companions, if I might play such a part under such circumstances.

The name of the husband in the play was Henry, and it was a delight to me during the rehearsals and at the performance to have Ruby take my hand, or put her hand upon my shoulder, and in tender tones address me by my own first name.

I remember how she looked upon the night when
we played the drama before the company. She wore
a curious gown of silk, in which golden tints shim-
mered and glanced among the brown; there was a
fluff of soft lace about the neck, and the bodice was
cut in such a way as to give to the robe a quaint old-
fashioned look. Her rich and splendid hair, dressed
by Julie, was twisted up into a knot and crowned by a
comb so oddly set as to complete the suggestion of
the olden time that her dress had supplied, and which
made her beauty glorious.

When she came down the stairs looking like a goddess, and greeted me as I stood there behind the curtain
waiting nervously for the play to begin, I felt some
sinking of the heart, "for how," I said to myself,
"shall such a homely, awkward, unworthy creature as
I ever dare to try to win that perfectly lovely woman?"
It seemed impossible then, and actually for a moment
or two the girl I had helped with her lessons appeared
to have belonged to a time long past.

But the goddess had no consciousness of her loveliness or of the shivering awe that had overcrept her
old tutor, for she greeted me with sweet and gentle
kindness, and she said she was glad to be in the play
with me because she had never acted before with a
man who was her friend.

Of course the performance gave delight to those who
were so fortunate as to have been Mrs. Purvis-Hyde's
guests. When Ruby first came on the stage there was
an involuntary exclamation from the audience, which
was the highest tribute to her beauty; and when the
play was ended Professor Midges came to me and said
that if Mrs. Purvis-Hyde would drop Deuteronomy

out of her *salon* for good and all, and take up Ruby
Bonner as a regular thing, she would occupy a first
place among philanthropists.

Well, the reason why I have told of the first acting
of the play is that the second acting was followed by a
notable adventure which might have brought sad consequences to our household. For it was inevitable that
so sweet a play with so sweet an actress should be
played again.

Among the guests was Mrs. L. Addison Merwyn,
wife of the celebrated city banker, whose country-seat
was just six miles across the hills from Happy Hollow.
Mrs. L. Addison Merwyn was a person who gave tone
to things just as Mrs. Purvis-Hyde did; but I have a
notion that there was an intensity and vigor about
the tone imparted to anything by Mrs. L. Addison
Merwyn which were greater than any quality that
could be found in the tone conveyed by Mrs. Purvis-
Hyde.

Mrs. L. Addison Merwyn was very rich and very
grand, and she treated me, when I was introduced to
her, with precisely that degree of courtesy which I
should imagine she would have thought due to a poor
young schoolmaster. She was gracious, even kind;
but she gave the impression at once that there was
distance between us. Actually I felt that there was
vast distance.

But I could not refuse when, after the play was over,
she urged us to repeat it a fortnight later at Meadowbrook, the noble home to which L. Addison Merwyn
returned day by day when he laid aside his gigantic
financial operations and sought repose. Mrs. Purvis-
Hyde was eager to have us go, and Julie and Ruby

were willing to go, and it would have been graceless for such an one as I to withhold consent.

And so it was arranged that Mrs. Purvis-Hyde should carry Mrs. Bantam with her upon the appointed evening, and that Julie should go with them, while Ruby and I should drive over in the buggy offered for the purpose by the kind-hearted A. J. Pelican.

The carriage of Mrs. Purvis-Hyde took the road right up the narrow valley or gorge that leads away from Happy Hollow to the outer world; but there was a way I liked better, for it was longer and lonelier, and there was a lovely view we should see in the twilight hour of the day.

On the hillside road.

This road ran slanting up the side of the highest of the hills that encircled the village, and it lay beneath the great trees, leafless, but with thick-clustered branches overhead, so that even in the light of the ending day there was gloominess not present in the open country.

The air was cold, but there were warm wraps in the buggy, and so we started up the hillside, soon reach-

ing an elevation from which we could look down upon
the houses and some of the movements of the life of
the village, and upon the lights which had begun to
gleam from the windows of the buildings.

For myself, I should have been content if the twilight could have lingered for hours, and if we should
not have reached the home of Mrs. L. Addison Merwyn until it ended. I was happy, and I think Ruby
was happy, for she talked with freedom and her spirits
seemed high.

Early in the journey I thought to be artful, and to
try her by praising Tom Driggs.

"But you were ahead of him in college," she said.

Then I contended (a mere pretence, I fear; so that
she might say even sweeter words of praise) that the
men of quickest minds are not always the ablest, and
so I took poor old Tom's part, with malice in my
heart for him; and she ended it all in a woman's way
by saying:

"He isn't handsome. I will write to him no more.
How good you must be," and she looked at me, "to
praise Tom Driggs to me!"

That seemed a significant thing for her to say, though
the full force of it did not come to me until afterward,
for my mind was in a kind of glow which made clear
perception difficult.

"If to be handsome," I said, "is to find favor, how
little shall I find?"

"But to be wise is better," she said, and then she
laughed a little bit, as if she saw that she had not been
wholly complimentary.

"Yes, to be wise! But who is wise?" said I.

"You are," she said impetuously, and making as

though she were half in fun. "Your knowledge is so great that sometimes it frightens me."

"I feel stupid and foolish," I answered, "when you talk in that way. Let me tell what I think of myself. I had a strange dream a few nights ago. It seemed to me that I took off my head and placed it upon a table. There was a small round bald place in the top, with a hole in it. I thought that I put my eye to the hole and looked in. The inside of the head contained only dust and cobwebs and a few stray feathers."

She laughed prettily and answered:

"But I can look into it without going to sleep, and I see there wisdom and—and goodness."

This praise should have pleased me, but in truth it made me feel half ashamed of the ignorance that I knew should be attributed to me, and of my deceitfulness in leading her to speak as she had done of Tom Driggs. More than all, the thought came to me, and brought a kind of torment, that if her feelings for me had been such as I wished them to be, she would not have praised me to my face; and then it seemed to me again that she must regard me only as a father or an elder brother. I resolved mentally to consider further, when I should be alone, the precise bearing and meaning of her talk upon our relations with one another.

Then I led her to speak of her life among the strolling players, of which, indeed, she had said little to me or to anyone in our house.

I remembered afterward that as she began to tell of her wanderings we came to a place just beyond Isaac Williams's house, where the road upon a level stretch was intersected by the brook through which we must drive, the bottom of the stream being rough with stones. It is the same brook that, far below this level, rushes through the town ; and as our horse waded into it, the water, still tawny from the washings of a recent storm, ran swiftly, but shallow, so that we gave no thought to it while we passed.

I did not learn from Ruby just how she began to act upon the stage. I guess her mother had to do with it, and this was why Ruby was silent upon that part of the matter. But she did tell me that A. J. Pelican and her father had been at school together in the same town, and because of this she had come under his direction, and he had cared for her.

"That horrid life!" she said. "That horrid play! It was never less than dreadful for me to stand upon the stage and to be stared at by the people in the audience. How I hated it, Mr. Sprat! But the applause was sweet to me sometimes. I could not help liking that, could I? Don't you think every one likes to be praised?"

"Absolutely every one likes praise. To be thought well of is almost the very strongest craving of human nature."

"Yes, and while I did not care for the thing I had to do, it was something, wasn't it, if when I must do it, I found I could do it well? The people about me were vulgar, but they were always kind to me ; and that was much, for it was a rough life, Mr. Sprat, going about from town to town, sometimes in crazy vehicles, and always staying at forlorn hotels. I shrank from the people who would look at me, often rudely, on the stage and off of the stage. It would all have been insupportable but for Julie. How I love her! I owe so much to her. I love her dearly."

"She deserves such love," I said.

"Do you notice, Mr. Sprat—or ought I to say it to you?—that Mr. Spiker admires Julie very, very much? Have you noticed that?"

"I do hope," she continued, "that he will just admire her, and stop there; but I don't see how anyone can help worshiping her, she is so lovely and good."

"Mr. Spiker is a very worthy man; worthy of a good woman," I ventured to say in behalf of my friend the editor.

"But Julie won't have him," said Ruby, very positively.

"Do you think that?"

"She will never marry; never! Marriage is so terrible. She is too good for any man. She and I will stay single all our lives, all! And after a while dear father will come back and live with us, and love me, and we will be happy."

"But there are many happy marriages," I said.

"There will be none for me. I have made up my mind," and she spoke with an air of strong determination. "But you will marry," she continued. "Men can always look and pick and choose, while the women must remain silent. It could be no other way, but do you think it is quite fair?"

"I will be single, too," I said, "unless I could get a woman I should much love."

"You will find her," she answered; "and some day you will be professor in a college, and you will write a book. How glad I shall be to read it, and how proud I shall be to say that I know the author, and that he is my friend!"

"By that time," I said, "you will be married to a rich man."

"I hate rich people. Never, never, could I marry anyone I did not dearly love. Far rather would I have a poor man who should love me so, and then I should be willing to die for him. But if dear father does not come, I must earn my living, Mr. Sprat, and what am I to do? I might sing, but there is small recompense for that. I am too stupid, as you know, to be a governess, or to teach school; perhaps Julie and I can join together and manage some little business; she is so bright and quick. I will do anything but go back to the stage again."

Then she fell silent for a time, and suddenly she said, with a tearful voice:

"Oh, Mr. Sprat, it is too hard to be dependent and helpless as I am! I wish, I wish you could tell me what to do."

I thought I could tell her a way out of her difficulty, in which I should prove her helper, but just then we came to Meadowbrook, and dismounting, entered the brilliantly lighted and splendidly decorated hall of L Addison Merwyn, Esq.

It is useless to tell of the play and the noble company that witnessed it; of the applause and admiration for Ruby, and of the eagerness of certain of the young gentlemen to be introduced to her.

When it was all over and we wrapped ourselves for our homeward journey, Mrs. L. Addison Merwyn gave me a limp hand, and said with a smile which was exactly of the kind that was fitting for a poor young schoolmaster:

"It was delightful, Mr.—ah—Sprat; *so* delightful,

and we are all so much obliged, and I do hope we shall see you again."

And L. Addison Merwyn himself just smiled and smiled and bowed and said nothing as we took our leave.

The night seemed very dark as, with Ruby beside me in the buggy, we followed Mrs. Purvis-Hyde's carriage along the curving sweep of the driveway in front of Mr. Merwyn's house, and then, through the wide gateway, came out upon the road.

The temptation was strong upon me to go homeward by the way we came, for the hour was not late, and as I could without difficulty perceive the white surface of the road, I felt sure I should have no trouble.

Ruby was not unwilling, and so, when we came to where the light shone in front of the Barley Sheaf Inn, we turned to the right, and permitted Mrs. Purvis-Hyde and our friends to go on without us.

Strangely, I had not thought of the thick-set trees that overhung the way further down, all along the windings of the hill which we must traverse for several miles of our journey. Thus presently I found, as we came within the woods, that I could no longer see the roadway. I had then an impulse to turn back ; but this seemed not brave, and while I considered it, and Ruby and I talked together, we came to a part of the road where I felt sure there was an unguarded steep descent upon one side. Then I felt really afraid to try to turn the horse lest we should be dashed over the precipice.

I drove very slowly, and leaned far forward, trying to peer into the darkness, stopping for a moment now and then that I might be sure. My anxiety was so

manifest, I suppose, that Ruby all at once became con-
scious of our peril, and she ceased talking.

I knew that safety lay in driving as closely as could
be to the hillside that towered above us to the left;
but this was not visible, and at last I proposed to Ruby
that I should descend from the carriage and lead the
horse. This seemed to terrify her, for she clung to
my arm and begged me not to leave her. I tried to
calm her fear, but at last I told her that I could not
any longer risk her safety by remaining in the buggy.
Thereupon she insisted that she too would get out and
walk with me.

I could not refuse this, for she would suffer no hurt;
and stopping the horse, I descended to the road, and
then helped her to alight.

While we were standing there, the sound of thunder
was heard, and I knew we should be fortunate to reach
home before the storm should break.

She held my arm very tightly as we walked far upon
the inner side of the road, I leading the horse by his
bridle. I spoke only to cheer and to encourage her,
and we seemed to be going bravely upon our journey,
when suddenly the storm broke.

Then I put her again in the carriage, and covering
her from the rain as well as I could, I threw the horse's
blanket over my shoulders, and went on through the
pouring rain, leading the horse along the way, which
soon was carrying a swift stream of water in the gutter
by its side.

Thus we went on in silence for half an hour, I think,
the storm raging about us, the rain descending in a
deluge, the wind roaring through the trees when the
noise was not smothered by the thunder-crashes. The

lightning-flashes sometimes, through the interlocking branches of the trees above us, showed dimly the path on which we went, and I could see, if I had not felt, that I walked amid mud and water.

After awhile we came out upon a level open place where the road could be discerned, and then for the first time I remembered that we must ford again the creek that we had crossed earlier in the evening.

As I got into the carriage I thought that the stream must be somewhat swollen by the rain; but I had had small experience with mountain torrents, and had I considered the matter I should not have believed that in so short a time the fording could have become dangerous.

I spoke to Ruby, as I knew we must have come near to the brook, and she answered with courageous words, but as again she held to my arm I felt that she was trembling.

Even then I had an impulse to turn back, and I would have done so had I known there was danger in the stream; but to return along that perilous hillside seemed then so dreadful that I thought we should be safe in going on.

The horse stopped, and I knew we had come to the verge of the stream, for we could hear the rush of water above the noise made by the falling rain. But I took the whip in my hand and strongly urged him on, and with a kind of a plunge he dashed into the current.

Before I could frame a thought the wild rushing torrent swirled the carriage around and overturned it, and I found myself with Ruby clinging to me in the stream.

I did have an instinct to hold to her, and with the

WRECKED!

swiftness of light, in inconceivable tumult, we were swept along and violently flung against a tree that had fallen half across the stream. This I seized and contrived to hold, finding footing upon the stones at the bottom of the creek, and by mighty effort I placed Ruby upon the trunk of the prostrate tree.

I tried to speak to her, but she did not answer, and so I knew that fright or collision with the tree had deprived her of sensibility.

It was a desperate situation, and standing there in the water, which I knew was rising, holding her above it by exertion which called for all my strength, I was bewildered and fearful. What to do I could not imagine. I was afraid to move to right or left lest I should lose my foothold.

But when the lightning flashed again I perceived that we were indeed but a few feet from the shore, and so, then, taking her in my arms, I dashed in the direction I knew to be right and got safely upon dry ground with my burden, on the side of the creek toward home.

I found afterward that the horse was drowned and the buggy literally torn to pieces. Ruby and I had a marvellous deliverance from a dreadful death.

To lay her upon the drenched ground was necessary, so that I could gather her up into my arms in such a manner that I could carry her. But whither should I carry her? What should I do? Both of us had all our clothing wet. I had not strength enough even under better conditions to carry her to her home, and my mind was half distracted, so that I could not employ my judgment clearly.

Perhaps she was dead; and I trembled as I took

11

her hand and found that the pulse was beating. Then suddenly I remembered that in the early evening we passed the house of Isaac Williams, the laborer, just before we came to the ford, and so with a flush of joy in my heart I lifted Ruby and walked with her down the road.

I was almost exhausted when I saw a light in a window just off of the road a little way ahead of me. But I summoned my spirit to further effort, and at last, pushing through the whitewashed gate up to the steps, I kicked open the door, and, putting Ruby upon the floor, fell over beside her.

Our entrance in such a fashion could not but startle the solitary inmate of the room, Mrs. Williams. She was badly frightened; but I knew her, and in a moment she knelt by Ruby's side with me, while I told her what had happened. Together we lifted the insensible girl and carried her to another room, where we tried to revive her. She was bruised about her arms, but not badly hurt, and while we dealt with her, consciousness began to return. Before she was fully restored she murmured "Mamma" once, and that seemed very, very sad to me; and then she exclaimed "Oh, save me, Henry!" and at last she opened her eyes.

Mrs. Williams promised that she would give dry clothing of her own to Ruby and then put her to bed, whilst I trudged on to Happy Hollow for help to bring her home.

With this intent I went to the outer room, and as I opened and closed the door, I saw, sitting by the fireplace in which a great fire of wood burned and roared, the figure of a man. He sat with his back to me, and I thought it was Dr. Bulfinch. I had upon my lips an exclamation of astonishment half uttered, when the man turned his head, the palms of his hands still held to the fire, and I saw that he was Simon Bulfinch.

I think I would rather have met almost any other man in the world at that place at that time.

Evidently he too had sought the house as a refuge from the storm. But upon what errand was this man out upon the mountain-road so late at night?

He knew me, and that evil smile came upon his face with the look of recognition. He did not rise, but turning again to the fire, he said quietly:

"How is she, Sprat?"

I knew then either that he must have seen me enter the house or that he had been listening at the door between the rooms. I thought it better, at first, not to answer him. But then, still without facing me, he demanded in an angry tone:

"Tell me at once, is she hurt?"

"Of whom are you speaking?" I said, concluding that I could not remain silent.

He arose and wheeled about and looking savagely at me, kicked his chair aside, saying:

"Boy, don't attempt any insolence with me!"

Then he strode forward, and actually made a movement to push me aside.

"Where are you going?" I asked, stepping before him and barring the way. It was manifest that he intended to enter the room where Ruby was.

He looked at me with mingled scorn and anger, his wicked eyes flashing, while his lips curled into a bitter smile, as he said:

"I must give an account to you, must I?"

"You must," I said, firmly.

No doubt I presented a forlorn spectacle, standing there hatless, my hair dishevelled, my mud-bespattered clothing wet and torn and disordered.

For a moment he hesitated. Then dashing at me, and striking me roughly with his open hand, he exclaimed:

"Get out of the way, you young fool!"

He had his hand upon the door before I could recover myself, but I would rather have given my life than that he should have entered that room, or that Ruby should have seen him, in or out of the room.

I threw myself upon him and he grappled with me. He was a powerful man, but I was younger, and I had not lost the skill as a wrestler that I had at school. He held me fast, and was no mean antagonist even for an expert at wrestling, and tired and forlorn as I was I realized that I had not an easy task upon me. But the horror of the thought that he should encounter that innocent girl to whom already he had wrought so much harm, gave me power, and soon I flung him on the floor and held him there.

He cursed me bitterly, and struck me with his clenched hands and strove to kick me; but I was his master, and when his struggles lost their violence I pushed him to the front door, and, opening it, I thrust him out as if he had been a venomous beast, and then closed the door and locked it.

I looked for him to return and try to enter that he might assail me again; but I saw him no more. In his heart he was a coward.

Then in a moment or two Mrs. Williams came out from the inner room, and I saw upon her face the token that she knew what had happened. Had Simon

Bulfinch had a habit of coming to her house? But she spoke not of him nor of the contest that she may have seen through the partly open door; for almost before she got into the room Ruby appeared also, dressed in strange garments, and with her face as white as paper.

What should we do now? I could not go to town for help and leave her in that house. Williams was away from home, and there was no one to send upon the errand. If we should remain there all night I should require other clothing also, and Ruby's friends would be much alarmed for her. While I considered these things and thought what was best to do, Ruby came to me and said:

"Oh, take me home! I must go home. Do not let me stay here."

Then she put her hand upon my arm, and for the first time, it seemed, realizing my condition, she added:

"We must not stop. You will die of wet and cold. Come, dear Mr. Sprat. Oh, come and let us leave at once."

"But, Ruby," I said, "the way is long and the road is flooded. There are two miles to town."

"I can walk," she said eagerly. "I am perfectly well. No harm can come to me—while you are with me," and she dropped her eyelids.

"We will go," I said, and seeking from Mrs. Williams a stout cudgel, "for Simon may waylay us," I thought, we bade farewell to Mrs. Williams and went out.

The rain had ended, but the sky was black with clouds, and the roaring of the brook could be plainly heard—that brook which had worked such havoc for us.

Ruby put her arm in mine, not caring for the wet sleeve, and clinging to me, we began the journey. For a time she was silent, but at last she said:

"And did you carry me?"

"Oh, yes," I answered, "I feared that you were much hurt."

"My father will love you for it," she said. "You saved my life."

And then we tramped along through the darkness, until presently, far off down the hillside and across the valley, there was a glimmer of lights, and I knew that we were safe, though the way still was long.

"It is Happy Hollow," I said, pointing to the lights.

Then she fell to weeping, and I heard her say "that dreadful man!" and I was sure she knew of my struggle in the Williams's house and who it was I wrestled with.

"It was brave and noble of you," she said through her tears; and while she spoke a carriage suddenly came upon us and some one called. It was Colonel Bantam, and Spiker was with him. They had come out to look for us. How glad they were to find us can be imagined.

We told them of our adventure in the brook, when we had put Ruby on the seat with the Colonel and I had climbed in by the side of Spiker, who drove the horses; but neither of us said aught of Simon Bulfinch.

Thus we came home, and when the welcomes from Mrs. Bantam and Julie and Elmira were ended, Ruby turned to me and said:

"Good night, my dear friend," and passed up the stairs with her aunt and Julie.

I would have gone to my room at once, for I was indeed quite ill, but Colonel Bantam would not let me go until, placing his hand upon my shoulder and assuming his grandest manner, he said to me and to Spiker:

" Sir, it was splendid, noble, glorious! Let me look at you. Look at him, Spiker! Hero is written upon every lineament! Like is drawn to like. I was sure you were brave when first I saw you. Professor! honor me by clasping the sword-hand of a veteran soldier of the Republic. With a thousand men like you at Fredericksburg I should have been in Richmond before sundown!"

Then I went to bed.

Upon the morning after our perilous adventure in the hills I found that I could not rise from bed. The night had been cold, and all my garments had been wet for several hours, and so fever came on. For several days I was quite ill, and it was by a narrow chance that I escaped pneumonia.

I fretted because of my absence from school and of my helplessness, for never before had I been so sick; but I found that the invalid may have some consolements. Mrs. Bantam was an assiduous and affectionate nurse; and Miss Mortimer had for me a bunch or two of flowers and each morning a gentle word through the open door; and more than once Ruby came in with her aunt and spoke of me as Andromeda might have told of Perseus. My action in saving her was indeed so much magnified by her friends that at last I felt shamefaced at hearing of it; but I was sure Ruby knew that I had done battle for her with an

enemy more cruel and dreadful than the wild mountain torrent.

So the days went on until I could sit in the great
chair by the window and watch the stir of the town
under the impulse supplied by A. J. Pelican. For the
boom seemed to have new vigor every day; and all
sorts of wonderful stories were afloat of lots that had
doubled their value twice and thrice a week; of the
eagerness of outside capitalists to invest their money
in almost anything that could be bought in Happy
Hollow; and of the discovery in the hills of metal and
building-stones and other precious materials of which
no Happy Hollower had ever dreamed in the years
gone by.

Elmira told me how the shares of the Improvement
Company had advanced in value, and with what eagerness they were sought for; and this seemed to me
comforting. I hope I am spiritually minded, but, after
all, isn't it true that the consciousness of an enlarging
revenue brings to the mind a feeling of bland, soft,
peaceful contentment?

The new horse-car line was opened while I sat in
my chamber, and as I saw the cars pass up and down
the street well filled with people, and observed how
the people themselves of late had acquired briskness
of manner and cheerfulness of countenance much beyond their wont, I thought myself fortunate that I had
come to Happy Hollow at such a time, and had found
favor with the conjuror who was calling so much
wealth into existence.

Dr. Bulfinch came to see me and brought Charley
with him. The Doctor was most kind in his assurance
that my mind could be at rest about my duties at the

school.   While we talked Charley squirmed.   He
squirmed upon his chair; then upon the edge of the
lounge, and then upon the chair again.   The squirm-
ing capacity of a boy who is waiting while persons
converse of things in which he has no interest has
never been expressed in figures, but it would count up
large.   Finally, at my suggestion, Charley squirmed
downstairs and began to run about the garden, while I
told the Doctor of my adventure with Simon Bulfinch.
The good man was troubled and sad, but he commended me warmly for holding Simon aloof from Ruby.

When Dr. Bulfinch had gone, Mrs. Bantam came in
and brought Ruby with her, and we had a nice talk
about Ruby's school, and about the marvellous things
that were befalling Happy Hollow.   And, after a while,
Mrs. Bantam began to tell of the Colonel's share in
them, and I found her disposed to give to him rather
than to A. J. Pelican chief credit for what had been
accomplished.

"The Colonel," she said, "is masterful.   He has a
largeness of mind that makes it painful for him to
stoop to detail, but when there are great things to be
done, and the scale is colossal, he is perfectly at home.
His intellect works with almost playful facility."

It was natural, then, for the dear old lady to drift
off to her favorite topic; and she said:

"There are few men like the Colonel, Mr. Sprat;
—none, in fact.   I often pity other women.   It seems
almost unfair to them for me to have taken him and
left the rest with no chance at all for him.   Do you
think it was too selfish, dear Mr. Sprat?"

" I wouldn't call it really culpable selfishness," I said,
and Ruby smiled at my answer.

"Many people, Mr. Sprat, think love is but an episode; it is life! The whole, absolutely the whole, of life. Without love there could be no life—no real life. Take Colonel Bantam out of my life, and at once I expire. There would be simply black darkness—the darkness of despair and death. If he should love another woman, I should instantly tear her limb from limb;" and Mrs. Bantam's eyes began to blaze; then suddenly they filled with tears, and, as her hand was instinctively lifted toward her back-hair, she said in imploring tones :

"Oh, Mr. Sprat, do you think Joseph ever *could* love another woman ?"

Ruby remonstrated with her for

"I should tear her limb from limb."

putting such a question to me, but I did not hesitate to assert that in my view conduct of that kind upon the part of Colonel Bantam could be confidently regarded as impossible. This seemed to comfort her, and she proceeded to say :

"You, Mr. Sprat, should have some of the sunshine

of love in your young life. Can you find no one to love?"

In the secret recesses of my heart I thought I could, but I answered that there was time enough for me to think of such a thing.

"No," insisted Mrs. Bantam, with sweet gentleness, "all time is wasted until love fills the life with radiance. Look around you and ascertain if there is no one whose heart would throb with your heart."

It flashed upon my mind, then, that she was thinking of Ruby, and to try her I said:

"Can you suggest anyone?"

"Let me reflect for a moment," she answered, laying her hand upon Ruby's arm. "Yes," she said, "I know of a lovely woman who would make your life happy."

"Who is it?" I demanded, and I confess that my heart beat strongly.

"Mrs. Purvis-Hyde," she said.

"Oh, aunty!" exclaimed Ruby. "She is a great deal too old for Mr. Sprat!"

"Hush, child! You are much too young to know about such things. Mrs. Purvis-Hyde is rich and handsome. You need to aspire, Mr. Sprat. Your motto should be Excelsior! My dear father always said to me, 'Edith, soar! Don't grovel'; and so I say to you, why not make that lovely woman of high station and generous income the object of your affections?"

Ruby's face was crimson by this time. She perceived the absurdity of the suggestion and of the entire conversation, and she proposed to her aunt to withdraw upon the pretence that I needed some refreshment which Mrs. Bantam should prepare. But, before they were gone, Colonel Bantam came into the room, and Mrs. Bantam gave him her chair, saying to me:

"The Colonel will care for you till I return." Then she and Ruby went down stairs.

"Magnificent woman, isn't she?" asked the Colonel, as he settled himself in his chair. "Magnificent" (and the Colonel's countenance fell), "but too much controlled by feeling. It is a womanly weakness, I know, but I have often pressed upon Edith the necessity for the infusion of a larger element of stoicism in her nature. I heard, sir, what she advised you with respect to that adorable and distinguished widow, Mrs. Purvis-Hyde. Adopt her counsel. You can get Mrs. Purvis-Hyde and collar (if I may be permitted to employ a somewhat vulgar expression) her incalculable wealth as easily as you can get a girl without a dollar."

"Speaking about marriage," continued Colonel Bantam, "I have just gone into a pool with Jason Hole, the Methodist minister."

"A pool? What kind of a pool?"

"Why, sir, there has been some rivalry between him and me in the matter of starting young people upon the joyous voyage of matrimony. There is no reason, sir, why the clergy should have a monopoly of this business when the laws of our country repose in the hands of the civil magistrate complete authority to bind loving hearts together; and so, as Hole asked five dollars for performance of the ceremony, I let it be known that the chief magistrate of the town would bring young lives into unison for four dollars. Thereupon this person Hole, with discreditable greed, dropped to three dollars. Considering the circumstances, sir,

was it not positively unavoidable that I should diminish my fee to two dollars? Hole met it and went
lower; he announced, almost publicly, that he would
throw the golden chains of conjugal union around the
loving pair for the paltry sum of one dollar. I am
almost ashamed to mention it. But, sir, no mere
clerical person, a non-combatant, can be permitted to
bluff me. My honor and the dignity of my office
were involved, and so, sir, to settle the matter once for
all, and to drive this unworthy intermeddler from the
field, I began to marry two couples for a quarter of a
dollar. Think of it!

"I supposed, sir, that this man Hole, whose conduct
had brought discredit upon his cloth, would succumb,
and we should hear no more of it. You will regard it
as incredible, but I speak the words of soberness and
truth when I tell you that he met me by the announcement that he would accept the fee suggested by me
and throw in a hymn-book and a blessing. He is
reported to have declared that I could not supply a
blessing. But, sir, when it comes to blessing, Joseph
Bantam in his capacity of Mayor of Happy Hollow,
can out-bless any minister that ever stood in the pulpit;
and I said so.

"At last, sir, vanquished at every point, he degraded
himself so far as to offer a free ceremony and six plated
teaspoons. I stopped the contest there. Apart from
the travesty upon decency and propriety by making
this solemn ceremony a matter of chaffering and bar-
gaining, my resources have fallen into such a condition
of dilapidation as to make rivalry along the line of
plated teaspoons impossible. I have had an interview
with Hole, therefore, and we have agreed to restore the

fee to the original figure, five dollars, and to pool and divide the proceeds."

When I had commended the wisdom of this arrangement, Colonel Bantam proceeded:

" I simply loathe these references to money matters, but the truth is that the losses inflicted upon me by this unnecessary contest have once more completely impoverished me, and I am in fact an involuntary bankrupt, with the wolf not far from the door. Would it be too great a trespass upon your good nature to let me have five dollars upon one of the blocks of Improvement Stock as collateral, and when my first dividend comes in we will resume the *status quo?*"

I handed him the money, and as he placed it in his pocket, Mr. Spiker knocked upon my door and asked if he might come in.

I thought Spiker seemed sorry to find the Colonel with me, but he sat with us and chatted pleasantly; and after awhile he told us that he had in the *Defender* office a practice of clipping from his exchanges sketches of the lives of prominent men, and filing them away in his obituary department for use when the persons referred to should die.

The Colonel commended the foresight thus manifested.

Spiker proceeded to say that the youth to whom this duty of procuring biographical material was assigned had lately clipped and labelled and pigeon-holed an account of the career of Martin Van Buren; and when Spiker asked him if he did not know Van Buren had been dead for many, many years, the young man expressed complete ignorance of the fact, and pretended to be painfully affected by the intelligence.

"Have you an account of my life in your collection?" inquired Colonel Bantam, with some eagerness.

"Oh, yes," answered the editor carelessly.

"Do you deal in a large, liberal way with my war record? I must have justice done to that."

"I guess so."

"The matter is far too important to be relegated to the domain of conjecture. You will permit me to examine your narrative, Mr. Spiker?"

"That would be very irregular."

"Irregular or not irregular, sir, no one can do justice to my achievements as a soldier but myself. I must see it."

"Impossible!" said Mr. Spiker, with a smile.

"No, sir; not impossible. It is necessary. I will leave no room for the malignant whispering of animosity when I can no longer defend myself. My record is mine. The story of my life is my own property. What, sir! do you deny me the privilege of examining the history of my own existence? Preposterous! I shall call upon the tribunals of justice to maintain my cause."

"All right," said Mr. Spiker wearily. "Call."

Colonel Bantam's excitement increased. He walked up the room, down the room, and around the room, as if uncertain what to do next. At last, with flushed face and voice husky with agitation, he said:

"I give you formal notice now, sir, that a *subpœna duces tecum* will be served on you to-morrow by my daughter, Miss Bantam, requiring you to produce my obituary notice in court!"

Colonel Bantam slammed the door as he went out, and Mr. Spiker looked at me and laughed.

When the Colonel was gone, Mr. Spiker rocked to and fro in the old-fashioned high rocking-chair with the red bombazine cushion, looking as if some matter of importance bore upon his mind. He was not gloomy, but he had an unusual air of solemnity, and he seemed abstracted.

" How is the *Defender* getting on.?" I asked, to rouse him from one of these spells of absent-mindedness.

"Oh, fair enough! Pretty fair! Not half as much cash business as there ought to be in a town like this; but I don't complain. By the way, Sprat, do you know anyone who has asthma ?"

I said I did not.

" Because I've just had to take four dozen of Wig-fall's Asthma Cure for an ad. But maybe I can trade them at Brindle's drug-store for soda-water and cigars. Funny way, isn't it, of running the mightiest engine of civilization? And of course you have no use for chemical fire-extinguishers either—the kind you carry on your back? I have taken in several more, and there hasn't been a fire in Happy Hollow for four years. However, they can lie there in my cellar as assets. I could start you in almost any kind of business from that cellar. I'd make the terms easy, too."

Mr. Spiker arose and walked around the room, looking at the lurid picture over the washstand of the eruption of Mount Vesuvius; examining the graining of my little mahogany secretary, glancing at himself in the glass, and softly half whistling at the time.

I was sure Spiker had something to say that he felt shy of saying.

Presently he sat again in the rocking-chair, thrust both his hands in his trowsers-pockets, extended his

12

legs at full length, fixed his eyes upon the carpet
between his heels, and said:

"Sprat!"

"Well?"

Then Spiker, gazing steadfastly at the carpet, remained silent for two minutes as if he were searching
for the right word. At last he said:

"Say, old man, I'm in love!"   And the editor's face
became as red as the roses upon the carpet.

"I congratulate you," I said, smiling.

"Very well; thank you; but then the question is
what am I going to do about it? Maybe she won't
have me."

"Have you asked her?"

"Not yet, but I'm going to. I'm gradually moving
up toward it. It's a ticklish business. Would you
mind helping me out?"

"I will do what I can; but who is the woman?"

"Miss Mortimer; Julie Mortimer. Sprat, I've got
to have her or life'll be of no use to me."

"Bad as that is it?"

"Bad or good, my boy, I'm in for it the worst way
you ever saw. I felt it coming on the first time I
looked at her in Pelican's show; and since she's been
hovering around the *Defender* office— Well, Sprat,
I'd rather let the *Defender* go into bankruptcy than
give her up. Perfectly lovely, isn't she? Did you
ever see such a charming woman? And smart, too!
Old man, I simply must have her, that's the whole
of it."

"But what can I do for you?"

"I want your advice," and Spiker felt around in his
coat-tail pocket and produced a paper scroll, tied with

a bit of string. Unrolling it and rolling it the reverse way to make it lie, he handed it to me.

"What do you think it is?" he asked.

"At the first glance," I said, turning the paper one way and then another, "it looks like a map of the townships of Blair County, only the names are all wrong."

"Man!" exclaimed Spiker, "that's a phrenological chart! It is a diagram, or lay-out, of my skull, drawn on a Mercator projection—that is, *flat*, you know."

"Funny, isn't it?"

"Not funny; interesting. That was drawn out for me by Professor Baffin, the celebrated phrenologist of Philadelphia, and I pay for it with a ten-line ad. on my inside, e. o. d., for three months. Now, Sprat, just run your eye over it," and Mr. Spiker pulled his chair over by mine and extended his forefinger to indicate the good points of the diagram. "Observe how strong the bump of philanthropy is, and here is the bump of acquisitiveness. Down here are the domestic propensities, so to speak, and you notice that all of them are abnormally large. That might impress her, don't you think?"

"Impress whom?"

"Julie, of course. I had it made for her. She can look at it before I propose and see just what kind of a man I am."

"Not a bad idea," I said, "but I notice that the bump of combativeness is very large, too. Maybe she won't like that."

"I had half a notion to ink that over; but I think I'll let it go. She knows very well I'm not quarrelsome, excepting with other editors, and that's really just a regular part of our business. How do you think she'll take it?" asked Spiker, rolling up the chart and tapping the arm of the rocking-chair with it.

"I hardly know; I never heard of anyone courting in just that way, but maybe it will go; it's original, anyhow."

"Exactly," said Spiker, "and she's just the kind of a woman to appreciate a bright, new thing. Do you think she cares for me, Sprat? Have you noticed?"

"I can't say that I have. You know I am really very busy, and I don't observe such things closely. But she's a fine woman. I hope you will get her."

"My life's just ruined if I don't get her."

"Oh, I don't know," I said. "I wouldn't feel that way about it. There are plenty of other nice women."

"Not for me," said Spiker, with some mournfulness.

"There's Elmira Bantam," I suggested. "Try her if you fail with Julie."

"Sprat, don't trifle with me!" What would I want Elmira for? Have you noticed lately she has got to tying up her hair with red tape? That is carrying the professional idea too far, in my judgment. Anyhow, Elmira will boss any man who marries her, and I'm not looking for a boss; I'm in search of a wife—some one to love. I'd hate to have a woman ordering me about."

"I suppose, really," continued Spiker, after a moment's reflection, "it would be a better stroke of business for me to marry somebody who has lots of relations instead of a woman who is alone, for then I might have a chance gradually to get rid of some of my tombstones and mantel-pieces among the members of the family; but I don't care for that; Julie is the woman for me, tombstones or no tombstones."

"I have a notion that she likes you," I said, with a purpose to offer the editor encouragement.

"It seems so to you, does it?" asked Spiker, with a gleam of hopefulness in his eyes. Then he looked despondent again and said: "But I don't know. Women are secretive and deceptive. You can never discover how they feel about such things until you ask them. I'll tell you, Sprat, I have half a notion to frighten her a bit if she shows any discouraging indications."

"Frighten her! How?"

"Why I have the census statistics at my office to show that there are ever so many more women than men in the country, and that, if every man of us should marry, there'd be thousands of women left over with no chance. The inference is, and she's smart enough to draw it, that each woman who has an offer had better jump at it, because if she doesn't she may be one of the too many. I'll show you the figures some time."

Mrs. Bantam came in with the refreshment she had made ready for me, and the editor replaced the Mercator projection of his head in his coat-pocket, while Mrs. Bantam began to express apprehension respecting the burglaries that had been committed three or four times since the boom had begun in Happy Hollow.

Mr. Spiker endeavored to calm her fears, assuring her that he would take care of any burglar who should be bold enough to try to enter the home of Mrs. Bantam.

Mrs. Bantam appeared to feel comforted.

"It is indeed reassuring," she said, "to have brave

men in the house; you, and Mr. Sprat, and the Colonel.
The Colonel is a host in himself. A mere burglar
would quail before him."

It is a very odd fact that we should have had a bur-
glar-scare in our house that very night. This may have
been due to the conversation upon the subject conducted between Mrs. Bantam, the Colonel, and Spiker,
with the result that their thoughts were strongly
directed to the subject.

In the middle of the night there was a tumult in the
second-floor hallway, and, hastily putting on some
clothing, I went out to learn what was the cause of it.
I found Colonel Bantam and Mr. Spiker standing in
the hall, by the bath-room door, and in the light that
came from the bath-room through the open doorway
I could perceive that both of them had white faces.
They were excited and trembling, and they could hardly
command breath enough for speech. Mrs. Bantam,
with a wrapper thrown about her, stood upon the landing just above the bath-room and held fast to the
banister. She was tearful and terror-stricken.

" Go down after him, Colonel," said Spiker, " and I
will follow you."

" No, no!" exclaimed Mrs. Bantam. " Do not go,
Joseph! He will kill you."

The Colonel turned and looked at Spiker as if to
convey the notion that consideration for the feelings
of his wife alone restrained him from dashing down
the stairs after the supposed burglar.

" If I had a weapon, I would go alone," said Spiker
boldly. He was sure there was no weapon within
reach.

" Let me go down, Edith," implored the Colonel,

showing at the same time a distinct purpose to remain rooted to the spot.

"I shall swoon if you do so," said Mrs. Bantam. "Your life is far too valuable for such a sacrifice."

The Colonel looked again at Spiker, then at me, as if to say:

"How can I go under such circumstances?"

"Let them take our things," said Mrs. Bantam eagerly. "The spoons are up stairs, and there is nothing below that is of any value in comparison with your precious life. I do wish we had kept the blood-hounds."

"You are a single man, Spiker," said the Colonel. "You take the lead and the Professor and I will bring up your rear."

"No," said Spiker firmly, edging back into the bath-room under the pretence of having to turn up the gas-light. "If the head of the house won't take care of his own burglars he can't reasonably expect me to do it."

"But you see how I am hampered," expostulated the Colonel. "To go down stairs is nothing, but to have the idol of my soul plunged into paroxysms of hysteria upon the staircase is more than I can stand."

"Call the police, then," said Spiker.

"He is asleep at the station," said the Colonel despondently.

"Are you sure there is a burglar down stairs?" I asked.

"Sure," said Colonel Bantam. "I saw him."

"So did I," said Mr. Spiker.

"Joseph," pleaded Mrs. Bantam, "don't think of such a thing as pursuing him farther. Let us all lock ourselves in our rooms and dare him to do his worst."

While Mrs. Bantam was speaking, Elmira leaned over the railing of the third-story staircase and asked :

" What is the matter ?"

" There's a burglar in the house," answered Mrs. Bantam, and Colonel Bantam, and Mr. Spiker and I.

" Wait a moment," said Miss Bantam's voice, floating downward.

In a moment Miss Bantam came down the stairs with a pink wrapper girded about her. She looked really handsome. She was as tranquil as if she were going to breakfast.

" How do you know there is a burglar ?" she asked.

" We saw him," answered the Colonel and the editor.

Elmira understood the situation at once. She glanced contemptuously at her father and at Spiker, and, I am sorry to say, at me.

" Let me have hold of something," she said, as she looked about for a cudgel. Finding nothing in the nature of a weapon, she entered the bath-room, seized a tooth-brush, and walked boldly down the front stairs.

When she reached the first floor she lighted the gas-burner in the hall, and then the Colonel and Spiker went down after her.

Without flinching, Elmira, with the tooth-brush held in front of her like a loaded pistol, entered the parlor and the dining-room, the sitting-room and the kitchen, looking under the sofas and tables, opening all the closets and examining the fastenings upon the cellar-door. Then, finding nobody, she turned out the light in the hall, leaving her two followers to come up in the darkness, and ascended the staircase.

Elmira's Burglar-Hunt.

·

"Did you find him, dearest?" asked Mrs. Bantam, as Elmira replaced the tooth-brush upon the washstand in the bath-room.

"Find him!" exclaimed Miss Bantam, scornfully. "There was nobody to find, and I knew it. How I should hate to be a man!" and Mr. Spiker looked as if he should wither under her glance.

"Pardon me, Miss Bantam," said the editor, "but there was a burglar down there, for I had a scuffle with him in the hall."

"So had I," added the Colonel.

"My room door was open," continued Mr. Spiker, "and I heard some one moving about in the darkness down stairs. I crept cautiously down the back stair-case here without my shoes, and I almost fell into the arms of a burglar."

"Why didn't you hold him, if you had him?" asked Elmira.

"We grappled and fought there for several minutes, when, finally, he broke away from me, and as he seemed stronger than I, I ran upstairs to call for help. I met your father out here on this landing just as I got here."

Colonel Bantam looked queerly at Mr. Spiker, and said:

"It is very strange. Did the burglar put his arm around your neck?"

"Yes."

"And you tried to throw him by locking your right leg in his left leg?"

"Exactly."

"And you said, ' Now I've got you, have I'?"

"Yes."

"Mr. Spiker," said Colonel Bantam, sternly, "you and I appear to have had some kind of frictional irritation between us ever since you made your home beneath my roof-tree. It is exasperating to the last degree. But do you know, sir, that I was the person you encountered upon the first floor? I had gone down to the pantry, sir, to obtain a drink of water, and when you descended upon me under the extraordinary delusion that I was a burglar, I not unnaturally thought you were a burglar, and I made, as you will testify, a resolute effort to throttle you and to hand you over to justice."

"You fled up one staircase," said Elmira to the editor, "and paw fled up the other."

Colonel Bantam was angry.

"The employment of the word 'fled' in that or in any other connection, with reference to a movement made by me, is not only in the last degree inconsiderate, but it borders upon outright impertinence! I first floored the burglar, and then came up to call Mr. Sprat to help me to secure him. Mr. Spiker, I will have further explanation with you of this unfortunate, and even mysterious, incident."

Colonel Bantam withdrew with Mrs. Bantam, and as Elmira went away into the third story, Spiker said to me:

"Sprat, trouble is brewing between that man Bantam and me. He has strained our relations to the point where a break seems inevitable."

Chapter XI

THE · STRIKE·

By the time I had fully recovered from my illness the signs were appearing of the swift coming of spring. Upon the distant hills and on the towering brown hill near by, whereon Ruby and I had so perilous an adventure, a faint tinge of green was to be perceived. The trees in our tiny park were covered with buds that swelled with a promise of foliage; the first narrow thread-like blades of grass had thrust themselves from the earth; the birds twittered and frolicked among the trees and bushes, and the brook that swept beneath the bridges was brimming with the melted snow that had lain upon the far upland.

It was comforting, after so long tarrying in the house, to be once more in the soft sweet air and in the warmth of the sunshine; and when school was ended I found delight during the afternoons in sitting in the park or slowly walking about while I watched the swift progression of the work of the Improvement Company. The buildings upon the main street were going up rapidly; the Water Works were nearly ready, and the two hotels just beyond the town were roofed in, with a promise of readiness for summer guests.

The horse-car line was in high favor with the people, and, indeed, I often found refreshment, and also gratification for curiosity, in riding upon a car out along the lovely lane that led to Grigsby's Bluff, where there was a noble view across the valley, and back again through the town to Purgatory Springs upon the other side.

Smiling prosperity appeared in every part of Happy Hollow. Everybody looked happy, nearly everybody expected to become rich. The boom started by A. J. Pelican lost none of its impetus; it seemed to become stronger day by day. As Mr. Spiker continued to declare in the *Defender*, destiny, beyond all doubt, had prepared a glorious future for Happy Hollow.

But in this perplexing world the law of things seems to be that nothing shall make an untrammelled movement toward higher and better conditions. A wise observer has said that the best of us zigzag heavenward, and the rule is that the path never runs straight toward any worldly goal that is worth striving for. So it was too much for even the most sanguine citizen of Happy Hollow to expect that the town should fulfil its lofty destiny without first encountering serious obstruction.

Trouble was in store for us; but the most gifted seer in Happy Hollow could not have foretold that it would come through the agency of the popular street-car line.

The demon who brought discord to Happy Hollow was Abram Hunsicker, walking delegate for the Street-car Laborers' Union of the metropolis.

Happy Hollow had but three street-cars; one to go up and one to go down, while the third stood on one of the turnouts waiting for the car that went down to come up, or for the car that came up to go down. Really it does seem as if our three little cars might have been passed by when Abram Hunsicker started out with a desire to create trouble. There were so many towns that had four cars, or forty —so many towns where people were more quarrelsome, and where the good times had lasted longer than in Happy Hollow.

The walking delegate.

But, no ; as soon as Abram Hunsicker and the Street-car Laborers' Union learned that there was a car-line in Happy Hollow out among the everlasting hills, Abram Hunsicker had an irresistible impulse to run up to the town to discover in what degree the unfortunate laboring man, engaged in operating the horse-cars, was being ground beneath the heel of the oppressor.

Abram Hunsicker, we learned at last, had very surprising gifts as a walking delegate. Put Abram in a group of happy and contented men, and within two hours he would send every man home discontented and miserable.

The driver of car number two, Albert Potts, was one of the most popular young men in Happy Hollow until Abram Hunsicker came up to look after the interests of the unfortunate workingmen; but within four days after Hunsicker's arrival all the other men employed by the street railway company refused to work until Potts should be discharged.

Mr. Pelican, busy though he was, had so much surprise and pain because of this conduct upon the part of men whom he had thought well satisfied with their work, that he made personal inquiry into the matter.

Why should the dismissal of Potts suddenly become so urgently and imperatively necessary to the peace of mind of his co-laborers that his co-laborers would rather go without money and bread than to fail to obtain it?

This was the question that engaged the attention of A. J. Pelican.

Jim Sturgis, driver of car number three, upon being interrogated, said the strike was ordered by the Car Laborers' Union.

"But Potts is a member of the union?"

"Yes, sir."

"Well, then, why does the union turn against him?"

"It's this way, sir. Al's Aunt Susan Hovey, who lives with Mrs Purvis-Hyde and does chamber work, is not a member of the Chambermaids' Union, and that, you see, makes all the chambermaids mad. And as

the Chambermaids' Union can't find no means of striking at Mrs. Purvis-Hyde, and can't nohow get at Al's
Aunt Susan Hovey, they have asked the Car Laborers'
Union to strike at Al's Aunt Susan Hovey in a round-
about sort of a way by hittin' at Al. That's the way
it began, sir."

"Do you think that's quite fair to Al?"

"Well, sir, it don't look jest that way, does it?"
But you know when you belong to a union, as Abram
Hunsicker
says, you've
got to stand
by the rules ;
and the rules
says Al has
to go unless
Al's Aunt
Susan Ho-
vey jines
the Cham-
bermaids'
Union."

"Has any-
body asked
her to join ?"

"Yes, sir. Abram Hun-
sicker seen her twice and
put the proposition to her,
and she said she wouldn't
jine unless they'd make her
corresponding secretary."

"She said Mary Jane Delaney's
bonnet was old fashioned."

"Won't the union do that?"

"No, sir; and I'll tell you why: Mary Jane Delaney

is the president of the Chambermaids' Union, and she won't let Al's Aunt Susan Hovey be elected corresponding secretary because Al's Aunt Susan Hovey, last February a year, at church one day, said President Mary Jane Delaney's bonnet was old fashioned."

"And so you men," said A. J. Pelican, "throw away your wages and stop the street-cars and make trouble all around because two women squabble over a bonnet!"

"We've got to do it, sir. The union says so. We only want to be reasonable."

A. J. Pelican resolved that Potts should not be dismissed, and he said so.

The next morning there was what Abram Hunsicker called a sympathetic strike. All the bricklayers, stone-masons, carpenters, plumbers, plasterers, hod-carriers, cart-drivers, mortar-mixers, and laborers refused to go to work.

The boom stopped suddenly, and A. J. Pelican was in a condition of much excitement and grave perplexity. He sent for Abram Hunsicker, who came into A. J. Pelican's office with an appearance of tranquillity which increased Mr. Pelican's irritation.

"This is a bad job, Hunsicker," he said, "that you have set up in the town."

"A good job, Mr. Pelican, I think."

"No; everybody was satisfied and happy until you came here to make trouble."

"That's always the way. The oppressed workingman is so used to tyranny that he never knows how the yoke galls him until somebody points it out. That's what I'm for. I'm a pointer-out."

"But, what has Al Potts got to do with his aunt and

the Chambermaids' Union ? What have the bricklayers
got to do with Al Potts and the horse-cars ?"

"Got a heap to do with them! We all stand together against the tyranny of capital. The thing runs
away back. Before you can lay a brick, for example,
you've got to be squared with the Clay-diggers' Union,
the Brick-makers' Union, the Lime-burners' Union,
the Sand-loaders' Union, the Water-pumpers' Union,
the Mortar-mixers' Union, the Hod-carriers' Union,
and the Bricklayers' Union. After a while we'll have
it fixed so you can't go to bed, or even wash your
hands, before you've got in touch with the Chambermaids' Union, the Cooks' Union, the Dish-washers'
Union, the Pillow-case-makers' Union, and the Toilet-
soap Union. The rights of labor have got to be protected all along the line."

A. J. Pelican reflected for a moment. Then he said:

"Don't you think that the unions ought to see to it
that a man does his work right when the rights of
labor have been protected all along the line ?"

"How do you mean?"

"Well, in half the buildings I am putting up the
window-frames are set crooked, and in all of them the
flues have been choked with brick-bats. Is that fair?"

"Oh, that's all right," said Hunsicker. "That is good
for the poor man. It makes more work, and that
means more wages."

A. J. Pelican had never closely considered wage and
labor questions, and his interest was excited by this
view of one of the involved matters.

"Do you mean to say," he asked, "that workingmen would be better off if they botched every job they
touched ?"

13

"Why, certainly!" responded Hunsicker, smiling at the ignorance of the capitalist; "because if every job was botched, then another gang of workmen would have good employment taking out the botches and fixing things."

"Suppose the second lot of men put in new botches, instead of taking out the old ones?"

"Fine!" exclaimed Hunsicker, striking the table with the palm of his hand. "That would make still more work."

A. J. Pelican meditated; then he said:

"Why not, then, arrange that as soon as a workman has made something—say a house—he should at once take it all to pieces, so that other workmen should make it all over again?"

"That would suit us. There couldn't be too much of that kind of thing."

"But, then," asked A. J. Pelican, "where would the employer come in?"

"Oh, he doesn't count. We don't mind him. He can take care of himself."

"But where do you think I could get money to pay wages with if I paid out money every week for work that was never finished, and so could never bring money in?"

"Why, you'd get it out of the bank, of course. And when the bank ran out, you'd get it out of mines or something, somewhere. We don't care where you get it. That's not our business. That's your end of the thing. All we want is that you shall get it somehow or other and pay it over to us. We only ask what is reasonable."

A. J. Pelican afterward confessed to me that this way

of looking at the matter was so startling and remarkable that, for a few moments, his head was not perfectly
clear about it.

"But," he said at last, "what if capitalists concluded
to refuse to go on paying out money for jobs that were
never completed? Wouldn't that be hard for the poor
workingman?"

"We'd have laws passed to make 'em go on doing
it," exclaimed Hunsicker. "That's part of our general
plan."

A. J. Pelican wanted time to think, and so he sent
Hunsicker away with the request that the whole body
of strikers should formulate their demands and present
them to him next morning.

At the appointed time a committee of four, headed
by Abram Hunsicker, appeared at A. J. Pelican's office
and handed him a paper containing a declaration that
the strike would continue all along the line until three
things were conceded:

First.—Susan Hovey must join the Chambermaids'
Union, or Al Potts must be discharged.

Second.—No carting of any kind must be done for
the Happy Hollow Improvement Com-
pany excepting by members of the
Haulers' and Pullers' Union, and this in-
cludes wheel-barrowing

Third.—Working hours must be reduced to eight a
day, and all wages advanced ten per cent.

These demands were read aloud to A. J. Pelican by
walking delegate Hunsicker; and, just as he concluded and was handing the paper to the capitalist,
Thomas Bolster, a bricklayer, and a member of the
committee, stepped forward and said:

"Our union also demands that you shall supply sponge-cake for lunch three times a week."

A. J. Pelican was already angry, and when he heard Thomas Bolster's request, he turned upon him with some fierceness and said:

"Don't you want me to hire a man to play the piano for you at your lunch-hour?"

"Add that!" exclaimed Abram Hunsicker, stepping over and trying to take the paper from Mr. Pelican's hand. "That's a good suggestion. Make it a hand-organ for convenience, and we'll accept it at once!"

A. J. Pelican sat by his table and read and re-read the specifications; and as he read and reflected—as the sense of injustice pressed more strongly upon him—he became more and more angry. At last, springing to his feet, he dashed his new curly wig violently upon the table and said:

"No, I won't do it! Do it! I'll see Happy Hollow bulged up from the bottom and made into a mountain first! Susan Hovey, and the sponge-cake, and the Chambermaids' Union, and the whole cantankerous thing can go hang; and so can you!"

And Pelican, tearing the specifications into shreds, flung them on the floor, dropped into his chair, put on his wig, wheeled around with his back to the committee, lifted his feet to the top of his desk, and looked out straight through the back window.

Abram Hunsicker laughed in a sardonic manner and said:

"Come along, boys. Now we'll tie up everything;" and so the committee walked out of Mr. Pelican's office.

Abram Hunsicker fulfilled his promise. He tied up everything that could be tied up. Operations were stopped upon the street pavement and the Water Works, as well as upon the buildings.

The park improvements were abandoned, the horse-cars remained in the shed; and the streets were thronged by idle men, who stood about and sat about looking as if they were by no means discontented with the conditions prepared for them by the walking delegate.

A. J. Pelican tried the experiment of bringing men up from the city and from the neighboring towns to take up the work; but the strikers always met the visitors at the station and sent them back upon the next train.

Then he called upon Colonel Bantam, as Mayor of the town, to give him protection in an attempt to start the street-cars; but the Colonel, keeping himself closely within his office, pleaded that he could do nothing with one policeman. To some of us it really seemed as if the old warrior who had held at bay the Confederate legions at Gettysburg had an odd shyness about facing a Happy Hollow mob.

A. J. Pelican then put into the *Defender* an advertisement calling for men to run the cars. Two brave fellows responded, and one of the cars was brought into the main street in front of the new Opera House. A crowd of strikers surrounded it, and when the driver refused to leave the platform they pulled him off, carried him struggling to the brook and ducked him there.

The other volunteer was discouraged and refused to serve, and so the car stood in the street through the night

The next morning Elmira Bantam came that way,

with her soul full of rage at the unreasonableness of the strike and at the cowardice of the men of the town. After looking at the car for a moment, she went into A. J. Pelican's office.

Presently Pelican came out, warm and angry, followed by Elmira. While Pelican went around to the stable for the horses, Elmira walked over to the Mayor's office. As Pelican again appeared, driving the harnessed horses, Elmira emerged from the police-station with 'Lias Guff, and the two bloodhounds in leash, walking behind her.

The mob of strikers observed Elmira's movement with curious interest.

While A. J. Pelican hitched the horses to the car, Elmira, with the air of a general marshaling his forces, placed 'Lias Guff and the bloodhounds between the tracks just in front of the horses. Then with a stern voice she ordered him to draw his club.

'Lias Guff did so, but the crimson hue of his cheeks was turned to pink. Plainly he was scared; but this may have been because the bloodhounds were restless and disagreeable. However, he held his head high and looked straight to the front, excepting that he leaned over for a moment to whisper to a bystander:

"Duty is my motter; and Wigilance."

When the horses were hitched A. J Pelican stepped around to the hind end of the car, intending to act as conductor. With stern resolution written upon her fine face, with her lips firmly set, her eyes flashing, her cheeks flushed, and her bonnet somewhat awry because of her unusual exertion, Elmira Bantam stepped upon the front platform. Taking in her hand the lines, she turned to the great crowd about the car and said:

"I am the counsel for the railway company. I represent law and order. You have no legal or moral right to interfere with the company's operations; and now as the men (the cowards!) are all afraid, I am going to show you that this car will run. I dare any man to try to stop it!"

Then Elmira Bantam said to 'Lias Guff:

"Proceed, officer!" and taking the whip in her right hand she applied it to the horses.

"Now let her go!"

The horses tried to start, but they could not move the car. Elmira whipped them again; she clucked with her tongue and made a kissing sound with her pursed lips and said "Get up," but, though the horses did their best, the car would not move.

Some of the men in the crowd laughed good-naturedly, and the proceeding seemed to be regarded as rather a fine bit of fun.

Elmira's face reddened. She turned about, and looking through the car, was just upon the point of asking A. J. Pelican if he knew what was the matter, when Abram Hunsicker stepped upon the platform and said;

" Excuse me, miss, but the brake is set."   Thereupon
he released the brake, twirling the handle around two
or three times, and said :

" Now let her go !"

Somebody shouted " Three cheers for Miss Bantam,"
and the crowd cheered and laughed.   But Elmira set
her lips more firmly and looked right over the top of
'Lias Guff's helmet as the horses went off at such a
pace that 'Lias and the dogs had to move along quickly
to avoid being run over.   The crowd cheered and
laughed until the car passed the turn in the road out
by Tulliver's farm.

'Lias Guff halted at the edge of the town, but Miss
Bantam and A. J. Pelican made the journey clear out
to Purgatory Springs.   As they came back 'Lias Guff
and the bloodhounds escorted them through Happy
Hollow, and the car went on to Grigsby's Bluff, returning finally to the town ; but there were no passengers.

When at last the car stopped on the turnout in
Main Street, Elmira threw the lines over the brake-
handle and said to A. J. Pelican :

" That is the way to do it !"

" Yes, miss, and it was mighty fine and bold for you
to undertake it, too ; but they wouldn't let a man run
the car.   It's all because you're a woman."

" If women had charge of everything there'd be a
good deal less foolishness," answered Elmira ; but,
indeed, she said afterward that her courageous action
really had accomplished nothing.

Actually nothing ; for the strikers still refused to
work, and nobody could be found to run the cars or to
take the places made vacant in the other departments
of Happy Hollow industry.

In the *Defender* Mr. Spiker mourned day by day
that so foul a blight had fallen upon so fair an enterprise as that which promised to bring prosperity and
greatness to Happy Hollow.   In his soul the editor
was angry and impatient with the workmen; but
editors must be careful; and it was interesting to
observe with what skill Mr. Spiker contrived to plead
the cause of A. J. Pelican and the Improvement Company while appearing as the champion of the workingman.

" It is impossible," he urged, " to exaggerate the
dignity of labor.   The horny-handed son of toil, who
eats the bread of honest industry, is the hope and the
mainstay of the country.   But the capitalist also, with
his keen vision, daring courage, and heaven-given intellectual force, is equally essential to the welfare of
society.   The interests of the two are, in truth, identical.
Capital and labor go hand in hand to bless one another
and the human race; and they never fail to work
harmoniously excepting when plotters against the peace
of both succeed in devising nefarious methods of
forcing them into hostile attitudes."

Meantime, Aunt Susan Hovey became in a large
way a person of importance.   Mrs. Purvis-Hyde pleaded
with her to surrender her claim to 'the corresponding
secretaryship of the Chambermaids' Union and to consent to become a mere member.   A. J. Pelican had
four interviews with her, and four with President Mary
Jane Delaney, in whose soul still lingered some of the
bitterness engendered by Aunt Susan Hovey's ungenerous reference to her bonnet.   Dr. Fury called at Mrs.
Purvis-Hyde's and talked the matter over fully with
Aunt Susan Hovey, representing that she owed a

sacred obligation to her fellow-creatures, who suffered because of her stubbornness.

Elmira Bantam had a warm argument with her, and Mrs. Purvis-Hyde thought had swung Aunt Susan Hovey around on the wrong side just as she was beginning to be swayed toward the right side. Even Abram Hunsicker undertook to discuss the case with her, and the talk among some of the people was that Aunt Susan Hovey's personal charm had been borne in upon Abram Hunsicker's mind to such an extent that he was getting to call upon her too often, unless his intentions were of a serious nature.

Whether it was the reasoning or the entreaty of her friends and advisers, or the influence of Abram Hunsicker's ardent manner, the fact was that one day all Happy Hollow was thrilled with joy by the announcement in the *Defender* that Aunt Susan Hovey had at last made up her mind to become an ordinary member of the Chambermaids' Union.

The sun seemed to shine brighter on that morning. All the people regained their cheerfulness. The workmen appeared in the streets in their overalls. The horse-cars were brought out and brushed up. The *Defender* had an exultant editorial explaining that Happy Hollow would now indeed fulfil its destiny. A. J. Pelican began to fly about the town again with the jingling harness and the brilliant carriage; and all the storekeepers smiled and greeted their customers joyously.

It was indeed strange that Aunt Susan Hovey's mind was not lifted up to vanity when she saw how much had depended upon her willingness to change it or not to change it.

But before two days had passed gloom again fell upon and enveloped Happy Hollow, for the announcement was made by President Mary Jane Delaney, who seemed to have an element of malignancy in her composition, that the Chambermaids' Union, at a special meeting, had peremptorily refused Aunt Susan Hovey's application for membership. Despair came into the hearts of A. J. Pelican and Emerson Spiker. The workmen removed their overalls and resumed their pipes and their gossip under the trees. The horse-cars were put back into the sheds, and despondency was stamped upon the countenances of the storekeepers.

"What's the matter with the Chambermaids' Union that they won't let her in?" inquired A. J. Pelican impatiently of Abram Hunsicker, whom he had summoned to his office.

"Why, you see," said Abram Hunsicker, embracing his knee with his interlocked fingers, "President Mary Jane Delaney says that the by-laws forbid anyone to become a member who can't repeat in the right way the union's motto."

"What is the union's motto?"

"Sweetness and Sincerity."

"Very well, can't Susan Hovey say it? What's the reason she can't say it?"

"She lisps," answered Abram Hunsicker.

"Lisps! What's that got to do with it?"

"Why, she says 'thweetneth and thintherity,' and President Mary Jane Delaney declares that thweetneth and thintherity won't go in the Chambermaids' Union while she's president. Women are queer, ain't they?"

A. J. Pelican did not even try to express his disgust; in words, at any rate. But he banged his wig on the table, and kicked over two chairs and got up and walked about the room. At last, pausing in front of Abram Hunsicker and shaking a forefinger at the walking delegate, he said:

"It's come to this, then: All the great enterprises in this town, involving millions of dollars, have got to stop, and the whole thing is to begin to go to ruin because Susan Hovey can't say 'sweetness and sincerity' as I say it. Is that so?"

"It's just about that way. That's the whole of it," answered Abram Hunsicker.

A. J. Pelican forcibly restrained his temper. He simply said:

"Pretty rough, isn't it?"

"Oh, I dunno," responded Hunsicker. "The rights of labor have to be maintained. We want nothing unreasonable."

"You won't call the strike off, then?"

"Can't do it, Mr. Pelican. The men would disown me."

"Can you do nothing at all?"

"Not till you give in about Al Potts, or President Mary Jane Delaney gives in about Aunt Susan Hovey."

"Could you bribe the Delaney woman, do you suppose?"

"I'll never help any capitalist to corrupt an honest laborer, never!" said Abram Hunsicker firmly.

"Will you call the strike off if I give Al Potts another job somewhere else?"

"No; not unless his aunt squares herself with President Mary Jane Delaney and the Chambermaids' Union. The men are dead set against Al."

A. J. Pelican resumed his seat and permitted his

mind to work with the problem thus presented to him. Finally he said to Abram Hunsicker:

"What do you say to arbitration? I've heard a good deal about it. I haven't much faith in it; but it might be tried."

"I don't mind it," said Abram Hunsicker, "if you'll let us pick out the arbitrators. That's all we ask. We're disposed to be perfectly reasonable."

"Well, maybe we can agree on just one. Who do you think of?"

"I'll step over and consult with the committee about it," said the walking delegate.

In two hours it had been arranged that Rev. Dr. Love, the Presbyterian minister, widely known for his services to the poor, should act as arbitrator; and Pelican and the committee signed an agreement to accept his decision.

Dr. Love consented to act, and for two days he was engaged in hearing testimony from the workmen, from Aunt Susan Hovey, President Mary Jane Delaney, Al Potts, Elmira Bantam, A. J. Pelican, Thomas Bolster, and everybody else who had anything to say.

Two days later the doctor made his decision, a part of which was thought by some persons to have been framed after consultation with Abram Hunsicker. The decision was as follows:

1. A. J. Pelican to yield in the trifling matter of sponge-cake three times a week for lunch; but the arbitrator urges the workmen to surrender this privilege upon the ground of the indigestibility of the cake as commonly prepared.

2. Al Potts to be promoted to conductor's place on the car-line when he pays all back dues. This promo-

tion being in consideration of the arrangement provided for in the fifth section, below.

3. President Mary Jane Delaney to accept Susan
Hovey's apology for the unfortunate reference made
long ago to an article of apparel; and the by-law referring to the pronunciation of the motto of the Chambermaids' Union to be temporarily suspended so that
Susan Hovey may be elected to membership.

4. The hours of labor to be reduced to eight, with a
reduction of five per cent. in all wages, or to remain at
ten hours a day with an increase of five per cent. All
transportation of materials, of every kind, to be done
by members of the Haulers' and Pullers' Union.

5. Susan Hovey to marry Abram Hunsicker, the
walking delegate of the Car Laborers' Union, if Susan
Hovey is willing so to do; thus securing her interest
in, and identification with, the sacred cause of the poor
workingman.

The decision made by Dr. Love ended the strike.
A. J. Pelican yielded everything, promising sponge-
cake three times a week and ice-cream once a month.
Albert Potts became a conductor upon the street-car
line. His Aunt Susan Hovey apologized to President
Mary Jane Delaney, throwing her arms around Mary
Jane's neck and asking her to be first bridesmaid at
her wedding with Abram Hunsicker, who was accepted
by Aunt Susan without a murmur.

Thus the great strike in Happy Hollow was ended,
and A. J. Pelican began again to urge the little town
toward better things.

Chapter XIII

Trouble in Happy Hollow

Happy Hollow had no bank, nor seemed to need one, until Mr. Pelican came to bring prosperity in a flood; but when the bank of Happy Hollow, with A. J. Pelican for its president, opened its doors in the late springtime, there was token enough that the bank was wanted. The money that had followed the president into the town followed him into the bank, and soon there was a long list of depositors and a mighty sum of deposits.

It was a grief to Colonel Bantam that he could not open a personal account in the bank; but there was a degree of solace in the fact that he owned blocks of the stock of the Improvement Company, which was the largest depositor. And thus also there was a kind of warrant for his practice of speaking of the institution as " my bank."

The Colonel had hoped to be chosen for the cashier's position, and had urged his claim upon A. J. Pelican and the directors; but without success.

·For the Colonel and for me and for the other members of our household life went along in the old smooth way, while the great capitalist did great things with his various enterprises, and Happy Hollow prepared for the summertime when the Sanitarium and the Aramink House should greet their first guests, and the lovely Aramink Lake should be covered with pleasure-boats.

Julie Mortimer had formed a friendship with Mrs. Bulfinch, and often went to the little house to tarry with her. Julie told me she had seen Simon Bulfinch there more than once ; and she told Mrs. Bantam, who related the fact to me, that she had seen Mrs. Bulfinch kiss her husband's picture and cry over it. Surely the most wonderful thing in all the world is the faithfulness of woman to her love for that which has become unworthy.

Mrs. Purvis-Hyde, also, was fond of Julie's society ; and to the grand house the fair woman went sometimes from the forsaken woman's house, to be entertained and admired and petted as her lovely person, her gracious character, and her remarkable gifts entitled her to be.

Far up in the Alleghany Mountains, at Hawksmere, Mrs. Purvis-Hyde had a cottage, and long before the summer came she had invited Julie and Ruby to come with her there to be her guests for a few weeks. And when I learned of this I secretly resolved that I should find refuge in one of the excellent hotels at Hawksmere during part of my vacation.

After the ending of the great strike Happy Hollow would have had peace but for the occurrence of several daring and alarming burglaries. Mrs. Purvis-Hyde's house had been robbed; Dr. Fury's residence had been broken open, and several of the stores had been plundered. Every one was uneasy and afraid, but no measures were taken to enlarge the police force or to discover the thieves. 'Lias Guff could not watch at night and do police-duty in the daytime, and the Council was not ready to give him a co-laborer.

Just after the robbery of one of the stores, the proprietor, co-operating with A. J. Pelican, obtained the services of a detective from the city. This officer, upon learning that there were two bloodhounds in the town, conceived the notion of employing them to trail the robbers.

They were taken to the store, and when it was supposed that they had obtained the right scent, they led the way out into the street. The detective and the storekeeper followed them with some eagerness, as they went hither and thither, until at last they burst through the gate of Colonel Bantam's garden, and discovering him upon the sideporch, tried to leap upon him.

The Colonel was both astonished and alarmed; but when the purpose for which the dogs were employed was explained to him he lost his temper.

"An outrage of the first magnitude," he said, "to permit an accursed beast with misleading instincts to attempt to place the odium of crime upon an old soldier of the Republic and the executive head of the municipality!"

The detective apologized, and added force to his words by expressing the opinion that the dogs, anyhow, were not bloodhounds.

In truth, Mr. Spiker's bloodhounds began to be regarded with diminished favor in Happy Hollow, and

14

the feeling against them became really bitter upon the part of some people when one morning, in front of the rectory, they encountered and slew Rev. Dr. Fury's dog that discriminated in so wonderful a manner in favor of Episcopalians. In trying to part the combatants the doctor was bitten upon the hand.

Mrs. Purvis-Hyde did not hide her anger.

"It is disgraceful!" she said to Mrs. Bantam. "If these horrid animals must follow the impulses of their bloodthirsty natures, why should they select as their victim a member of the sacred ministry? Why not bite some of the denominations that are around us?"

At last arrangements were made that the burglary matter should be dealt with by relieving 'Lias Guff from duty in the daytime and requiring him to patrol the streets at night.

This was satisfying to the householders, but 'Lias Guff regarded the plan with disfavor. He said to me plainly that he did not like to go about at night, and for one thing, he had always thought he should hate to encounter ghosts.

"Do you know how you can tell a ghost, Mr. Sprat?" he asked as we talked of the matter.

"No."

"Why, a real ghost never casts no shadder. That's the way to tell 'em, and that's the reason they go around at night when shadders is scarce."

But 'Lias Guff had Duty for his motto, and when nocturnal service was required of him he did not flinch. That he was faithful to his duty seemed to be demonstrated by his adventure with Mrs. Meeker, the wife of the Baptist pastor.

'Lias Guff, coming near to Mrs. Meeker's house late

at night, perceived a person upon the roof of the front porch. Without waiting to ask questions, the policeman fired at the figure twice and was answered by a woman's screams. Upon inquiry he found that the person at whom he had shot was Mrs. Meeker, and by the time this fact had been disclosed half the people in the neighborhood were in the street

Mrs. Meeker was sitting upon the porch-roof sobbing, and in response to repeated questions she related in a broken voice that her husband was away from home and that, after retiring, she heard a mouse in her room. In alarm, she had crept through the window to the porch-roof, and the shutter had then blown shut and locked itself upon the inside.

Some one brought a ladder, and 'Lias Guff began to ascend it with the gallant purpose to bring Mrs. Meeker down. But she would not have it.

"Do not come up here, officer," she said. "Do not dare to come up here."

"Why not, ma'am? You can't stay there all night."

"No, but I want you all to go away except Mrs. Brown, and I'll come down by myself."

This request was acceded to, and Mrs Brown received the unfortunate woman at the foot of the ladder and took her home for the remainder of the night.

It appeared that Mrs. Meeker, rising and wishing to leave the room in haste, had put on Mr. Meeker's pajamas and a pair of gum overshoes, and not unnaturally she wished to have as few spectators as possible when she reached the ground.

These are but trivial incidents of the life of a little town, and they are recorded chiefly because the burglaries and the excitement created by them have direct bearing, as will be seen, upon some of the personages in this narrative.

But, after all, the great events in town or city are of rare occurrence. Life everywhere is upon the whole a matter of small happenings and of things that seem unimportant. Thus, if we are to tell at all of Happy Hollow, why should we pass by in silence the storm that arose in the village from that discussion between Dr. Fury and Dr. Bulfinch, at Mrs. Purvis-Hyde's soiree, concerning the authorship of Deuteronomy?

The sentiment of the people was divided along denominational lines, and the feeling that was warm when the controversy began, became hot when the different ministers had preached vigorously upon the subject.

Dr. Fury's view was that Deuteronomy was written by some unknown person long after the time of Moses.

Dr. Love, of the Presbyterian Church, held with Dr. Bulfinch, who was one of his deacons, that the book was actually written by Moses.

Rev. Wm. Meeker, the Baptist minister, believed that Deuteronomy was the oldest of the five books, the rest of the Pentateuch having been derived from it.

Rev. Jason Hole, the Methodist, was neutral, not caring to commit himself.

The members of the various congregations followed their ministers, and the more they talked about the subject the more angry they were, until there was danger that all social and business relations in Happy Hollow would be made difficult because of the bitterness of the people.

Colonel Bantam would not range himself with any of the parties. To me in private he declared that " The whole thing is humbug;" but whether this was a reference to the dispute among the people or to the book of Deuteronomy remains concealed.

The views of Felix Acorn, though unimportant, were pronounced.

"There never was no Moses, nor no ark made of bulrushes. I put it to you, sir," he said, as he prepared to shave me, "would a king's daughter go a-swimming in a river and picking up and carrying home stray babies? Now, would sech a woman do that? They're trying to impose on us. You don't believe, sir, do you, that them Israelites walked through the Red Sea on dry land? Never! And the sea ain't red, neither. The Bible ain't true, and I can prove it."

"How can you prove it?"

"Why, sir, from cover to cover, it never mentions cats once. Not once. Mentions all kinds of other animals, but skips cats. Now, sir, we know there was cats in them days. We know it positive, because they've dug out thousands of cat-mummies of the Bible times, and if that book was true would it have named all the other things that walks on four legs and forgot about cats? No, it wouldn't; and there's the way we see we're being imposed on.

"The same with other things. No whale never swallered no Jonah; and Joseph's coat hadn't many colors; and there wa'n't no flood and no animals in the ark. There wa'n't no ark. And there never was no Jupiter, or Nepture, or none of them people, and Columbus never discovered no America."

"You reject everything then?"

"Yes, sir, everything, or pretty near everything. You don't believe in Santa Claus? No, sir, I knowed you didn't. It's cruel to impose on children that way.

And this thing about the phœnix rising from its ashes.
No burnt bird never rose from no ashes, now did it?
And Crœsus wa'n't so very rich; if ever there was a
Crœsus; and my opinion is that there wa'n't.

"And the talk about a man having a soul," continued Felix. "There ain't no soul. A man's made
of four elements: earth and air and fire and water;
and he has luck or no luck just as the planets happen
to strike him; and when he lets go and dies, his elements is just swallered up and that's the end of *him*.
I don't even believe in microbes."

One afternoon as I walked in front of the Pelican

"I say he did write it."

Arcade I saw Cossack the grocer and
Brindle the druggist talking together
upon the sidewalk and violently gesticulating. As I
came near they grappled, and for a moment or two
there was a vigorous combat; but I seized Cossack and
pulled him away, while 'Lias Guff held Brindle fast.
Cossack hardly noticed me, but struggling to free himself that he might fly at Brindle, at last he extended his
arm, and shaking his fist at the druggist, he exclaimed:
"I say he did write it."

"And I say he didn't!" shouted Brindle in reply.

Then Cossack made a more violent effort to free himself, but I held him fast while 'Lias Guff led Brindle away toward his drug-store.

Then Cossack, pulling down his waistcoat and setting his hat on straight, looked at me to see who it was that had restrained him, and then turned to go up the street.

"Who wrote what?" I ventured to ask.

"Moses; Deuteronomy," he answered, rather sulkily. "I'll teach that Episcopalian drug-person that he can't cram any of his heresy down the throat of an orthodox Presbyterian like me."

As for Dr. Bulfinch, he was not only indignant but alarmed that notions about the Scriptures which he regarded as wholly wrong should have such wide circulation among the people and be sanctioned by the pulpit.

He happened to overhear one of his boys, Thomas Bowser, speaking in a light way to another boy about the authorship of Deuteronomy, and that very afternoon Thomas Bowser found his way to the Doctor's study, and was urged by a vigorous application of the rod to acquire new views of the authenticity of that portion of the Scripture.

"The poison," said the Doctor to me, warmly, "infects even the young. The very babes in arms after a while will have their minds warped about the Pentateuch."

I did not smile, but it seemed an odd fancy that the little ones who had not begun teething and were still happy in brandishing rattles, perhaps, should be in peril of having erroneous opinions upon this subject.

The editor of the *Defender*, as usual, steered a middle course. He referred to the subject in several of those dexterous editorials in which one thought he could discern an expression of opinion, but which left one in complete doubt as to what the writer really believed.

Mr. Spiker was vexed about the whole controversy. In his office one day he said to me:

"It's a shame, Sprat, to have the town all gone wild about Deuteronomy. I hate these theological questions. Now, tell me, Sprat, what possible difference can it make to Cossack, bustling about among ham and crackers, or to Brindle, when he stirs up soda-water or measures out ipecac, who wrote Deuteronomy? Here you have everybody in a jangle over Moses—an absolutely dead issue; and I'll bet you half of them believe the Golden Rule is some kind of a thing to measure feet and inches. If heaven is shut against a man who believes wrong about Deuteronomy most of us are lost any way; and, if it isn't, then I say drop the subject and stop fretting, and try to be honest, and pay your bills—your subscription bills, anyhow."

Inevitably, Mrs. Purvis-Hyde's interest in the controversy was eager, and her opinions were those of Dr. Fury.

"Dr. Fury *must* be sound," she said to me, "because he gets his information about it from the Fathers."

"How did they know?" I ventured to ask.

"How did the Fathers know, do you mean?"

"Yes."

"Why, they had tradition; and they knew old men who had known other old men, who had known other still older men, who had known very much older men, who—; but you understand what I mean—; a beautiful, unbroken chain, just like the Apostolical Succession, only going away back until you come to very, very, very much older men who were personally acquainted with Moses. That's the way we know it. We lean on the Fathers. Dr. Fury leans on the Fathers. I lean on them. The Historic Episcopate leans on them."

A part of the blessing of the peacemakers surely is that, by keeping the peace for themselves, they never acquire that habit of pugnacity and that heating of the blood which impels to contentiousness. Thus the spirit of strife having been awakened in some of the really good Christian people of Happy Hollow by a controversy which ended in each person holding fast to his original opinions, it was almost inevitable that there should be further strife concerning another matter.

Mrs. 'Lias Guff worshiped in the Presbyterian Church, and her worship had some of the characteristics of fervor. Mrs. Guff was a very small woman with a very large voice. As her husband's voice had diminished to mere unsonorous huskiness, there was a theory that Mrs. Guff, by some means, had superimposed his voice upon hers; and really it was surprising that a woman with so diminutive a body should have the ability to produce tones of such volume and depth. Mrs. Guff did not come far short of the power to sing bass—a power which has always been supposed beyond reach of any member of her sex.

It was a matter of complaint among the other worshipers that Mrs. Guff always sang *fortissimo* and always sang Balerma, no matter what was the metre of the hymn. Balerma, at the best, when it fits with precision the measure of the sacred song, is not a soul-

elevating tune.   Balerma is in a degree melodious, but
it is jerky.   It is built upon the iambical plan; that is
to say, it has one short foot or note, and then one long
note; so that when you sing it you give the impression
that you are trying to catch your breath between two
long notes.   Or perhaps the construction and operation
of Balerma may better be indicated if we say that there
is a short hop, a long jump, a short hop, and then
another long jump.   It may be inferred, therefore, that
Balerma lacks smoothness; Balerma does not glide;
Balerma is impetuous and fidgety, and to persons who
love flowing music, irritating.

Unfortunately Mrs. Guff's natural musical gifts were
out of all proportion to the volume of her voice, and
she had had almost no chance at all to enlarge her
powers by culture.   But Mrs. Guff, in the ductile
period of childhood, while she attended Sunday-school,
had succeeded in obtaining a firm grasp of Balerma,
and had trained her vocal cords to reproduce it.   It
was her one tune, without which Mrs. Guff would
either have been condemned to silence or to discord, so
far as the service of praise in the sanctuary was concerned.

And Mrs. Guff was not the kind of woman to keep
her single talent wrapped (if metaphor may be strained
to express the fact) in a napkin.   Whether the hymn
called for from the pulpit by Dr. Love were long metre,
short metre, sevens-and-sixes, eights, elevens, or a
compound of these and other figures, Mrs. Guff always
sang it to Balerma, and she sang it vociferously, with
all her stops out and the wind-pressure up to its limit.
She never sang without being in earnest; she never
skipped any verse that Dr. Love asked to have omitted;

she never had a cold; she never failed to come to church; and she always had a notion that both Dr. Love and the congregation admired her singing.

Indeed, Dr. Love and the members of his flock had been long-suffering and patient with Mrs. Guff. They recognized with pleasure the intensity of her enthusiasm; they shrank from wounding her feelings; they could not bear to ask her to try to reduce her voice to *piano*, if not to *pianissimo*, even if such reduction had been possible. They persuaded her to move to a pew in the rear of the church; then they shifted her into the gallery; then they put her up near to the sixteen-feet pedal pipe of the organ; but wherever she sat Mrs. Guff's interpretation of Balerma overswept and flooded and submerged everything of a sonorous nature in the church.

Finally, at a meeting of the deacons, Dr Love appointed a committee to wait upon Mrs. Guff to remonstrate tenderly with her, upon the ground that mere unselfishness required that she give other members of the congregation a chance to participate in the singing.

At first Mrs. Guff was astonished. Then she became indignant; and when Deacon Slack unwisely offered some observations reflecting upon the inadaptability of Balerma to absolutely every kind of hymn-singing, Mrs. Guff lost her temper, and gave formal notice that she would continue to sing Balerma; that she would now sing louder than she had ever done; and that she would hereafter sing it while the choir sang the anthem during the taking up of the collection.

The committee reported to another special meeting of the deacons, and in a spirit of half-panic a resolution was passed declaring Mrs. Guff's pew vacant, and instructing the treasurer not to rent another pew to her.

Upon the next Sunday Mrs. Guff came to church early, and taking a seat in a front pew she sang through all the hymns; and then with a glare in her eyes, she stood up and sang Balerma to her favorite verses while the choir struggled through the anthem.

The next time service was held a guard composed of the deacons and the sexton stood at the front door and refused to admit Mrs. Guff to the church.

Mrs. Guff had an impulse to stand upon the steps and to make the welkin ring with a continuous and vehement performance of Balerma, but her better judgment suggested that Elmira Bantam should take the matter to the civil court, and thus the foundations were laid for the case of " Amelia Powers Guff *versus* the First Presbyterian Church of Happy Hollow."

It was a case suited in quite a remarkable manner to Miss Bantam's convictions and enthusiasms. She was never happier or more intense than when she was called upon to champion the cause of members of her sex who had suffered wrong, and so Mrs. Guff walked home from the attorney's office with the assurance that unless justice had forsaken her accustomed seat in Blair County, the Presbyterian Church would rent a pew to Mrs. Guff, and Mrs. Guff would sit in it and sing Balerma.

Dr. Love called upon Miss Bantam at an early day to ascertain if a compromise could not be made, so that the church might be spared the scandal that would ensue upon the appearance of the matter in court. But Miss Bantam was firm.

"Your pews are for rent, aren't they? For rent to anyone?"

"Yes," said the Doctor, "but there is a tacit understanding, of course, as a part of the contract, that the occupant of the pew shall not indulge in any unseemly behavior; shall not, in fact, interfere with the orderly conduct of the service."

"Unseemly!" said Elmira Bantam. "Does this pious woman sing any hymns but those in your regular hymn-book?"

"No."

"She sings them only when they are formally given out to the congregation, which is invited to sing?"

"Usually, yes, but she always sings too loud."

"How loud is too loud?" inquired Miss Bantam.

Dr. Love was unable to say.

"Is there anything in the constitution or by-laws of the church indicating that a member must sing more or less loud?"

"No."

"The matter is always left to the discretion of the individual singer?"

"I suppose so, but in this—"

"And Mrs. Guff, in the exercise of this lawful and necessary discretion, sings more loudly than you like?"

"Not my like or dislike," answered Dr. Love.

"Just how loud does she sing?"

"Really there is no term that would exactly express—that is, no method of measuring precisely the degree of loudness."

"Then how can you be sure about it? How can you go into a court of justice and under the solemn obligation of an oath declare that she sings too loudly when you cannot tell how much too loudly she sings or how loudly is exactly loud enough ?"

"I suppose we must be guided in such a matter," said the Doctor, "by usage, or by the consensus of opinion of the congregation."

"No," said Miss Bantam, firmly, "for perhaps all the rest of the people may have a habit of singing too softly; or it may be that something has prejudiced them in favor of singing softly; and, at any rate, Mrs. Guff's judgment as to the right degree of loudness may be sounder than that of the rest of the congregation   You admit there is no standard."

"But she drowns the voices of the other worshipers."

"She is but one of two hundred.   Will you venture to tell the court that the other worshipers combined cannot overcome the voice of this one old woman ?"

Dr. Love hesitated for a moment, and then he said :

"And she always will persist in singing Balerma, too."

"Very well; is not Balerma one of your authorized tunes ?   It is in your hymn-book, isn't it ?"

"Yes."

"And you sing it sometimes ?"

"Often."

"Well, then, Mrs. Guff wishes to sing it oftener; that is all.   It is clear to me, Doctor, that the church has no case.   If Mrs. Guff were unruly or profane; if she persisted in singing the 'Star Spangled Banner' and 'A Life on the Ocean Wave,' and such things, you might exclude her; but the courts will never allow you to shut the doors upon a helpless old woman because she sings your own hymns to your own tunes, and merely offends your taste by singing loudly; never!   I shall apply for an injunction upon the church at once."

The view of the matter taken by 'Lias Guff, in a conversation with me one afternoon in the park, was that of a loyal husband.

"Amelia Powers Guff's singin' is a gif'. The elves give her the gif' of song in her cradle, and she's faithful to it. The sun was in Cancer when she was born, and people born when the sun is in Cancer is always faithful and has gif's for singin'."

"A gift to sing Balerma?"

"Anythin'. The Guffs make no trouble, but Amelia Powers Guff will exercise her gif' if she has to quit her own church and hold with the Methodists. A rollin' stone gathers no dross; but her gif' is to sing loud, and I don't see why, if Dr. Love can holler loud in his preachin', a little ewe lamb of his flock can't sing loud if she has the gif'.

"Amelia Powers Guff has sung that one chune goin' on forty year. She's sung it at her uprisin' and at her down-settin'; she's sung it to soothe me in sorrer and to cheer me when sad. It was her gif' and she used it. Better one chune and be faithful, than many chunes and be unfaithful and never live up to 'em. She's always knowed them notes like you know your catechism."

"You didn't have the gift?"

"I had it, but a cat drawed my breath when I was a baby and fast asleep But I sing sometimes to myself—deep down inside you know.

"What makes the little birds sing, and the bull-frogs? It's the fairies. You know birds and bull-frogs is kin anyway. Rail-birds turn into frogs in the fall and dives into the mud and stays there all winter; and when you hear the frogs in the spring, that's them a practisin' for when they'll be turned to birds agin.

"All brute animals likes music," continued 'Lias Guff, "except them Presbyterian people at Dr. Love's church. I've seen a snake in Madagascar beat time with his head like he was a stick in the hand of a drum-major, whilst a man played on the fiddle.

"Snakes is queer anyway. Snakes is devils just as rail-birds is frogs. I seen a hoop-snake once put his

tail in his mouth and chase a boy, rollin' round and round, up-hill, and he'd a ketched that boy and e't him if the boy hadn't a rab-

The hoop-snake.

bit's-foot in his pants' pocket. You've seen the jynt-snake, of course?"

"The joint-snake?"

"Yes, the jynt-snake. I've knowed 'em, when they seen a man a-comin', to break themselves into four lengths, and each length run a different way to hide in the grass till the man'd go by, and then they'd come out and all hitch together agin. I seen one jynt-snake oncet that couldn't find one of his lengths, and he had to go away crippled without it. William Jones, one of my old mates, told me he had seen one take off one of his lengths and play on it like a flute; but I never seen it done, and I don't believe what I don't see.

"But you bet, sir," said 'Lias Guff, returning to the case of Mrs. Guff, as he prepared to leave me, "that

Miss Elmira'll fix them Presbyterians. She's a smart
woman, ain't she? I've noticed, sir, if you'll let me
say it respectful, that you've looked tender at her."

" You are mistaken."

" Werry well, sir, if I'm mistaken, then I'm mistaken,
but I haven't spent forty years with Amelia Powers
Guff without realizin' that a man who hain't a wife for
his bosom might as well have no bosom. Life ain't
worth livin'; and happy is the bosom, say I, that gits
Miss Elmira Bantam, if her hair is borderin' on red."

Upon application from Elmira Bantam, the court
issued a temporary injunction requiring the First
Presbyterian Church not to interfere with the attempt
of Amelia Powers Guff to participate in an orderly
manner in the services.

On the Sunday following Mrs. Guff went to church
and sat in a pew in the middle aisle, and found the first
hymn when it was announced. The organist played
Balerma before the choir began, and Mrs. Guff, hearing the tune, closed the hymn-book and refused to sing.
Later in the service Dr. Love gave out four other common metre hymns, and the choir sang each of them to
Balerma, and another hymn was sung to the same tune
in place of the usual anthem. Mrs. Guff remained
silent through it all, and then walked out during the
benediction and went over to arrange with Rev. Jason
Hole to join the Methodist Church.

Miss Bantam withdrew the case from court.

Chapter XIV

The Black Sheep

Before the theological and ecclesiastical excitements had fully passed, and Happy Hollow, excepting for the never-failing interest maintained by A. J. Pelican's boom, had lapsed into tranquillity, Simon Bulfinch's wife died. She has not often appeared in this narrative, for indeed I never met her above twice, and I heard little of her excepting now and then a word from Mrs. Bantam, to whom Julie spoke sometimes of the forlorn and desolate life of the poor woman.

Julie was with her in the last illness, nursing her constantly, and caring also for the needs of Charley and of the dwelling house. Mrs. Bulfinch's constant longing was for her husband, whom Julie Mortimer found and urged to visit his wife. Simon came now and then to see the invalid, and made a pretence of affectionateness which deceived her, but did not at all impose upon the clear-headed woman who attended her.

When the end was near, Julie, upon Mrs. Bulfinch's entreaty, sought Simon once more; and when he came Mrs. Bulfinch told him she was sure she was dying, but that she should be perfectly happy if he would put his arms about her. This Simon did, and held her while

226

she faintly smiled at him and seemed indeed satisfied. But Julie said that even while the woman who loved him so deeply and had suffered so much for his evil conduct was passing away, Simon's face showed perfect indifference. He behaved as if he were an actor in a comedy, smiling at Miss Mortimer as she stood by the bedside, and even once whispering to her a jibe at the devotion manifested for him by his wife.

Simon Bulfinch seemed to have had the hope that when his wife had gone he might find some means of taking possession of the house and its contents and of exercising control over Charley. But the day of the funeral had not passed before he learned that Dr. Bulfinch's power over the property and the boy was absolute and indisputable. The boy became his uncle's ward, and the property remained in the Doctor's hands to administer until Charley should be of age. Mrs. Bulfinch's father had taken Simon's measure before his daughter married; and his wisdom and foresight now had clear demonstration.

Charley, of his own choice, became a member of the Doctor's household, and this filled Simon with bitterness and fury. The sole purpose of life with him seemed now to be to harass and insult the Doctor. He adopted an odd method of doing this. I have said that in face and figure he closely resembled his brother. Now he assumed a costume precisely like that usually worn by Dr. Bulfinch, and dressed in this manner he appeared nearly every day upon the streets of the village in a condition of semi-intoxication.

I have been startled more than once when I saw him swaying in his walk upon the pavement, or half-lying upon one of the benches in the little park, by the first impression that this was Dr. Bulfinch himself; and it was therefore not remarkable that some of the stupid people who were to be found in Happy Hollow, as

The black sheep.

they are to be found in every community, should accept the report that Dr. Bulfinch had become intemperate.

Where Simon dwelt, where he hid himself when he was not before the public, nobody seemed to know. I inclined to suspect that the house of Isaac Williams, out upon the mountain-side where I found him in that night of tempest months ago, was his abiding-place.

It was his favorite practice to waylay Dr. Bulfinch in his afternoon walks, and to jeer him and fling insulting epithets at him, the more virulently if any of the town's people were within hearing.

By the middle of June the great Aramink House out upon the border of the sweet Aramink Lake, which mirrored the great hills and lay placid and beautiful at their base, was ready for its summer guests. It was but a little distance from the edge of the town; and one afternoon when the sunshine was glorious and the air pure and soft and warm, and all the hills and fields were rich with their covering of green, I walked out to the place with Dr. Bulfinch.

We had looked through the great house and admired its equipment, and then we came out to the border of the lake and strolled along by the water-side until we reached a point where the lake emptied itself into the stream that ran right through the town. A little bridge was here—a bridge without parapet or railing, over which vehicles and pedestrians might pass the stream to reach the other side of the lake without using a boat or going clear into the town.

While Dr. Bulfinch and I stood upon the bridge admiring the view up the lake and down the stream, and talking about school-matters, I saw Simon, manifestly not wholly sober, coming toward us.

I had an impulse to turn the Doctor away that he might not see his brother; but we could not escape Simon unless we should go to the further side of the lake, and this Dr. Bulfinch was indisposed to do.

Simon had sought him out and came rapidly toward us. As soon as he reached the bridge he assailed the Doctor with venomous language which I shall not repeat. He stood in such a posture that we must either stand still, retreat, or push by him at close quarters. Dr. Bulfinch made no reply to his evil words, and both of us moved forward, intending to pass the man and go onward to the village. As we came to him, Simon, nearing the edge of the bridge, and no doubt made more angry by the Doctor's silence, lifted his arm as if to strike his brother. At that moment either his foot slipped or, his body not being under control, was swayed by his gesture, for he tumbled backward into the lake and went under.

The water there is quite ten feet deep, and I doubt if Simon Bulfinch could swim. Assuredly he did not swim then. I do not know the thought that was in the Doctor's mind when the man went over. The thing was done so suddenly and without expectation that anyone might be forgiven for hesitating. Probably the Doctor's first thought was that he could hold out a hand to Simon when he came to the surface. But in truth when Simon's head appeared again above the water there was evidence enough that he could not clasp a hand or any other thing, even if he could be reached.

In a moment Dr. Bulfinch flung off his coat and hat and plunged into the water. That *he* could swim was plainly apparent. When Simon came up again the Doctor, old and weighted by clothing as he was, seized him by the collar of his coat and pushed him toward the bridge. Thereupon I lay flat upon the bridge, and leaning over caught Simon's clothing and held him while the Doctor clambered out of the water.

By this time two men over at the hotel, who had seen the man fall, came up to help us, and Simon was dragged out and laid upon the bridge. He was quite insensible, and the Docter, wet as he was, addressed himself to the task of restoring him. The Doctor knew precisely how to do this, also, and in twenty minutes Simon opened his eyes. The men from the hotel a few moments later lifted him and prepared to carry him to the house. As they did so Simon saw the Doctor beside him, and gathering all the little strength that he could command he raised his head and spat upon him. Then the head dropped backward and Simon fainted.

Dr. Bulfinch, against my remonstrance, would have Simon carried to the Doctor's house, where, when he had been dried and reclothed he was placed upon the Doctor's bed, while a physician was summoned.

That night he must have recovered fully, for when the Doctor came down stairs in the morning after a night almost sleepless, the front door was wide open, many of the fragile things in the library had been wrecked, and Simon's room was empty.

I could not repent that Dr. Bulfinch had saved the man's life; nor could I have mourned had it happened that he should have fallen into the lake when no one was near to rescue him

But a worse fate than drowning was awaiting him, and near at hand, too.

We were coming close to the end of the school year, and teachers and scholars were glad of it. In the bright June days the boys often turned their eyes from their books, and looking through the open windows of the school-room at the trees and the grass and the flowers, felt longings for vacation time. For the young the summer days should be play-days, and for the teachers, days of refreshment and refitting for the tasks of the school time.

Under the influence of the reign of love, stimulated by diligent application to the backs of the boys of love's symbol, the rod, most of our pupils had climbed fairly well the hill of knowledge, that tough old declivity, and could declare that they had really learned a little of the necessary, but quite inferior, variety of wisdom that the schools supply.

One of the things Dr. Bulfinch most desired to teach the boys was the art of reading their own language with proper articulation, emphasis, and inflection, and in this purpose he had my hearty sympathy.

And so, upon every Friday the afternoon session was given up to recitations, which the boys always

alluded to as "speaking pieces." Those who have
heard boys in the privacy of the school-room trying to
speak pieces will have conviction that, excepting in the
rarest cases, the hardest task of the teacher is to in-
struct the mind how the tongue should be used.

In truth, the task generally is beyond the power even
of the teacher whose own mind and tongue have been
trained, and who has acquired, from long and painful
experience with somnolent preachers and other dull
public speakers, a conviction that human utterance
rightly guided by intelligence is one of the pressing
needs of the race.

The boys in our school were permitted to choose for
themselves the pieces they should speak, and the range
of their choice was narrow. The youth who ventured
to select any bit of prose or verse that had not a hundred or more precedents behind it was regarded by his
companions as eccentric beyond the limits of their
patience.

Dr. Bulfinch and I have listened to "The Psalm of
Life" and "Excelsior," to "Bingen on the Rhine" and
"Casabianca," and later, to "Barbara Freitchie" and
"Sheridan's Ride," presented with such variety of
utterance and gesture that we have wondered how a
new boy could invent any new awkwardness of manner
or blunder of emphasis.

Often I have sat upon the front bench while a boy
persuaded himself that he was reciting "Excelsior,"
and tried to put myself mentally in the speaker's place
that I might conjecture if that stumbling, stammering
lad had the smallest notion of the poet's meaning.
Mr. Longfellow did not deserve such a fate, but remorse would have embittered his declining years could

he have known what unoffending pedagogues have suffered from the "Psalm of Life" and "Excelsior."

There are nervous men in the profession who, upon recitation day, finding that they were doomed again to form a mental picture of that intrepid but un- reasoning young man who insisted upon mounting to the Al- pine summits amid snow and ice, have felt that they would gladly assassinate him and take the chances of the scaffold if they could get at him be- fore he began his wintry and slippery ascent.

The Doctor was long - suffering, but sometimes he grew petulant and sarcastic. One day when a boy rose to give the third recital of "Excel- sior" upon that after- noon, the speaker re- peated four times the opening lines—"The shades of night were falling fast"—and at the end of each repetition stopped and looked weakly about, as

"The shades of night were falling fast."

if he expected to find the second line written upon the walls or the windows, or coming in at the front door.

"Joseph," said the Doctor at last, "if the shades of night fell no faster than your utterance indicates, the miracle of Joshua must have been repeated; but I doubt it. You seem to fail to seize the broader sentiment of the poem. Strange, too! for you have heard it not infrequently."

Joseph gasped once or twice and then, clutching at the missing line, he went on

Three boys having dealt treacherously with "Excelsior," a fourth boy came upon the platform and, with an air of having found a hitherto undiscovered jewel of poesy, began to say, "The shades of night were falling fast."

"Stop!" shouted Dr. Bulfinch. "Stop! not four times! Not four times in one day for 'Excelsior'! It is a glorious poem, conveying invaluable moral lessons, but we need to digest what we have already taken into our mental constitution. Give us more time, Thomas. Besides, Thomas, you appear to misapprehend the very title of that lovely composition. You give it as 'Eggselsior,' whereas Mr. Longfellow entitled it 'Excelsior,' a Latin word signifying higher. Have you no other piece in your memory to favor us with?"

"No, sir," said Thomas, gloomily.

"Very well," replied the Doctor. "Report to me in my study at quarter past three."

When Hosea Blinn began to tell about that surprising boy who stood on the burning deck (how very tiresome that boy is!), Dr. Bulfinch interfered:

"You spoke 'Casabianca' last Friday, Hosea, did you not?"

" Yes, sir."

" And the Friday before ?"

" Yes, sir."

" If my memory does not mislead me, you spoke it so long ago as September, and many times since."

" I don't remember, sir."

" But I do !" thundered the Doctor. " It seems to me that I have burned into my mind the image of Hosea Blinn standing here declaiming about the heroic performance of Casabianca. I fear you are acquiring it as a habit, Hosea, and that if I permit it to proceed, you will pass on down to an advanced old age repeating 'Casabianca.' Stop it now! Learn something else. The human mind craves variety. The kingdom of song contains other gems than this, little as you suspect it. Search for them, Hosea, search, I say, and try to find another or prepare to meet me in my study."

While George Grass was relating Mrs. Norton's piteous story of the " Soldier of the Legion " who lay dying in Algiers, he drew his sleeve over the end of his nose three or four times, until Dr. Bulfinch interfered :

" George," he said, in a stern voice, " is that intended for an explanatory gesture ?"

" No, sir," said George, mournfully, doing it again as if to prove that it was not.

" Because," said the Doctor, " if it is so intended, it seems to me to be irrelevant. Discontinue it, if you please, and go on. You were saying, if I recall your words, that 'the soft moon rose up slowly.' Begin again there."

George took up the narrative at that point and with

evident effort kept his sleeve from his face. Several times his arm made an involuntary movement in that direction, but he grasped it quickly with his left hand and pulled it down.

"I observe," said Dr. Bulfinch, as George concluded the recitation, "that you speak of Bin-gen with the 'g' soft, as in 'gingerbread.' That is incorrect pronunciation. Do you know what Bingen is?"

"No, sir."

"Make a guess, George."

"It's a place where they make soft gingerbread."

"Come to my study at quarter past three," said the Doctor, "and we will consider the matter further."

The practice of visiting the Doctor's study at quarter past three had an unfortunate consequence upon Dr. Bulfinch's fifty-ninth birthday. I think the Doctor was liked by the boys in spite of the vigor of his right arm and his severe interpretation of the law of love.

At any rate, upon the suggestion of Polly Hopkins, whose conscience had never had complete satisfaction since his famous combat with the master, the boys collected some money and bought therewith Shakespeare's Complete Works in three volumes bound in muslin of a violently red color; and a committee of three was charged to give the books to the Doctor on his birthday.

I had not been acquainted with the enterprise, or I should have arranged it differently; but the boys wished to surprise the Doctor, and so the committee headed by Polly Hopkins, who carried the books, visited the study upon Thursday afternoon at quarter past three.

Five other boys were in the room when the committee entered, and one of the five at that very moment
was the victim of strenuous flagellation. The committee sat down to wait until the regular exercises should
be ended.

But Dr. Bulfinch had warmed up to his work when
five boys had received the benediction of the rod, and
he was always intensely in earnest while performing
this particular service. So, as the last of the five fled
through the door, the Doctor, holding the rod in his
right hand, and looking warm, beckoned with his left
hand to Hopkins to come forward and take a thrashing.

Hopkins, never at his ease in that room and in the
presence of the wielded rod, rose to his feet and began
to. try to explain to the Doctor that his errand was
rather that of a bearer of tokens of peace than of a
malefactor to whom stripes were due.

But Dr. Bulfinch was impatient; he never would
permit argument from a boy who had been ordered up
at quarter past three, and so it happened, most unfortunately, that the surprise prepared for him turned out
to be a surprise for Polly Hopkins and the committee.

"Come here, sir!" said the Doctor sternly, with outstretched hand, as Hopkins attempted to speak; and
the boy, overawed and frightened, dropped the Complete Works of Shakespeare in three red volumes and
came forward.

When the Doctor had brought him in complete sub-
jection to the reign of love, Hopkins made another
effort to remove the misapprehension under which the
Doctor labored, but again he was silenced until the
Doctor had thoroughly flogged the other members of
the committee.

Then there was another and very painful surprise. The scarlet volumes lay upon the chair, and the three boys stood about them much inclined to cry, and yet with a grim resolution to stand fast by their original purpose to celebrate Dr. Bulfinch's fifty-ninth birthday.

When the Doctor had put the rod in its resting-place over the mantel and had expressed with a sigh his feeling of gladness that his task was done, he turned about and was astonished to see the boys still lingering in the torture chamber.

He was startled.

"What's the matter, boys? Why don't you go?"

Choking down a sob that would come into his throat, Polly Hopkins at last began the formal address that he had prepared and committed to memory.

" Honored teacher; the pupils of the Happy Hollow Classical and Mathematical Academy, appreciating your noble and unselfish efforts to lead them along the ways of learning and to train them up in the way that they should go, have felt that on this your fifty-ninth birthday—have felt that on this your—your fifty-ninth bi—have felt" (here Polly Hopkins's memory broke down completely) " like giving you Shakespeare's Complete Works in three magnificent red volumes;" and Polly Hopkins seized them and held them out toward the Doctor.

Dr. Bulfinch was filled with consternation and remorse when he discovered the mistake he had made. For a moment he hardly knew what to say. At last he spoke to Hopkins:

"Thomas, my son, do I understand that you and the other boys in the school have prepared for me a birthday present?"

"Yes, sir," said all the members of the committee.

"And this is it?" said the Doctor, looking at the books.

"Yes, sir," responded the committee.

"And none of you were sent here for punishment?"

"No, sir. We came to give you the Complete Works of Shakespeare in three volumes."

"And in my stupid blindness I flogged all three of you?"

"Yes, sir," said the committee promptly.

Dr. Bulfinch was troubled. He put the books upon the table, sat in his chair, and with his hand to his chin considered the matter. When he looked up again he had tears in his eyes, and Polly Hopkins and the other members of the committee had to bite their lips to keep from breaking down.

"I hardly know," said the Doctor, as if he were speaking to himself, "I hardly know how to—or rather, what—exactly in what manner to— Boys, I am most grateful; far more grateful than I can tell you, for your beautiful gift and for the affection that prompted all the boys to remember my birthday. Say so, Thomas, to all the boys in the school. And now—I can't quite ask you to forgive me, Hopkins and Blinn and Prosser, that is not enough. It was really terrible for me to misunderstand you on such an occasion."

Dr. Bulfinch again put his hand to his chin, while he reflected.

"Did I hurt you, Thomas, just now?" he asked.

"Not very much, sir."

"I must have done so, Hopkins. I am feeling particularly well and strong this afternoon. And you, Prosser, I dealt strenuously with you, my boy, did I not?"

"I've had it worse, sir," answered Prosser bravely.

"Hosea," said the Doctor, turning to Blinn, "I think I bore on hardly in your case."

"No, sir," replied Blinn, with an almost reckless purpose to be cheerful, "I didn't even feel it."

"Hah!" exclaimed the Doctor, his professional instinct asserting itself, "I must remember that when you come up for discipline. You had nothing under your jacket, Hosea, for you were not expecting—"

"Not a thing, sir."

Dr. Bulfinch meditated for awhile, and at last he said:

"How many blows did I strike you, Thomas?"

"Sixteen, sir. I counted them."

The Doctor arose, removed his coat and waistcoat, and took down the symbol of love from the place above the mantel Handing it to Polly Hopkins he said:

"Thomas, I want you to strike me sixteen times on the back, sixteen for yourself, and sixteen each for Prosser and Blinn. Hit hard, Thomas, I must suffer humiliation for the wrong I did you."

When the presentation committee filed out of the Doctor's study and hurried down stairs, there was not a boy of the three who did not feel that the Complete Works of Shakespeare in sixteen volumes bound in scarlet and gold would fail to represent the degree of admiration with which Dr. Bulfinch's pupils should regard him.

On one of the last days of the session an unusually large number of boys waited in the doctor's study at quarter past three for the rod which could not be spared without spoiling the child.

I do not know how it came to pass that the victims

were so many. It may have been that the high spirits produced by the nearness of the holidays impelled the boys to unusual misconduct; it may have been that Dr. Bulfinch had a purpose to whip the boys in an anticipatory manner, so to speak; to flog them ahead, to cover the holidays, so that the faults yet uncommitted, but latent in the depraved natures of his pupils, should have retribution prepared for them.

At any rate, the boys sat upon the chairs upon that unfortunate afternoon, and I sat with them to prevent the escape of any.

While Dr. Bulfinch was engaged in punishing one boy, the door of the room opened and Simon Bulfinch appeared. He stood and watched the Doctor for one minute, and then he said:

"Swish, swish, swish! Flagello, flagellare, flagellavi, flagellatum, verb of the first conjugation, signifying to wallop. Boys, it is good for you; it is wholesome, wholesome for young and for old. Swish, swish, swish!"

Dr. Bulfinch, still holding the boy by the collar, suspended the whipping, and, with a white, stern face, turned to Simon

"Don't pause, dominie," said Simon, smiling. "Give him some more. Let the reign of love continue its gentle sway. You are waiting for your turn, Sprat, aren't you? Then the dominie ought to have a turn."

The waiting boys looked scared as the intruder continued his ribald talk I should have tried to thrust him from the room, but the Doctor with a motion of his hand restrained me.

"Next!" exclaimed Simon, as the Doctor released the boy he had been whipping and sent him away.

16

"Come, boys, step up for punishment; and when you have all been punished we shall see about punishing the old man. His turn is coming."

"Have you no shame, Simon?" said the Doctor at last. "Go away from us, and stop this scandal."

Simon laughed, and, turning to the boys, he said:

"You would think him a nice clean old Christian gentleman, wouldn't you? Scandal, boys! If we wanted scandal we could get it by telling on him!"

"Leave the room," said the Doctor, angrily.

"And I will tell on him," continued Simon. "Why, boys, do you know that this man who is flogging you stole money while he was at college—stole it with that very hand that holds the rod!"

Dr. Bulfinch sat down by the table and buried his face in his hands.

"See!" exclaimed Simon, "he doesn't attempt to deny it. He can't deny it. He daren't look you in the face. Boys, what do you think ought to be done with a thief that poses as a saint? Whip him, I say."

For the second time in my life the duty devolved upon me of casting out Simon Bulfinch. Without caring for what the Doctor thought I seized him suddenly and flung him into the hall.

The Doctor raised his head, and with white, trembling lips he said:

"Boys, you are dismissed," and the scholars, awestruck and silent, went out of the room.

Chapter XV

On A Summer Night

Every boy who heard the accusation made against Dr. Bulfinch by his brother Simon helped to spread the news throughout the school, and the scholars carried it to the village, so that within a few hours all the people in Happy Hollow knew what had happened.

Most of them were disposed to regard the matter with indifference because of their confidence in Dr. Bulfinch and their knowledge of the worthlessness of Simon, but always there are people who love a bit of scandal more than they love fair play and people whose experience with their own moral constitutions incline to make them suspicious of any man who has a reputation for uprightness.

Besides, this report of the Doctor's misconduct in early life came to the ears of the folks in Happy Hollow just after the reports had crept about that the Doctor had become intemperate; and what more natural, some people said, than that a man who had been dishonest in his youth, and probably also intemperate,

should find at last the effort to be virtuous too much
for him, and should begin to drop backward toward
vice?   There were men in Happy Hollow who in their
own lives had found virtue slippery to the fingers and
friendship with evil entirely easy and comfortable.
Every one of these persons believed Dr. Bulfinch guilty,
and all of them no doubt felt a little glow of pleasure
in entertaining that belief.   When you are weak and
foolish and wicked it is agreeable to know that you are
not lonely.

Dr. Bulfinch had true friends who feared that the
scandal might hurt his school, and there were brethren
in his church who, wisely or unwisely, considered that
the Doctor's church-membership required him to make
some answer to the charge, even if it were offered by
a malignant half-inebriate vagabond.

There is something to be said for that stern system
which requires a professor of religion to keep his good
name spotless or else to give an account of himself to
his fellow-professors; but I have always felt that, if I
should be called to sit in judgment in such a manner
upon a human creature, I should be so filled with a
sense of my own deficiencies that I should be ashamed
to pretend to be a minister of justice.

Dr. Bulfinch was summoned to appear before a tri-
bunal composed of the church officers, and with characteristic loyalty and humility he consented to obey
the call.

"I came late to the session that night," said Cossack,
the grocer, in giving me an account of the proceedings,
"and so I didn't hear Doctor Bulfinch's statement; but
the presiding officer told me when I got there that the
Doctor had owned up to taking some money while he

was at college. It was this way," continued Cossack.
"The Doctor, just a young fellow, you know, was
treasurer of a college society, and this rascal Simon,
his brother, came along and made him believe that
Simon would have to go to prison unless he could
raise a hundred and twenty dollars quick. And Simon
told the Doctor that if he would let him have it he
would pay it back in two weeks. So the Doctor, like
a fool, hands over to Simon out of the society treasury
the dollars he wanted, and of course Simon never returned a cent. The Doctor tried in various ways to
raise the money, but he couldn't do it, and pretty soon
it was wanted by the society, and the Doctor confessed
and they turned him out.

"Very well, what does Dr. Bulfinch do but go to
work in a saw-mill or somewhere that summer, and
earn a lot of money, and pay the society back twofold—gave 'em twice as much as he took!

"Now, Mr. Sprat, when I saw the poor old man
setting in the pew there at the meeting with his eyes
turned to the floor and his face ghastly; and when I
heard that he never really stole any money, but was
cheated by his brother because he wanted to show a
kindness, and then actually paid back double the
money, I couldn't help myself, but I exclaimed ' Gosh,
brethren, is that the whole of it? You're not going to
condemn one of the sheep of this fold—a holy man—a
saint, I think, on any such case as that? I'm not,
any way. Paid it back twice! Simple interest'd have
squared the thing in the grocery trade and ended it;
and if we don't call it square and stand by this good
man we ain't fit to be called Christians?'

"That's about what I said, and said it warm, too,

and the poor old Doctor a-setting there with his eyes shut and the tears just bursting from under the lids and a-rolling down his cheeks. Sprat, if you and I were to be overhauled by a church committee for every little crooked thing we've ever done, where would we be, Sprat? Where would the church committee be? I know where some of 'em would be. There's men among 'em, Sprat, that wouldn't bear examination under a microscope; just forlorn old sinners, like you and me and the rest of us; you understand.

"Well, sir," continued Cossack, gaining in earnestness; "when I set down it was clear enough that the meeting was going to let the Doctor off and tell the town that he is a true Christian; but what does brother Prosser do but look at me and say: 'I now move that we take up the case of brother Cossack,' says he, 'and proceed to call him to account.'

"What for?" says I.

"'For saying "gosh" a moment ago,' says he, 'for saying "gosh" in this sacred edifice at a solemn meeting.' 'What's the matter with "gosh"?' I asked. 'It is a pagan form of profanity,' says brother Prosser, 'used by unbelievers when they swear, and entirely unbecoming to the lips of an officer of the Christian church' He said it is derived from Josh, who is a heathen god in China, and a bad sort of god at that.

"Well, then," said Cossack, still with fervor in his manner, "I up and says: '"Gosh" is a familiar phrase in the grocery trade, and as harmless as the prattle of a little baby. It means the same as when a man says "My!" or "Do tell!" or "Well, well, well!" or "I declare!" or any other innocent exclamation of astonishment.' And then I went on to say that I'd heard it used in Sunday-school when I was a boy, and by ministers, and I'd want to hear some better reason than brother Prosser's guess about a Chinese josh before I'd take it back or apologize.

"And then Dr. Love he asks, 'What Sunday-school did you hear it in, brother Cossack, and what minister have you known to use it?' and I said I'd wait until my case came up before I put in my evidence; for to tell the truth I don't exactly remember the particulars about the Sunday-school and the ministers, although I'm positively certain about it, and the facts may come to my mind, and besides, I wasn't going to be caught in a trap.

"And then, to wind the thing up, I says: 'And anyhow, Dr. Love and brethren, there's been fuss enough in the churches over the Deuteronomy business, for I nearly got into a fight about it myself with Brindle of the Episcopalians; and then there was a row over Mrs. Guff's singing; and now if you're going to try to discipline a faithful member who tries to do right and to live up to his profession, because in a moment of excitement caused by the persecution of an innocent man he happens to use a harmless, little, playful word like "gosh," it seems to me there's just no use at all trying to have peace and brotherly love.'

"'What I say,' says I, going right on and freeing my mind, 'is, let's disband the church and fight it out like the world's people. Let's sand our sugar and water our syrup and put bread-crumbs in our black pepper, and sell intoxicating liquors by the jugful.'

"Then Dr. Love advised to let the matter drop, and we all went over and shook hands with poor Dr. Bulfinch, who was very hearty with me, and I told brother

Prosser that what he wanted, besides more grace, was to steer for home and look up 'gosh' in the encyclopedia, or one of those all-round dictionaries."

This was Cossack's version of the story of the full acquittal of Dr. Bulfinch. The Doctor himself never spoke to me upon the subject. He was acquitted by the church, but I could perceive that the whole business had brought anguish to the soul of the good old man.

He was the kind of man to keep his sorrows to himself and bravely to bear his own burdens. But who indeed can give much help in such a case to the burden-bearer? And then, just at that time I was selfishly busy with an important matter of my own, and in youth the sorrows of others sit lightly upon us if our minds are filled with our own delights. In truth, I was much occupied during the week in which the trial was held by consideration of my feelings for Ruby, and of the methods by which I might properly express them.

Our house faced the street, with a little space between the front door and the gate. At the side of the house, as I have already said, was a covered porch, stretching the length of the building and looking out over a lovely garden, with clumps of trees and shrubs, and here and there a bed for flowers.

I sat in a rocking-chair upon the porch one sweet summer evening with Mrs. Bantam not far from me, and Ruby in the chair midway between. After a time Mrs. Bantam left us and went over to the house of the neighbor next door to make a little visit; so Ruby and I were there with no one near.

It was a perfect night. The soft wind came up from the southwest and blew upon us, carrying the fragrance of the roses in the garden, and gently rustling the leaves of the trees and the vines that overcrept the trellis upon the porch-pillars.

There was not complete darkness, for the stars were out, and there was a faint glimmer of the street lamps a hundred yards away; but there was silence, excepting when we heard the tinkling of the bells of the car-horses down the street; or the rattle of a light vehicle which swept quickly by our house; or the step of a pedestrian. The katydids and the crickets chirped among the trees, and now and then a tree-frog sent forth his harsh note; but the hush of the night was upon us save for these intermittent sounds, and as I sat there alone with the woman I loved so much I felt sure the time had come to discover if indeed she loved me as I hoped.

Ruby was in good spirits, full of laughter and bright talk, and without any thought that serious things were to be said to her.

We spoke of all the people of this story who were dear to us; of Colonel and Mrs. Bantam, of Julie and Spiker and Elmira, and laughed a little bit about Aunty Bantam's affectionate enthusiasm for her husband. And then we turned the conversation somehow to the difference in age of some of our married friends.

"And how old do you think I am?" I asked Ruby at last.

She laughed lightly and said, half in fun, but speaking as she had been used to speak of that matter:

"You seem very, very old to me."

I was vexed "I don't want you to think me old," I said. "I am but twenty-nine, and that is only ten years older than you are."   ·

"Only ten years!" she exclaimed. "But that is very much older, isn't it? I feel as if I should be ready for gray hairs in ten years."

"Nonsense, Ruby! Twenty-nine is a charming age for a woman. She is young, but she is mature, and with her character formed. A man and his wife should have just about that difference between them," I ventured to say.

"It is too much," she said demurely.

"What difference do you think is best?"

For a moment she did not answer. Then she said:

"Truly I think it is unimportant. But, indeed, I know nothing at all about it. How should I know?"

"It can make no difference," I said, "if they love one another, can it?"

"I suppose not," she answered, "but I cannot tell." Her voice had fallen low. She suspected that I had a purpose in such talk; and then she said nervously, "I wish aunty would come home."

But I was resolved not to permit this opportunity to pass by unimproved. I would know the best or the worst before we parted.

"Ruby," I said, "shall the difference in years shut me out from you? I love you, my dear."

Her answer was to put her hands quickly over her face and to begin to cry.

I never know what to do when a woman cries in that manner. Why does she not speak? Does she mean yes or no?· or that she cannot decide? or that she is hurt or pleased, or just torn up about it? Women cry for so many different reasons.

But, having spoken my mind and my heart, I could not be silent further.

"Do not cry," I said. "I cannot tell if I have hurt you or made you happy. I love you dearly, my Ruby. From the very first; when I saw you in the green room; when you walked with me to school; out on the mountain, where I was mad to risk your life that I might have the sweetness of your company. I love you now more than ever, and you will come with me and be mine, won't you dear?"

"It cannot, cannot be! Never!" she said, sobbing, and with her face still covered by her hands.

"You do not say you do not love me," I said. "You cannot say that. I shall not despair until you do say it."

"Do not urge me," she said. "Oh, be kind to me as you always were. Pity me. I cannot answer you."

"How can I hold my peace?" I said. "Be my wife, Ruby dear, and I will make your life happy."

"I know you would try to do so," she said, taking her hands from her face. "You are a kind, good man. You have always given me more than I deserve. I owe you so much. How can I grieve you?"

"You owe me nothing," I answered. "There is no question of obligation. If you love me, you love me. If you do not, it is better that I should have you say so now, however painful the words may be."

"I cannot accept your love. That is all I can say," she answered, with her voice full of tearfulness. "But please, oh, please, do not let this take from me your friendship. Let us be always as we have been. Let us forget that you spoke to me. Some day I can tell you all. But not now! Not now!"

I took her hand and kissed it, and she was willing that it should linger for a moment in mine.

I was filled with grief and disappointment, but hope was far from gone. Sitting there with her I could not measure her words or consider the situation with a clear mind, but, overpowering every other thought and feeling, was the remembrance that she had not said that she did not love me.

And she wished me to be with her still as a friend, a helper, and a companion.

I saw plainly enough, when I had time for reflection upon the matter, that a woman who felt no and meant no, would have said no. Either Ruby was uncertain about herself, or she loved me and had some reason for concealing the fact.

I was not sorry that Mrs. Bantam should return to us almost as soon as Ruby had finished speaking the words that I have quoted.

The old lady suspected nothing, and as she had much to say, the way was made easy for Ruby and for me to speak now and then of common things.

But what perverse spirit infested Mrs. Bantam's mind and impelled her presently to say:

"I called at Mrs. Purvis-Hyde's this afternoon, Ruby, and she asked in the kindest manner about you. She inquired about Mr. Sprat, also, in what seemed to me a most interesting way. Why don't you spend an evening there sometimes, Mr. Sprat? It would be lovely. She is a gifted woman, and she adores intellect. She told me so"

"She is a charming woman," I said.

"Perfectly charming, and quite equal to the most advanced thought. She makes an idol of culture, and yearns for the society of the gifted—of children of genius."

"But I am not gifted; and then, she is much older than I am."

"Not much," said Mrs. Bantam, persuasively. "Only a few years. Perhaps ten or fifteen. And ten years' difference is very little, isn't it, Ruby, my love?"

Ruby scarcely murmured a reply that I did not hear.

"You wrong yourself, dear Mr. Sprat," persisted Mrs. Bantam. "To find both a mother and a wife in one lovely intellectual woman would be a twofold delight. I say nothing of Mrs. Purvis-Hyde's large financial resources. Gold is but dross when love reigns. You need love in your young life, dear friend. It would lift you to a higher plane. What shall we say of life without love? What *shall* we say? Merely that it is a form of death. Shall I begin the campaign for you? Would you be willing that I should with the greatest delicacy and discretion try to ascertain what Mrs. Purvis-Hyde's feeling for you is? She will reveal herself to me."

I entreated Mrs. Bantam not to engage in such an investigation, and so she passed to other subjects of conversation, until at last the time came for aunt and niece to retire.

Mrs. Bantam went bustling into the house when she had said good-night; but Ruby lingered for an instant as she reached the open door, and extending her hand to me, while she smiled as if she could hardly refrain from weeping, she said:

"Good-night, my dear friend. I thank you so much for your friendship. Forgive me if I have wounded you. Oh, forgive me!"

And then I kissed her hand again and said:

"Good-night, Ruby! Even your friendship is precious to me. Good-night!" and she went away from me.

I had time enough in which to reflect upon her words and my own situation. For I sat there during several hours; and while the night grew stiller and the south wind swept more strongly across the garden, and the belated gibbous moon, creeping slowly upward, threw faint shadows and little glints of soft light upon the lawn, I said to myself that I should have Ruby for my wife.

I knew nothing of such matters from experience, and I had no vain feeling about my powers of attraction; but every man has sometimes, deep down in that mysterious consciousness which does not deal with logic and which is not subject to direct control, convictions which are immovable; and there my immovable conviction was that I should win my sweetheart at last.

It was past midnight when I rose from my chair to enter the house. The night was so lovely that I had an impulse to linger upon the porch; but I resisted it, and turned away from the shrubbery and the moonlight and the fragrance of the flowers. As I placed my hand upon the latch of the door I was startled by two reports of a pistol, followed by the scream of a man's voice, and the sounds seemed to come from a place not far away.

While I hesitated whether to go into the house or to try to discover what had happened, two men hurried by me in the street, plainly bent upon investigation, and at once I went out and followed them.

We had not walked two blocks away before we saw

a man lying flat upon the pavement, while by him stood
'Lias Guff holding another man, and two great dogs
ran around and about the group, sniffing the pavement,
wagging their tails, and now and then barking in a
queer, half-muffled way.

"I was a-layin' in on Prosser's porch," said 'Lias
Guff, when we asked him what was the matter, "and I
guess I must have fell asleep, for when I feel sleepy I
always gits out of the moonlight so it won't blacken
my face, and while I was layin' there either asleep or
thinkin' about somethin', them dogs begun to bark, and
I set up, and the fus' thing I knowed, out comes that
man on the pavement there through Prosser's side
winder yer, and this man a-follerin' him, skeered, I
reckon, by the dogs a-barkin'.

"So then I hollered for that man there to stop, but
he didn't, and this man didn't, so I drawed my pistol,
not ezzackly intendin' to fire at him, but before I
knowed it, somehow, the thing went off, and that man
dropped; I must a hit him by accident; and them
dogs jumped on this man and would've e't him if I
hadn't come up and pulled 'em off. They was tryin'
to rob Mr. Prosser's house, and they would have robbed
it if me and the dogs hadn't been yer tryin' to keep
out of the moonlight, all good and ready for burglars;
and if you want to know whose been a burglin' in this
yer town you don't have to look fur, for there is the
men."

Prosser and half a dozen of the neighbors were out
in the street by this time, and as we gathered about the
cowering wretch who stood helpless in the grasp of
the big policeman, we were all astonished to find that
it was Felix Acorn, our barber.

Then we turned to the man who lay prone upon the sidewalk. When we touched him we thought him dead, and so he was. Two of us lifted him to look at his face, and it was the face of Simon Bulfinch. That career of guilt and shame was ended. We placed the body upon Prosser's porch until daylight should come,

The burglars.

and then Felix Acorn was led away to the lock-up. He was sullen and not inclined to talk, but he did say:

"Simon led me into it. I didn't do nothin'. He did all the burglin'. I had to be imposed on, as usual. I'm always imposed on. There is no fair play, nowheres, nor no chance for a poor man."

As 'Lias led him up the steps of the station-house and began to open the door, Felix turned about, and looking at the dogs which stood behind him as if to guard him while 'Lias fumbled with the keys, he said to me, sadly:

"Say, Mr. Sprat, them's no bloodhounds; and bloodhounds is not bloody; and real bloodhounds is not hounds at all; they're mastiffs.   It's just all humbug, like everything else."

Then Felix Acorn went into his cell, and I walked homeward, not sorry indeed that, even through shameful, sorrowful means, Dr. Bulfinch should be for ever relieved of the burden that his brother Simon had imposed upon his life. ·

17

Chapter XVI.

A Storm in the Household.

Late in June Madame Bertolet's Academy for supplying higher education to young ladies under exclusively church influences concluded its operations for the school-year, and Ruby went off at once to Hawksmere. She went thither with Mrs. Purvis-Hyde and Mrs. Purvis-Hyde's companions and retinue, including her coachman and the prancing horses with the jingling chains, to remain until September.

And so our house for me was desolate. Julie stayed with us, for some reason unknown to me; perhaps her duties upon the *Defender* restrained her; perhaps she was kept at home by dislike for dependence upon Mrs. Purvis-Hyde's hospitality; but while she and Mrs. Bantam and Elmira and the Colonel and Emerson Spiker were not poor company, I found domestic life almost devoid of interest if Ruby were not with us to participate in it.

The first dividend of the Happy Hollow Improvement Company was due in September, and the surface-indications in June were that it would have large proportions. Colonel Bantam's expectations regarding it were, however, exaggerated beyond the point of reasonableness, and long before September came he had expended, in imagination, an amount of money far exceeding the total cash value of his blocks of stock.

What a happy provision of nature it is that men who can never learn how to accumulate wealth, nearly always have that hopeful disposition which permits them to enjoy continually receding expectations of wealth!

One evening, when all of us but Elmira Bantam were at home and upon the porch in the coolness and the darkness, Colonel Bantam entered the house, lighted the gas in the library, and in a few moments asked us to come in and inspect some drawings he had had prepared.

The drawings, of crayon, were placed upon the mantel and upon the centre-table in positions which permitted them to be seen to advantage. They represented a design for a statue of Colonel Bantam as Mars, the god of war; a sketch for a marble group in which Colonel Bantam figured as the angel of mercy, setting the prisoners free (in his capacity as magistrate); a drawing for a painting showing Colonel Bantam advising President Lincoln about the Emancipation Proclamation, and presenting the Colonel in full length with his face to the spectator, while the President was crouched in a chair and half hidden by the Colonel's figure; another drawing for a great picture representing Colonel Bantam holding the Bloody Angle at Gettysburg, and plainly indicating that our brave soldier had been almost completely deserted by his comrades upon that exciting occasion; a sketch for a full length portrait of Colonel Bantam which should be hung in the Mayor's office, and a design for a marble mausoleum in which the Colonel would have his war-worn remains deposited when the battle of life for him should be ended.

We examined these drawings with much interest, while the Colonel explained to us that he had induced an artist in the city to prepare them for him, so that he could give the orders for the groups and the pictures and the mausoleum to the sculptors and the artists so soon as the dividends of the Happy Hollow Improvement Company should be paid and pocketed.

"My thought, Edith, my love," he said to Mrs. Bantam, "was to have the mausoleum made large enough for two, so that in death we should not be divided; and to have a medallion upon the arch over the door, bearing your profile and mine. Do you care, love, whether the accompanying inscription is just 'Bantam,' or a monogram indicating 'J. and E. Bantam'? The mere name of Bantam, I think, is glorious enough. If I should go first——"

"Oh, do not speak of going first, Joseph," said Mrs. Bantam, immediately giving promise of tears and derangement of her back hair. "When you go I go. I shall not survive you an hour."

"The angel in that picture has very large wings," said Miss Mortimer, in a spirit possibly too critical.

"Wings!" exclaimed Colonel Bantam. "Necessarily wings. How else will you indicate the angelic nature? Real angels may not possess pinions of that type, and if you press me closely I might be compelled to confess that they are an anatomical impossibility; but we must yield in a measure to convention. Omit the wings from that picture and Joseph Bantam would present the unseemly spectacle of releasing prisoners while he wore something like a bath-robe."

Miss Mortimer very good-naturedly acquiesced in the Colonel's opinions.

"The wings," he said, "might be abbreviated, and they might be expanded, and the rather pronounced appearance of feathers might be softened down; but when you remove the wings from that picture you surrender the whole case; you lose everything."

"There were other Union soldiers at Gettysburg," I ventured to remark, as I examined the picture of the frightful conflict at the Bloody Angle.

Colonel Bantam frowned. "Others, of course," he said. "Some others. But they were not in focus in the picture; and besides, in a work of art of this nature, what one wants is definiteness. Fill the centre of the picture with a miscellaneous jumble of figures, and the mind is confused. It can hold on to nothing. My picture of the incident represents me with historical accuracy. If other men want to have themselves represented, no doubt there are artists who can be bribed to do it; artists who are accustomed to dealing in a reckless manner with fact."

I am truly sorry Emerson Spiker should have come in while we were examining the pictures. Our household had always been fairly harmonious, but already a feeling of bitterness had appeared between the Colonel and the editor, and both had got into a frame of mind that made them indifferent to one another's sentiments. .

When Mr. Spiker had glanced at the drawings he laughed in a manner which the Colonel was quick to resent.

"There would seem to be, sir," said the Colonel, with a dangerous look in his eyes, "but little in these admirable works of the artist to supply inspiration to hilarity.

May I ask, sir, the precise nature of the provocation to this, I had almost said indecent, outburst of mirthfulness?"

Mr. Spiker did not make direct reply. Turning to Miss Mortimer, he said:

"Now, if you had those wings there would be a delightful picture; but Bantam—"

Spiker's idea of a monument for the Colonel.

"Well, sir; but Bantam! What about Bantam?" demanded the Colonel angrily. "Are all angels women? What do you know about angels? I should like to have you understand, Mr. Spiker, that when an old soldier of the Republic takes a fancy to have wings he will have wings; as many wings as he wants; four wings; sixteen wings; fourteen hundred thousand wings; without condescending to obtain the permission of a mere journalist, sir!"

Mrs. Bantam, lifting her hand to steady her hair, sat down upon the sofa and began softly to cry.

"Is that a church, Sprat," asked Spiker, pointing to the design for a mausoleum, "or is it a design for a new opera house?"

"It is a mausoleum," I said; and that I might help to restore good feeling, I added, "and a very handsome one, too."

Mr. Spiker continued to find in the exhibition food for amusement.

"It is my mausoleum, sir," said the Colonel sternly, and with the air of a man whose temper, loosed from restraint, would soon impel him to do rash and dreadful things. "Mine and Mrs. Bantam's. Do you find it stimulating to the risibilities, sir? Is it supremely and unbearably ridiculous to you, sir, that a scarred and maimed veteran of the Civil War should prefer to be interred under circumstances of distinction in an honorable tomb than to be chucked under ground, as you probably will be, sir?—and the sooner the better in my opinion."

"Absurd!" said Mr. Spiker to me, without looking at the Colonel.

For just a moment Colonel Bantam, livid with rage, hesitated; then with a sweep or two of his arm he gathered the pictures into a bunch and rushed into the street, slamming the front door with such violence that the house trembled.

Leaving Julie to console Mrs. Bantam, who sobbed while she struggled to push her hair from her face, I went again upon the porch, rather angry indeed with Spiker for irritating the Colonel so needlessly and cruelly.

The next morning Spiker received from Colonel Bantam a fiery letter, in which the Colonel conveyed an intimation that unless the editor should speedily supply a written apology for his insolent conduct, he would be challenged to meet the Colonel upon the field of honor.

To this Mr. Spiker sent an insolent and irritating reply; which evoked a more furious letter from the Colonel. The correspondence continued for several days, each of the combatants covering pages of paper with acrimonious language, and meeting three times a day at our table, where they refrained from speaking to one another.

This was very trying to me and for the ladies of the household, but Julie and I and Elmira endeavored to maintain a cheerful spirit and good-humored conversation for the sake of Mrs. Bantam, whose despondency kept her always upon the very edge of tearfulness.

The Colonel spoke little, but said grace with much less than usual fervor, and then he would savagely thrust the fork into the chicken and assail the joints of the fowl with the knife with an air of ferocity that would have diminished an appetite less keen than mine. When he helped Spiker, he always had the plate passed first to me, under the rather hollow pretence of ignoring the editor.

As Spiker's soul was bitter, and the Colonel had no notion of forgiveness, I felt that the affair would reach a very disagreeable climax. It came in an unexpected manner.

One day Spiker gave in the *Defender* what pretended to be a laudatory description of the Colonel's drawings and of his military career, but was plainly intended to ridicule the designs and his pretensions as a soldier. Accompanying the article was a reproduction of an advertisement from a magazine sixty odd years old which Spiker had found in an old book-store in the city. It was an advertisement of Perrine's food for infants, and it contained a picture styled "A Perrine's Food Child," representing "Joseph Bantam at the age of two" vainly trying to bite his own toe.

Colonel Bantam was almost insane with rage when he saw this unkind article and the picture; but there was something worse for him in the paper. On that same day, under the head of " Personals," the following words appeared:

" J. B. Your darling letter received. My love for you unabated."

Mrs. Bantam, unhappily, saw this advertisement, and most unreasonably leaped to the conclusion that it was addressed to the Colonel.

She would not be comforted; but she did not expend herself upon grief. From 'Lias Guff, who had often talked to her of such things, she obtained a love-philter which she placed one morning in the Colonel's coffee, de-

"A Perrine's Food Child."

termined at any hazard to hold him faithful to her.

The Colonel found the taste unusual, and upon his peremptory demand that he should be informed of the reason, Mrs. Bantam fell upon the floor, vociferously weeping, and confessed her guilt.

Colonel Bantam, very white, looked at her lying prostrate, and hardened his heart. Steadying himself by holding the back of a chair, he said:

" This ends it. The die is cast. All is over. I shall be a fugitive from my own domicile. I am not insensible to the impulses of affection, but I sternly refuse to permit my higher emotions to be stimulated by the action of chemicals upon my digestive tract!"

Then the Colonel walked with a lofty air to the hallway, took his hat from the hook and vanished. He began to lodge in a room adjoining the Mayor's office, and Mrs. Bantam was a broken-hearted woman.

I went down to see him that very afternoon to try to persuade him to forgive Mrs. Bantam and to return home.

"Professor," he said, "in a moment of mental aberration I counselled you to marry Mrs. Purvis-Hyde."

"I remember," I said.

"Well, don't do it! With my reason fairly under control, I now formally retract that ill-timed suggestion. You are single. Happy man! Remain so. Let the words of a bitter sufferer from the torments of the conjugal relation have weight with you. Refrain! The ancients manifested high sagacity in framing that fable of Pandora which represents the inferior sex as the source of all trouble. Sir, I say *all* trouble! Absolutely all! Celibacy alone is bliss. If you would fly from it, fly from it to the grave. Seek death rather than involve yourself in the toils of accursed matrimony."

I began to speak of Mrs. Bantam's genuine affection for him, and of her sufferings.

"No more!" he said, waving his hand in front of his face as if to dispel some hideous vision. "No more of her! My love for her is extinct. A love-philter; hah!" and the Colonel laughed hysterically. "Sir, when a wife falls so low as to believe that the conjugal tie can be strengthened by paregoric or essence of peppermint, or some other nauseous compound from the pharmacopeia, the case is hopeless. She is insensible to the potency of spiritual influences. I draw the line, sir, at application of drugs in affairs of the heart.

I shall have the proportions of the mausoleum changed so that it will hold but one person—myself."

I persisted in urging him to return.

"No, sir; no! Let us hear no more of the matter. Spiker's presence in that house would be sufficient to exclude me from it. When he enters the door I go out. It is monstrous, sir, the conduct of that irresponsible scribbler! No true soldier could tamely endure it. The man who assails my military career strikes at my heart. Consider, sir, have I drenched the earth with my blood to be held up to derision by a brainless journalist who doesn't know a bayonet from a canteen? My laurels, my friend, were won upon the field of glory, amid the wild terrors of the battle-storm, not by shedding ink from a fountain-pen. No, sir, Spiker and I are enemies. Only the responsibility of my office as chief magistrate restrains me from seeking his heart's blood.

"And that reminds me, Professor," said the Colonel, diminishing the ferocity of his manner, "that while I am homeless I am also not far from a condition of absolute financial destitution. The marriage-fees are now rare, and my salary is not due until August first. It is most repellant to my feelings to allude to such things, but the sternest necessity compels me to ask you if you could conveniently let me have five dollars for a few weeks. Do not consent unless the transaction commends itself perfectly to your feelings, and depend upon it you shall have a first lien upon my next salary payment."

I gave him the money.

"This," he said, as he put the money in his pocket, "will keep the wolf from the door—the station-house door—for a time. On August first I shall promptly give you a *quid pro quo ;* but I may add that unless the Improvement Company does the liberal thing in the matter of dividends in September, I shall be compelled to put my affairs into liquidation and go into the hands of a receiver."

Elmira Bantam, with quite characteristic good sense, always refrained from interfering by word or act with the strictly personal matters relating to her father and mother. I am sure that she thought both of them had behaved foolishly in this instance, and that Mr. Spiker had been unnecessarily harsh in his judgment upon the weakness of her father. But she held her peace.

She thought, however, that the Colonel should come home and forgive and solace the wife who with yearning soul awaited that return and the happiness it would bring to her.

Elmira had several conversations with her father, but he was obdurate, and at last, finding persuasion of no avail, she undertook a line of action which she thought might be more effective. She actually brought suit against him, in his wife's name, for desertion, and asked that he should be compelled to contribute a sum every week to her support.

"I dislike to prosecute paw," she said to Miss Mortimer, " but he has no right to leave maw, and when maw asks me, as an attorney, to bring suit against him, I cannot for a moment permit filial considerations to stand in the way of professional duty."

Colonel Bantam was very angry when the summons came to him ; angry that Elmira seemed to have turned against him, and scared by the promise that he should be compelled to pay money into a household which, in recent years, had been sustained by the payments made by Mrs. Bantam's boarders.

"A father's curse upon that most ungrateful child!" said the Colonel to me. "Was it for this that I had her trained for the legal profession? For this I permitted her to become a practitioner of the laws of her country? Shame upon her, sir! I warn her now that I shall cut her off with a pittance unless she retraces her steps. I will not patiently endure persecution from my own offspring. I shall recast my will to-morrow."

But the Colonel thought better of it. Within a week of the time when Elmira had laid the foundations for an action, Colonel Bantam came to me and said, laying his hand upon my arm:

"Professor, I have relented. I can stand it no longer. Separated from my soul's idol I find myself yearning for her. I have learned that life apart from her is intolerable. Lead me home, that I may forgive her and confer upon her my blessing."

When we reached the house I entered, and finding Mrs. Bantam alone in the library, I motioned to the Colonel to remain in the hall, while I went in to prepare her for his return. He stood just outside of the library door, where he could hear everything.

Mrs. Bantam sat by the centre-table, her hair all loose upon her back, and in her hand she held a photograph of her little boy who died many years before. On the table were his tiny shoes and some broken playthings. The poor woman, in her grief for her desertion, had taken these relics from their hiding-place and was trying, vainly I thought, to obtain from them some sort of consolation.

She was kissing the picture as I came in. She greeted me sadly, and said:

"Look at my darling, Mr. Sprat. How sweet and pretty he is. Is he not the very image of his honored father? If he had lived, dear friend, perhaps now he would be a minister or a great statesman; perhaps a brave soldier like the Colonel. But now my heart is broken; broken! I shall never know what it is to be happy; never!" and again she began to kiss the picture passionately.

Before I could say a word the Colonel dashed into the room, and clasping her in his arms, lifted her from the chair and pressed her to his bosom. Mrs. Bantam gave a little shriek, and would have fainted, had not the Colonel held her.

"I am a villain, a base wretch!" he exclaimed. "Why did I not fall upon the field of battle rather than that I should wound my darling?"

"No! No! Not that! Oh, not that!" said Mrs. Bantam, frantically embracing him. "Not that, my darling Joseph."

"My queen! My love! My life," said the Colonel, kissing her as she turned her face upward to him. "A heart of steel would melt in the presence of such devotion. I am yours. Your own Joseph; yours for ever and ever and ever!"

"You will not leave me again, my Joseph?" she asked, almost piteously.

"Never! I swear it! No power on earth shall separate us. We will die together; my darling, my only one!"

"Professor," said the Colonel, still holding Mrs. Bantam in his arms, and turning his eyes to me, "we learn

the most useful lessons of life from experience ; sometimes sad experience. I counsel you to take warning
from this affecting incident. When you love, love un-
selfishly ; let nothing persuade you to wound the feelings of your heart's idol."

"You advised me not to marry, you know," I said
with a smile.

"In an evil moment I did. Erase the suggestion
from the tablets of your memory. It was the passionate, reckless utterance of an angry man. Believe me,
bliss is to be found alone in the perfect love of wedded
life. I shall now let the original design of the mausoleum stand ; so that it will hold two."

"Heed the Colonel's words," said Mrs. Bantam,
speaking with her head upon her husband's breast.
"They are words of wisdom. The grave would be
welcome to me if the heart of Joseph should be given
to another."

"I would not speak of that again, my darling," said
the Colonel with a shade of annoyance coming upon
his countenance. "Let bygones be bygones. For me,
there is but one woman ; it is you, my love. All other
women might be swallowed up in one vast convulsion
of nature, and I should maintain perfect tranquility if
you were by my side."

Mrs. Bantam looked up at him fondly and seemed to
tighten her hold upon him. Presently she said :

"And you must forgive Mr. Spiker, Joseph."

A spasm of pain passed over the Colonel's face. I
thought he would thrust Mrs. Bantam from him.

"That reptile ?" he said.

"For my sake, Joseph," she pleaded.

"He deserves death," he said.

" Forgive him, darling. Make the sacrifice because you love me."

Colonel Bantam remained silent and seemed to be thinking the matter over. There was an internal struggle; but his good angel got the better of it and at last he kissed Mrs. Bantam and said:

" Your word with me is law. I forgive the scoundrel."

I went out to find Spiker and to urge him to play his part in the general reconciliation. After much persuasion he consented for Mrs. Bantam's sake.

" But, Sprat," said the editor, as I prepared to leave him, " what an intolerable old humbug the Colonel is !"

And so that night at dinner, when the Colonel and the editor had shaken hands, and the Colonel had kissed Mrs. Bantam and Elmira, and restrained his impulse to kiss Julie, he said grace sonorously and .heartily, and asked Spiker if he preferred the white meat or the dark meat of the chicken.

The storm had blown completely over.

Chapter XVII

The Cloud-Compeller

"**This** afternoon," said Colonel Bantam at the breakfast table one morning, "I make my experiment in the production of rain."

The country suffered from drought. There had been a few small showers in recent weeks, but for much more than a month the rain had not fallen continuously, and vegetation showed the need of it.

"My theory," said the Colonel, "is that artillery firing, rightly conducted, produces precipitation of moisture. I never witnessed more tremendous rain than we had after the cannonading at Gettysburg. The very windows—no, not the windows, the sluice-gates of heaven were opened. It was always so after a great battle."

"Why," I asked, "does the rain fall upon such provocation ?"

"I am not familiar with science, excepting military science, sir," replied the Colonel. "But I conceive the facts to be these: Artillery firing produces concussion of the atmosphere. The atmosphere is largely charged with moisture. This moisture is held in minute globules, as butter is held in cream. When you churn the cream you violently disrupt the globules and release the fat. When you supply the impact of concussion to the globules in the atmosphere, you shatter them and release the rain. I judge, sir, that is how the consequences are persuaded to ensue."

"There is nothing in it," observed Mr. Spiker.

"Nothing in it!" responded the Colonel hotly. "It is strange indeed how often presumptuous ignorance sets itself against knowledge and wide experience. I have seen the effect, sir, upon a hundred battlefields. I will demonstrate to your satisfaction this very day, sir, that there is something in it, a big something, too."

"I'll lay a heavy wager that the weather will be dry as a bone to-morrow," persisted Spiker.

"My habitual and temperamental aversion to gambling in any of its forms," said the Colonel, "alone prevents me from accepting any wager that you or any other venturesome person may be rash enough to lay. Professor," said the Colonel to me, "if you should accept the challenge the prize is yours, unless indeed you shall be barred by having bet upon a certainty.

"We have brought a brass cannon over from Purgatory Springs," continued Colonel Bantam; "A. J. Pelican, with his accustomed public spirit, has contributed the ammunition, and at three o'clock the exercises begin. Edith, my love, see that the windows are all closed by three-thirty, and do not venture out without your umbrella and overshoes."

The little cannon had been placed in an open space

in the park, and its brazen mouth was turned upward toward the hill-tops.

At quarter to three Colonel Bantam pushed his way through the crowd, followed by 'Lias Guff, who brought the red-flannel-covered cartridges in a wheelbarrow.

"Professor," said the Colonel, as he reached the place where I stood, "I know little or nothing of mechanics; I have never, for example, been able to comprehend the mechanism of so simple an implement as an umbrella; but artillery is my plaything. I handle it as a min-

The cloud-compeller.

strel manipulates his instrument. Officer," he said to 'Lias Guff, "charge the piece and ram home!"

While the officer was engaged in performing this service, Colonel Bantam addressed the crowd:

"Observe, if you please, fellow-citizens, that we have above us a cloudless sky; absolutely cloudless; you see only the azure of heaven. Prepare, I warn you, for a change. Officer, put on the cap. Are you ready?"

Colonel Bantam retreated five or six paces, probably

that he might better study the general effect of the operation, and then he exclaimed, " Fire !"

There was a great roar from the cannon, and the hills in a moment sent the overlapping echoes flying back to us. " Continue firing," said the Colonel, and twenty times the little cannon sent out its vociferous entreaty to the blue heavens and brought the reverberations to us from the hills.

" Is that," said the Colonel, pointing to the western horizon, as the echoes of the twentieth shot died away, " is that a cloud over there, Professor ?"

It was a cloud; and soon a black cloud; a thunder-cloud. In truth, there was within a short time evidence enough that, for one reason or for another, Happy Hollow would soon be blessed with rain.

Colonel Bantam was in a condition of high exhilaration. He smiled and rubbed his hands and laughed quietly to himself; and then, as 'Lias Guff drew away the cannon and another man removed the wheelbarrow, the cloud grew bigger and bigger, and the rolling distant thunder seemed to be sending its antiphon to the music of the cannon.

The crowd began to disperse, and Colonel Bantam, linking his arm in mine, limped slowly toward home.

" That perfectly asinine editor, my dear Professor," he said, " has learned a wholesome lesson this afternoon. Is it any wonder that our unfortunate country should have so low an average of intelligence among its people when the public press, which should be an educational instrument, is in the hands of such inconceivable stupidity ?"

Upon our way home the Colonel encountered several of his fellow-citizens, whom he stopped to tell of his cannon-firing and to point to the swiftly darkening sky. He tarried so long that when we reached the corner of the street near to our house rain-drops fell, slowly at first; then quickly and heavily, and at last we ran, and as there was trouble with the latch on the gate, both of us were wet as we gained the front door. But Colonel Bantam did not care for wet clothing. As we dashed the water from our hats and hearkened in the hallway to the roar of the rain upon the pavement outside, the Colonel said to me:

"Professor, when I undertake to do a thing I do it. I don't trifle with it. You are a young man; let me warn you never to be satisfied with half measures."

We went into the front parlor and stood at one of the windows to watch the storm. The rain fell in sheets, filling the gutters, covering the street surface with yellow rivulets, and pouring in cataracts from the edges of the roofs across the street; while at short intervals the gloom that overhung the town was illuminated by dazzling flashes of lightning, each quickly followed by a crash of thunder, and then by long rumbling detonations.

Colonel Bantam was really gleeful. I think I have never known him to enjoy anything so much. This was his first own personal thunderstorm, and he felt responsible for all the uproar and the downpour.

"A good many globules seem to have been broken," I said to him as we looked at the flood.

"Im—mense!" he exclaimed. "I never had a greater success. How wonderful, Professor, is the intellect of man, the lord of creation! He dominates and sways the elements. He speaks with imperious voice, and the mighty tempest breaks forth. By the way, where is Mrs. Bantam? I hope she did not venture out."

Anxious that his wife should share his triumph and express her admiration for his achievement, the Colonel left the room and hurried upstairs. In a few moments he returned, and stood again by my side, gazing at the storm.

"Is she at home?" I asked.

Colonel Bantam laughed lightly.

"She has drawn a feather-bed into the middle of the floor of the guest-chamber, and is reposing there with her head buried in the feathers. Mrs. Bantam, Professor, has pursued that practice for thirty-four years whenever there was a thunderstorm. Timid, shrinking creatures! How fortunate for them that they have our bold and manly hearts to rest on! It is mere superstition, too, sir. There is no quality in feathers to ward off lightning. The fowls of the air are fre-

quently annihilated by it. I have often said to Mrs.
Bantam that if it could be done without hurting her I
wish she could be struck
some time while enshrouded
in that feather-bed."

"She should be brave

Mrs. Bantam's refuge from
the storm.

during her own husband's thunderstorm," I ventured
to say.

Colonel Bantam was not displeased.

"You are right, sir; you are right! you do not
exaggerate. The town owes this glorious rain to me.
Was it not Jupiter, sir, who was known as the cloud-
compeller? I think so. If my dividends are large
enough I shall have a design made for a statue of me
in that capacity."

The storm seemed to increase in violence as we
talked.

"This," said the Colonel, still looking through the
window, "sends me to Congress. All the farmers in
the county have suffered in the most alarming manner
from drought; the cattle in some places have wanted

water; many wells have been dry; the ministers everywhere have persistently and ineffectually prayed for
rain; at the critical moment Joseph Bantam demands
it at the cannon's mouth, and lo, it comes! Yes, sir, I
go to Congress for this. And Spiker! how insignificant he now appears! A man of that kind, Professor,
really needs a care-taker."

The thunder and lightning soon were gone, but the
rain continued to fall heavily.

Colonel Bantam came to the dinner table in a joyous frame of mind. Spiker reached home late, and
went at once upstairs, manifestly to remove his wet
clothing. There was a merry gleam in the Colonel's
eye when he heard the footsteps of the editor.

I thought Spiker seemed gloomy when at last he
entered the dining-room and took his seat at the table.

Mrs. Bantam shared the Colonel's exultation over
his remarkable performance, and, speaking of it, she
was saying when Spiker arrived:

"Under happier circumstances the Colonel's commanding intellect would force him into pre-eminence."

Mr. Spiker made no reference to the rain; but when
Colonel Bantam had put a slice of roast beef upon the
editor's plate, the Colonel stepped over to the door
that opened upon the side porch and unlatched it for a
moment and sniffed the air:

"The rain continues," he said, "and how delightful
and fresh is the perfume of nature as she satisfies her
thirst."

"Is it raining?" asked Mr. Spiker, in an indifferent
tone, but with a slight affectation of surprise, and without looking up from his knife and fork.

"The *Defender*," said the Colonel, with a triumphant

smile, will have to-morrow, of course, a full account of the wonderfully successful experiment in the park?"

" The rain would have come anyhow," said Spiker, sullenly.

" It is amazing," responded the Colonel, "to what extremities ignorant prejudice will carry a man. When the skilled physician rescues him from disease, he says he would have got well anyhow. When the trained mariner steers the ship through the wild tempest safe to port, such a man says she would have come safely home anyhow. No!" exclaimed the Colonel vehemently. " It rains because Joseph Bantam's brain unloosed the torrents from the skies and subdued stubborn nature to his will."

The rain came down without cessation all night and all the next day. I met the Colonel as he came into the house just before dinner on the second day.

" Grand, isn't it?" he asked, as he removed his hat and put his umbrella in the great jar.

" I should think we have had enough," I answered.

" The human mind," he said, " is never satisfied. Two days ago the thirsty earth gasped for moisture. Now we complain of too much. Be patient, Professor, and all will be well."

He spoke like a man who could stop the rain by lifting his hand.

There was hard rain all the second night and all the third day. As the Colonel looked from the window with me on that third evening he said:

" Perhaps it would have been as well, Mr. Sprat, if I had fired only ten guns instead of twenty. It did not occur to me that the concussion might have excessive force."

Colonel Bantam was beginning to be troubled, and he was in no mood for trifling conversation when we assembled at dinner. I thought Spiker indecorously joyous.

"Still raining, Mr. Sprat!" he said. "Noah would have cared for this. That globular theory seems to me to have been overworked."

"Sir," said the Colonel sternly, "the regular average rainfall for June has not yet been reached. We were an inch and a quarter short at three o'clock."

"That's all very well," responded Mr. Spiker, "but the creek is up over its banks, the first floor of the Aramink House is under water; they are taking people out of the houses in boats in the lower part of the town, and they tell me that over in the valley barns and hay-stacks and piles of lumber and chicken-coops are sailing down the river past Grigsby's Bluff faster than you can count them. Some men never do a thing without overdoing it. The farmers are mad all through, and I heard a report as I left the office of a serious washout on the railroad."

Colonel Bantam was pained; as his mind contemplated the ruin in the valley and reflected that the farmers would accept his own theory that he was responsible for the storm, he saw his hopes of a career in Congress shrivel up and disappear.

"For my part," persisted Mr. Spiker, "I never heard anybody complain very much of the drought. Nobody cares for rain just as harvest-time begins. If people would just let things alone we should be much better off. From what I hear I calculate that this flood will cost the county half a million dollars in spoiled crops and other property destroyed."

"Every benefactor of his race," said the Colonel, with an angry look upon his face, "is the victim of wicked ingratitude. It was so always. The Israelites wanted to stone Moses; Galileo was imprisoned; Goodyear starved to death; Joseph Bantam brings the gracious rain from heaven to refresh the parched earth, and he is reviled because there is a superfluous quart or two. It is hard to bear such baseness patiently; I will withdraw."

The Colonel rose, left the room, took his hat, and opened the front door. He was about to go down the street, but instead of doing so he came back into the house, closed the door, replaced his hat upon the rack, re-entered the dining-room, resumed his seat at the head of the table, and smiled at Mrs. Bantam.

"What is it, love?" she asked.

"It has stopped raining," said the Colonel.

In truth, Mr. Spiker had by no means exaggerated the dimensions of the harm that had been done by the storm. The Aramink House was so much injured that it could not be opened at the appointed time, and so the guests who had thought to come went to other places, and the whole season was spoiled. The dam that held back the lake was broken, and the lake turned into a dreary mud-flat until repairs could be made; the new park was badly damaged; part of the track of the horse railroad was torn out over by Purgatory Springs, and, upon the whole, the Happy Hollow Improvement Company, the town, the steam railroad, the farmers, and the county lost much more than the sum named by the editor. Colonel Bantam trembled for his September dividend when he heard how the Improvement Company had suffered, and no doubt mourned the day that he undertook to make experiment with concussion and the globular theory.

One week after the great Bantam deluge Mr. Spiker said to me one morning, with mystery in his manner, that he was going to the city that day upon important business. He returned in the evening, and when he came upstairs in our house I would have passed him in the hallway; but Spiker took hold of my arm and pulled me into his room, shutting the door.

"Sit down there, Sprat," he said, pointing to a chair; "I have something terrible to tell you."

Spiker's countenance, and even the tone of his voice, indicated that he was the subject of violent emotion.

He sat upon the lounge, face to face with me, but at first he put his elbows upon his knees and buried his face in his hands, as if he could not trust himself to speak.

Then suddenly he raised his head, and flinging wide his arms in a gesture of despair he exclaimed:

"It's all over, old man! It's all over!"

"Your matter with Julie, you mean?"

"Yes, it's all over, Sprat. I shall lose my mind. I'm afraid I shall go crazy!"

"Oh, you take it too hard," I said. "You will recover in time. Many a man has been refused before."

"Yes," he said, with a strange laugh. "Refused, yes, plenty of men. But, my friend, that hasn't happened to me; not that."

"I don't understand you, then. Certainly you are not agitated because she has accepted you. What's the matter, Spiker, anyhow?"

"I've had the refusing to do," he said.

"Well, I give it up until you are calm enough to explain yourself."

Mr. Spiker arose and walked about the room for two or three minutes, then standing before me, he said :

"Last evening, while we were sitting out here in the garden, I proposed to her."

"Did you show her the Mercator projection?" I asked.

"Don't speak of that, Sprat! It looks to me now just like foolishness. Something about her said, 'Don't try that!' A queenly woman, Sprat! A wonderful woman! But she's lost to me. She was solemn and tearful when I spoke to her about my feelings, and she made no answer. I am not skilful at such things, but, of course, I pressed her to speak to me, and, to my astonishment, she turned to me with her eyes filled with tears, and said simply, 'I wish it could not have happened so!' 'But,' I said, 'you do not say no, and you have only to say yes, and all will be right.' 'I cannot say either yes or no,' she answered, 'because there is more than just that. You do not know all How could you know?' 'I don't want to know,' I said 'Nothing shall take you from me but your own direct refusal. Nothing else can separate us' 'Ah, yes!' she answered, 'but something else will separate us.' 'It is impossible!' I said. 'I love you too dearly to let you go for any consideration.' 'No,' she persisted, 'it will be your own act. You will refuse me.'

"Sprat! I saw that something unusual was the matter, and I was filled with dread. I did not know just what to say. But at last I answered, 'Tell me the worst. I must know it.'

"'Will you go to the city to-morrow?' she asked.

"'Yes,' I said, and then she named an hour at which she would meet me in the railway station in town. She was there at the time fixed, and with her I walked silently through the streets until we came to a small, but very nice, two-story brick building. She rang the bell, and the door was opened by an elderly mulatto woman, nearly white, in fact, in a tidy blue frock, and with the appearance of a superior servant

"We entered the house, and when Julie had closed the door, she took the mulatto woman by the hand and, turning to me, she said with a sweet voice: 'Mr. Spiker, this is my mother.' A negress, Sprat! Julie a negress! Black blood in her veins! Think of that! Julie has supported her mother by her labors. This is where she went so often when she mysteriously disappeared from here; to the city to see her mother! Who would have suspected that she was a negress? I was smitten dumb; I could say nothing; and while I stood there, almost paralyzed with grief and disappointment, Julie came to me, and taking my hand, she said, softly and sweetly: 'Good-bye, Mr. Spiker, good-bye! My mother was a runaway slave, and in her flight she carried me in her arms, as many a time I have carried the child in the play. I am faithful to her; and—and—yes, faithful to you! Good-bye!'

"Sprat, I went from the house almost insane. I am almost insane now. But she acted fairly, didn't she? She could have deceived me. Suppose she had not told me, and I had married her! But was it fair not to tell us long ago, and to let me fall in love with her? I don't know. She acted nobly at the last. A negress! She will never come back here. It is over.

What will Ruby do, do you think? What shall I do with the Woman's Department? I can't have the public know that a negro woman edits it, can I? That splendid woman! So beautiful and gifted and generous! Think how she cared for Ruby; how she shone at Mrs. Purvis-Hyde's 'uplifters' and everywhere else! And now she turns out to be the daughter of an ex-slave woman!"

The next day Mrs. Bantam received a long letter from Julie asking that her clothing and other property should be packed and sent to her, and bidding an affectionate farewell to Mrs. Bantam, Elmira, the Colonel, and me. She would not return to Happy Hollow.

When the day was ended we sat together in the parlor after supper, and we could not avoid speaking of the strange revelation that had been made. All of us were sad, for we missed Julie much; she had filled the house with brightness, and by her gentle good humor and kindness had endeared herself to every one.

Mrs. Bantam, of course, was tearful and partially dishevelled.

"She is so lovely!" said Mrs. Bantam, "and so kind and good. Is it not painful beyond expression, dear Mr. Sprat, to reflect that her ancestors were naked savages who bounded about in the regions of equatorial Africa, perhaps cannibals, eating one another and behaving in a perfectly inhuman manner? But I shall never forget her kindness to Ruby, cannibals or no cannibals."

"It is ridiculous, maw," said Elmira, "to talk in that way. Your own ancestors ran around in the woods of Germany without clothing, and very likely ate one another."

"I know, my child," said the Colonel, "but, as members of the proud Caucasian race—"

"Paw!" said Elmira sharply, "please do not be perfectly absurd! The jails around here are full of members of the proud Caucasian race, and there are more Caucasian rascals running at large here than ten times as many jails would hold. Julie is a brainy woman, and fit to govern nine-tenths of the Caucasians I am acquainted with."

"Brainy, yes," responded the Colonel, "and she is unsurpassed in her power to touch the springs of feeling, but shall we permit our admiration for her intellectual gifts to impel us to fly in the face of Scripture? Shall we attempt with impious hand to set aside the edict uttered by the venerable patriarch against the descendants of Ham? I shrink from such a course."

"I thought you said you were a Fire Worshiper," I whispered to the Colonel.

"I am, sir, but my nature is not revolutionary. I would not consent to override and sweep away the social usages of sixty centuries. For the race which my own arm helped to deliver from the bondsman's chain I would do still more; but the line must be drawn, sir, against the Ethiopian when he attempts to invade the hearthstone of the higher race; or, rather, in this case, when *she* attempts it. I say, sir, it must be drawn, and I draw it."

Miss Bantam simply said " Pshaw!" and took up the evening paper.

The Colonel felt like speaking further:

"Cupid," he said, "plays sad, sad pranks! This is one of the most familiar of facts; but, sir, Cupid has no business to meddle with ethnological questions. It cannot be tolerated that Cupid should contemptuously disregard Noah's justifiable reprobation of Ham. Cupid, sir! Ham, sir! The two are obviously incongruous. Let Cupid stay here and Ham there; apart. Their spheres of influence are and should be widely separated."

Miss Bantam could stand no more. She laid down the paper and rising, said:

"The only question is, Is she a lovely, gifted, good woman? She is, and for me, I stand right by her!"

The Colonel was about to reply, but Elmira withdrew from the room and went upstairs.

"I am so sorry, too, for poor Mr. Spiker," said Mrs. Bantam. "You have never loved, Mr. Sprat, I think you said, and therefore you can form no conception of the intensity of the feelings where the flood-gates of passion have been opened and the soul is filled with love's delirium. Love, my dear Mr. Sprat, is a devouring flame; it is ecstasy. I tremble for Mr. Spiker. Will it not be dreadful if we shall be compelled to watch him slowly wasting away? And suppose his reason should totter upon its throne? Words cannot express how this would pain me."

"Your anxiety is needless, Edith," said the Colonel. "Give yourself no uneasiness about Mr. Spiker. He will waste nothing but provender. Whatever reason he has will not totter a particle. He chuckles to-day, no doubt—yes, chuckles, to think that he has escaped marriage with a colored woman."

"How can you speak so ungenerously, Joseph?"

"Because, madame, I know Spiker. He is deficient in the finer sensibilities. He has a heart of stone.

19

Shed no tears upon his account. He will return to his sanctum without a pang, and continue to stupefy mankind with editorials as deficient in intelligence as they are wanting in literary grace. Dr. Bulfinch himself could not parse one of them. I warn you, Professor, to keep your eye on Spiker. My own eye looks clear through him. I take him in at a glance."

"You wrong Mr. Spiker, Joseph," insisted Mrs. Bantam. "He really loved Julie. I know it."

"Women, Professor," said the Colonel, turning to me, "are always weak when matters relating to the affections are involved. Edith's own noble nature impels her to believe that even the most unworthy are capable of the higher forms of affection. Show a woman a pair of lovers and she says good-bye to her judgment; she will believe anything. But, sir, as one who is always master of himself, and who looks at such things in the cold light of reason, I assert that, Ethiopian though she be, Julie is as much above Spiker as the Matterhorn is above Happy Hollow."

I was sorry for Spiker and for Miss Mortimer, and I knew Ruby would be sorry. Our school was over, and I determined to go to Hawksmere to see her, not only that I might tell her of Julie, but that I might try again if she would have me for her husband.

Chapter XVIII

At Hawksmere

ON an afternoon in the early part of July I went to the city, and at night I took a train in which I travelled until the morning. Dismounting then at a little station almost surrounded by vast heaps of hemlock bark, I entered the stage, and pulled by four stout horses, began to make the steep ascent along the winding way to Hawksmere.

Hawksmere is upon a mountain top. When one has climbed for hours by steep roads through the forest the summit is reached, and there, lying in a cup resembling the crater of an extinct volcano, is a pretty lake, a mile and a half long and half a mile wide. Sixty feet above the margin of the water the spaces upon two sides are occupied by hotels and pretty lawn-bordered cottages; whilst upon the other sides the ancient forest lies thick and deep about the lake, the great hemlock trees with twisted and knotted roots and trunks thrusting themselves out over the water. Beneath the shade of the overhanging branches the boats may move from one end of the lake to the other ; or if the rowers be weary, or would have seclusion and peace, the boat may be thrust under the very roots of the great trees, close to the red earth of the shore, and there in the cool air and the deep shadow one may read, or think, or talk with a companion, or watch the gay scene out in the golden sunshine that floods the lake.

For there the little steamer runs to and fro filled with pleasure-seekers, and row-boats and sail-boats pass from place to place, or lie at anchor for the patient fishermen.

It is a charming place for an idler on a summer day, and it becomes more charming if one shall have such company as I hoped to have when I went there.

I reached the town in the morning, and when I had fixed my quarters at the hotel, I considered if I should go at once to Mrs. Purvis-Hyde's cottage in pursuit of Ruby, or if I should accept the chance of meeting her upon the lake or at the bathing-beach.

I thought at last that I should find pleasure for myself and perhaps should not displease her if I should come upon her suddenly, surprising her among her friends as they mingled with the throng upon the water or at the beach. And so I started down to the path that enters the great forest, and skirts the lake a little distance from it and a few feet above it, clear about the whole circumference.

This is a walk full of delight at any time; but on that morning the sun was shining in a cloudless sky;

" Let me be ever the first, the truest, the nearest and dearest."

the air was cool with freshness that the lowlands rarely
know, and it was fragrant with the scent of the pine
and the hemlock, and of the ground whereon pine
needles had fallen and lain undisturbed for centuries.
The earth was soft to the footfall, and elastic, so that
the pedestrian felt every movement was without effort.

I strolled along, catching glimpses here and there
through the trees of the shining surface of the lake,
and counting with a feeling of elation upon meeting at
the beach far ahead of me the woman for whose presence I longed. But, as I stopped for a moment not
far from the edge of the water to examine a great fun-
gus upon the trunk of a fallen hemlock, I heard a
voice near to me, and it was a familiar voice. Stepping forward a little distance, I looked downward, and
there lying in close beside the moss-covered bank was
a boat, and in the boat sat Thomas Driggs, clad in a gay
shirt and white flannel trowsers, with a belt about his
waist and a Panama hat worn slouching upon his head.

Tom sat upon a thwart in the middle of the boat,
reading aloud, and in the stern upon a bundle of
cushions facing him sat Ruby Bonner, placid, smiling,
comfortable, knitting or doing some other kind of
woman's work, while she listened to Tom.

All my soul flamed up within me at the spectacle.
My heart beat vehemently. I felt my face flush, and I
was filled at once with grim misery. " Here," I thought,
" is the end of it all! Now I know why she would not
hear me when I told her that I loved her. She has
maintained correspondence with Driggs. Far better
would it have been for me if I had not come here.
There will be no more peace for me this summer or in
this life."

I did not wish to stay there spying upon them, or listening, but I could not help hearing that which Tom was reading. It was in the Courtship of Miles Standish. Driggs had found it at last. Just as I began to turn to go away he read these lines, and I thought with quite scandalous fervor:

" Yes, we must ever be friends; and of all that offer you friendship
  Let me ever be the first, the truest, the nearest, and dearest."

I thought I saw Ruby look up from her work and smile at him as he uttered these words; but perhaps I was mistaken, for my brain was in such a whirl that I almost lost consciousness, and did not know but that my trembling knees would give way and I should swoon there in the forest.

I turned about, and though I seemed to have no strength left, I ran directly away from the border of the lake, forsaking the path, and buried myself deep in the wood.

For some of us it is not hard to understand how men may seek relief in self-destruction. It comes to a man now and then that all life in him and about him and ahead of him is thick darkness. The very sunshine is gloom. Hope is extinct, and existence now a burden—existence in the time to come a horror not to be faced or endured.

I went stumbling along among the prostrate trees, the tangled laurel, and the rotted remnants of the ancient hemlocks, not knowing how I went or whither I went, or if the branches scratched my face or tore my clothing; or I went ankle-deep in the morass that here and there lay sodden in the shade of the woods. All my past life seemed useless; all my present life a

wreck, and the years to come—years without the love
that had illuminated all my soul—an intolerable stretch
of dreary wandering over desert land.

It would have been a relief to curse Driggs and to
curse the woman who had so finely hidden from me
her preference for him; but even in the fury of my
rage I could not venture to do that. I hated him with
bitter hatred, and for her my heart was sore that she
should have thought such a man more worthy than I.
I knew he was not.

"I would have lifted you up," I said, as if she were
present with me, "to such a height as his love can
never reach. You stoop to him and he will keep you
on his lower level. How mightily I would have loved
you until my love should have given you glimpses of
holiness. Yes; it is that; it is holy; for it is a sacrifice, and I would willingly die for you, my dear.

"Too old," I said bitterly, as I rushed along. "She
thought me too old! Too old at twenty-nine; and that
abominable Driggs is twenty-seven. Twenty-seven and
stupid, and infatuated with shoes and soap. Too young
you are, my Ruby, to perceive that a girl's foolish
fancy may wreck a woman's life!"

I had gone far before the violence of the bodily exercise had in a measure tamed the wild passion of the
soul; and when calmness began to come again to the
perturbed spirit, I thought to take note of where I was.
It is an easy thing to be lost in that vast, far-stretching
mountain-forest, and I had heard tales of wanderers
who had never returned, or who had been found and
brought back after bitter suffering.

So then I sat down upon the protruding root of a
tree to find breath, to wipe the moisture from my face,

and to consider. Even then only by violent effort could I turn my mind from that scene in the boat and reflect upon my situation. No matter how hard I tried, my thought would slip back again to my own misery; and before me always was the picture of the lovely girl smiling upon the man who seemed to plead with her that he might be her nearest and dearest.

I sat there long, thinking of it all, and when at last the cool wind had refreshed me and the rest had given me larger strength, I thought of going back again to the hotel. I was resolved to leave Hawksmere by a night stage. I would not try to see Ruby. I would not permit her to know that I had been there. But I remembered that I could not go away until the morning.

Looking about, I found that I did not know by what way I had come. I had not the least notion whether the village and the lake lay in this direction or in that. I might have walked five miles for aught I knew. In half-delirium one does not count paces.

I sat down again to try to exercise cooler judgment upon the matter. To go in one direction might be to have to spend a week in the forest without food. Perhaps to die there. To go in another might be to find my way out at the end of a ten miles' tramp. The sun could not guide me, for actually I did not recall if Hawksmere lay east or west, or how it lay. The place had not been familiar to me.

At last, after long reflection, I determined to find and to climb the highest tree near to me. Perhaps then I should discover some token which would show to me the right direction.

My climbing days were long past, but I had not for-

gotten how to climb; and so, with hard toil and strenuous effort, and much damage to my garments, I went
up and up a great tree, higher and higher, until I could
look out over the
top of the forest
which lay beneath,
a billowy mass of
green, with here and
there the naked
branches of a dead
tree thrust out from
the verdure. There
was not much hope
in the first outlook,
but at last I caught
sight of a moving
object, far, far away
to the southward,
and when I had
looked long and
closely I made it
out to be the flag
over the great hotel.
As I watched the
moving thing I be-
came sure of it, and
I noted that the vil-
lage lay in just the
opposite direction
from that which I

There was not much hope in the first
outlook.

should have taken if I had not thus examined the
field.

So, noting carefully the objects upon the ground

beneath the tree, that I should make no mistake when I descended, I came down, and then I bent my mind to the task of walking, so far as I could, in a straight line, that I might not fall victim to the propensity to go in a circle.

I reached the hotel in the middle of the afternoon, and went to my room to repair damages and to rest. I was weary in body and in soul; but I held firmly to my purpose to go away in the morning.

When the sun was down and the dusk began to gather where the trees stretched their branches over the lake, I went down stairs and out upon the porch of the hotel, not thinking to find anyone I knew. Indeed, I wished to be alone. I could hardly bear to face the people assembled in the house. But there, upon the porch, sat Thomas Driggs, with his chair tilted backward and one of his feet planted high upon the post that upheld the porch-roof. It was the attitude in which he had talked to me while we tarried upon the porch of the Metropolitan Hotel upon the day when I first came to Happy Hollow. Thomas Driggs's mind seemed to work with more ease when his heel was on a higher level than his head.

He was surprised to see me, but he did not seem glad. He greeted me politely, but I thought there was a trace of sullenness in his manner.

When he had explained to me, still with his foot lifted against the post, that he had abandoned the soap business and was now engaged in selling oils, he was silent for a moment while he twisted his moustache, and then turning his head toward me with a scowl upon his face he said:

"You did up that Miles Standish business finely for me, didn't you?"

I asked him what he meant.

"You know well enough what I mean, Jack," he answered. "I didn't recall the Miles Standish story when you wrote to me about it; but it is plain enough now that you had made up your mind at that very time to try to undermine me with Ruby Bonner."

"That was only a bit of fun," I answered good-humoredly, despite the offensive nature of his words.

"Yes, fun for you and death for me. I thought that, as an old friend, you'd play fair, any way. The girl was mine if I could have been with her, and I never imagined that an old classmate whom I trusted would go back on me and try to cut me out."

"Have I cut you out?"

Thomas Driggs laughed bitterly, and began again to twist his moustache.

"I guess you know," he said.

"I know nothing," I answered.

"You poisoned her mind against me."

"Never!" I said. "I praised you to her."

"Some men know how to make praise more deadly than slander! Much good your praise was to me."

"Doesn't she care for you?"

Thomas hesitated before replying. Then, turning his head and looking out over the lake, he said:

"Threw me over this morning."

"Refused you? Ruby did?" and a great joyous hopefulness swelled my heart.

"I should say so! Turned me down flat Said she never dreamed of such a thing as marrying me. And I know why."

"Well, why?"

"Because you've run me out and put yourself in

my place. The girl is fool enough to be in love with you."

"Tom, you are crazy."

"Now, look here, Jack, it's perfectly useless for you to sit there and try that hypocritical business with me. I can see through you just as if you were made of glass. You can hardly keep from chuckling. I like a man to play decent and fair. You know mighty well she wants you, and she wants you solely because I had to be away earning my bread. I wouldn't have knifed you in that way."

"I pledge you my word, Tom, I thought she cared for you. I thought so until you told me she had refused you."

"Oh, very well. It makes no difference. I must accept your word, of course. But the game is up for me. There's no use of me trying her again. She said no with a big N and a big O. That's over; and I suppose, in fact, there are other girls to be had. The earth's full of 'em."

I trusted he might discover some consolation for himself in that reflection. But, in truth, I did not care much, for how could I find room in my soul for mourning, or even for pity, for this foolish young man, when it was overflowing with joy because of the revelation he had made to me?

Pure love, they say, is pure unselfishness; but to me it seems that the passion, in its early stages at least, involves a very considerable element of self-complacency and self-enjoyment. I went away from poor old Driggs exultant, but with secret shamefacedness, for how could I recall that useless sudden outburst of passionate anger in the morning, and that headlong flight through the woods, without perceiving that I had acted like a fool?

That very evening I went to Mrs. Purvis-Hyde's cottage, and Ruby, in a gentle, quiet way, seemed glad to see me. But Mrs. Purvis-Hyde and three of her friends sat upon the porch through all of my visit, and I could not speak with Ruby alone.

Mrs. Purvis-Hyde was kind, and she asked me to come again and to be with them upon the lake next day and in the excursions she should make here and there. I could perceive that her quick wit discerned my feelings for Ruby, and her graciousness inclined her to favor my suit. If I had been a solid Episcopalian I think she would have promoted it actively. As I looked at her, and saw her interest in the matter, I smiled to think how she would have regarded Mrs. Bantam's suggestion that I should endeavor to make her mine.

During the next four or five days I tried in every way I could think of to detach Ruby from her companions and to have her to myself; but in this I could not succeed. Either she would invite some one or two of the company to go with us; or Mrs. Purvis-Hyde would suggest it with an air of having just thought of it, although I could see that she was pretending, or Ruby had a prearranged plan in which I must join with others, or she refused to go at all.

I began to despair, for it was plain enough she had a resolute purpose that I should not obtain another chance to speak to her alone; and, while it was pleasing to be in her company when with others we rowed upon the lake, or drove upon the mountain roads, or explored the forest, or visited the bathing-beach, I

could not be satisfied to see her thus while my heart
was bursting with a desire to learn from her whether
Tom Driggs had guessed aright that she loved me.

One night, when the moon hovered over the little
lake, and the water, stirred by the faint breeze, shim-
mered in the silver light, Mrs. Purvis-Hyde and two of
her friends, with Ruby and me, walked down to the
boat-house, where a dozen boats lay; and I thought
to manage to have Ruby alone in a boat with me. So
I persuaded her to step into one and to seat herself;
and then I swung the stern away from the landing and
pretended to be busy bailing out and fixing the row-
locks and choosing the oars; so that, when I was done,
Mrs. Purvis-Hyde and her companions were fixed
comfortably in a larger boat wherein was no space for
Ruby or for me; and so perforce we must stay where
we were. For appearance' sake I asked one of the
company to come with us, but this person was comfortable and contented, and so we remained alone, and
the two boats started up the lake together, leaving a wake
that rippled in the soft light that fell upon the water.

It is not easy for boats to keep together under such
conditions. It is very easy to fall apart if there is no
desire for company. And so I rowed our craft slowly
over to the eastern side of the lake, where the hemlocks
stood black against the lustrous sky, and as we moved
along Ruby talked brightly and cheerily; but I thought
I could discern a tinge of dread in her tone. Perhaps
it was my own consciousness of a determination to
speak to her that gave me this notion.

After a while we came to the point where a great
stone twenty feet wide lay with its foot in the water,
while ten feet above the water the bare surface formed

a kind of platform. Upon the top of it some voyagers, now departed, had left the glowing, flickering embers of a fire which we could plainly see, and on either side of the fire were rough seats, while the grim forest lay but two or three yards distant at the rear.

"Let us stop here, Ruby, and renew the fire," I said, and without waiting for her to answer I ran the boat against the shore and fastened it. She was willing to follow me, and soon the fire was roaring again with the dry hemlock branches that we heaped upon it, and the crimson of the flames went over the water to meet and to contrast itself with the pale splendor of the moonlight.

We talked idly for a little time, and then, as the flames began to burn less fiercely and to die downward, I sat upon the rough bench facing Ruby, and I said most gently:

"I have tried to be alone with you, Ruby, but it seemed to me that you avoided me."

She looked at me with trouble in her face.

"Shall we not rejoin our friends?" she said, glancing out upon the lake.

"Stay with me here but for a moment," I pleaded, "only for a moment, until the fire has burned out."

She folded her hands upon her lap, as if she had agreed to remain, and she fixed her eyes upon the embers.

"Ruby," I said, "forgive me for speaking to you again, but we cannot go on in this manner. It is torture—torture for you and for me. You have only to say a word and I will go away from you for ever."

She waited for a moment before replying, and then, as if she could hardly speak at all, she said:

"No; I cannot say that."

I remembered in what summary manner she had dealt with Tom Driggs, and I took courage.

"By accident I saw you in the boat with Tom Driggs on Tuesday; I thought you favored him, and I rushed away frantic with pain."

"I am sorry to have hurt you," she said, almost tenderly. "I do not care for him. I could not help being with him; he urged me so."

"You are sorry to be with me?"

"No."

"It will be frightful to part from you, Ruby, but better that than to be near to you and shut out from you. Better for both of us."

"You must not leave me," she said, and made a little motion with her hands as if she had an impulse to hold them out to me. "Where shall I look for friendship? I am alone; alone and desolate," and she wept.

"I believe you love me," I said boldly.

There was no answer, but more tears, and her hands upon her face.

"Now, if that be true," I said, resolved to end the matter there, if it were possible, "there is a reason why you feel impelled to hold back from me—some other reason than my unworthiness. You wrong yourself by not telling me everything."

Still she did not answer.

"The matter is so serious for both of us, Ruby, that even at the risk of hurting or offending you, I must speak. If you love me, then to remain silent will be to wreck our lives. I shall try to guess why you cannot give me your confidence."

She did not bid me be silent; so then I said:

"I know that you have suffered through one who

was dear to you. I know it all. You feared to have me know it, didn't you?"

She nodded mournfully, her face turned half away from me, as though she looked across the lake.

"But I knew everything; and you thought I should have shame for it and for you, if the facts were revealed? Forgive me if I must say that."

She wept bitterly.

"Well, it is not so. That you should have suffered for such a reason makes my love for you tender with unspeakable compassion. The thought of your loneliness and your sorrow has filled me with anguish. I will consecrate my life to you if you will accept it, and my great love will bring you peace. And now, Ruby, tell me; the worst you feared for me to know, but that which I have long known—was it this that kept you from me?"

"Yes," she said in a trembling voice

"Then we will put it by, and we shall be as if it were not, excepting that you shall speak to me always of any sorrow you may have. You do love me, my Ruby, don't you?" and I went over by her side and took her hand in mine.

"Yes, dear Henry," she said, looking up at me, with her eyes still wet with tears.

"My love, my Ruby, my wife!" I said. "How you have suffered! But now we shall have happiness, or blessedness, which may perhaps be better."

"I have been so desolate, Henry," she said; "orphaned and forsaken; and if you had not loved me—! Did you think it strange that I laughed sometimes? but my heart was always sad."

"But now, dearest, there will be peace."

20

" Yes. Why did you bless me on that night long ago, Henry? That was strange and mysterious. In my room that night I wept, and yet I was glad."

"It was a message," I said, "from one who loved you. I will tell you some day how it came."

She looked at me with wide-open eyes, as if she half suspected that her mother had been there; and then she said:

"I loved you first when you laid your hand upon my head. It was more than a simple blessing."

While we talked the fire burned down to coals and then to ashes, and the moon swung over to the western side of the lake, and the boats were turning their prows homeward. So then, a happy man, I put my dear one in the boat and swiftly we swept across the water with the light of heaven pouring down upon us; and as we went a voice called to us from another boat. It was Mrs. Purvis-Hyde, who asked us if we should go home with them; and so we rowed with her to the landing and walked to the cottage. Much to my surprise I found A. J. Pelican sitting upon the porch. He had come up to Hawksmere in the evening stage, and, calling at Mrs. Purvis-Hyde's cottage and finding everybody away, he sat down to wait for us. Mrs. Purvis-Hyde greeted him courteously, and I wondered a little bit why Mr. Pelican should have chosen that place for his short vacation.

Mrs. Purvis-Hyde was a wise woman, and so she said nothing to Ruby or to me of our separation from her on the lake, but she looked at me as we stood in the flare of her hall-lamp and then at Ruby, and I could discern that she knew, as well as if I had told her, that Ruby had joined her life to mine that very night.

Chapter XIX

A Little Grey Man

I tarried at Hawksmere until the first of August, having such pleasure as I had never known in any other vacation time. Mrs. Purvis-Hyde learned of my engagement with Ruby, and gave it her strong approval, besides supplying all kinds of opportunities such as lovers would be sure to covet.

When July was ended I must return to Happy Hollow to make preparations for the school session and to attend to some personal matters in the city. Colonel and Mrs. Bantam had gone away for a brief holiday at the seashore, and Elmira was in the White Mountains with some of her school friends. So our house was closed, but I thought to stay there while I remained in the town and to seek food at the hotel.

I had a key to the side door of the dwelling, and carrying my bag, I walked thither from the station, expecting of course to have all the house to myself.

When I had passed the front gate and come around

into the garden I found a man sitting upon the top step of the porch. He was a small man, about sixty years old I guessed, and he sat there with his feet upon the second step, his elbows upon his knees, his hands extended, and his fingers touching while he twirled his thumbs. He was dressed in a rather shabby grey suit, with a grey slouched hat, which was pushed backward slightly from his forehead, as if he felt warm. His full beard and his hair were grey, and his eyes seemed to have the same color.

He looked not at all like a vagrant person, and yet his attire conveyed the impression that he was not a man of thrift. From the first glance I had at him he puzzled me.

When I came to the porch he looked at me for an instant and nodded, but he neither moved nor spoke. He just sat there crossing his thumbs and looking at me in what I thought a timid way. I had a queer impression that if I should speak harshly to him I should frighten him, but indeed there was something in his look which would have deterred me from doing so if I had had an impulse of that kind.

I stopped in front of him, supposing that he was a stranger who had perhaps wandered into the garden to seek a place for rest, and that he would now explain himself, apologize, and take his leave.

But he had no notion of going away. While I stood before him he retained his position and looked shyly at me as if he expected me to speak first. I hardly knew just what would be best to do about him; and I was vexed at his silence and his immobility, so that I began to wonder if he were not merely insolent.

Then I took the door-key from my pocket and advanced toward the steps. When he saw the key he said, still with his finger-tips touching and his thumbs slowly revolving:

" Live here ?"

" Yes," I answered.

" Hah !" he exclaimed, withdrawing his gaze from me and looking at the ground. He seemed to be considering something.

" Bantams away ?" he asked.

" Yes."

Then he began another meditation which lasted for a few moments. Looking at me as if the question required all his courage, he asked:

" Who are you ?"

I told him; and again he looked downward and engaged in reflection. Raising his head, he inquired, and he spoke as if he could hardly force himself to utter the words:

" Is—where is—do you—you—do you know Miss Bonner—Ruby ?"

" Yes."

" She—is ?"—

He seemed really unable to complete the sentence; and so I told him that she was at Hawksmere with a friend, and that I had come from there that very day.

At this he looked at me more keenly than he had done at all before, and I saw that the man was trying to take my measure. I discerned also that he was not timid nor weak. There was force in the soul that looked out from those sharp grey eyes.

My curiosity was now awakened, and while I would much rather have ended the matter and gone into the house, I could not be satisfied until I knew who the

man was and what was his purpose in coming there.
He was silent again for a little while, and then, sitting
in the same posture, with his fingers spread and his
thumbs in slow motion, he said quietly:

"I am Amos Bonner; Ruby's father."

I do not know why I did not suspect it. No doubt
my reader has done so; but, in truth, the thought never
came into my mind, and when the little grey man revealed himself I felt the blood rush into my face, and
I was so confused that I could hardly reply to him. I
suppose the shock of the surprise had something to do
with my feeling, but more, the consciousness that my
relations to Ruby were still hidden from him.

However, the feeling passed quickly, and I greeted
him heartily. He did not offer to shake hands or to
move from the porch-step. But he asked me, still in a
hesitating way, about Ruby and the Bantams and Elmira and myself, and about Dr. Bulfinch's school. I
did not tell him of the death of Simon Bulfinch. I
could not guess how he would receive an allusion to
that man.

I invited him to enter the house; his house.

"Closed, isn't it?" he asked; and when I said that
it was, he waved his hand toward the door and said:

"No, you go in and I will wait here."

When I came out he had arisen and was sauntering
about the garden, but I am sure his mind was not
fixed upon the things about him. My return seemed
to awaken him from a reverie.

"I am going to the hotel to get dinner," I said to
him. "Will you go with me?"

"Yes," he answered, and joined me as we passed
through the gate.

We walked to the hotel almost without conversation, and Bonner's silence annoyed me. It is so hard to talk with a man who will not do his share that I gave it up at last and let him alone. I know now that Bonner was one of those inarticulate men who, however full their minds and hearts may be, cannot easily interpret thought or feeling in speech. I am sure that such men suffer more keenly than those who can express themselves in words.

"When will Ruby come back?" This was all that he asked of me, and when I told him that she had proposed to stay in Hawksmere until September, he did not reply.

While we dined I made no attempt to talk with him, and when dinner was done, and I paid the bill, he saw the operation and gave no sign that he would pay for himself. I began to fear that Colonel Bantam's assaults upon my slender finances would have reinforcement.

We strolled back to the house, and on the way Bonner said to me:

"Where's Pelican?"

"You know him?" I asked, but I had no need to put such a question; I remembered that as boys they had been friends.

"A little," he answered softly.

"Shall we call there? He may be at his office."

"No," answered Bonner coldly, "I don't care to see him."

So we came to the house, and Bonner seated himself again upon the porch-step. I resolved just to leave him alone. I opened the door, and then turning to him I said:

"You will stay with us, I suppose?"

"Yes," he answered.

"Then I will leave the door unlatched, and you can go in and out as you please."

"I was about to pass into the house when I heard him say: "Henry!" and I paused. "Henry," he said, "send a telegram to Ruby to come down to-morrow, but don't name me." The free use of my first name appeared to me odd, but he was an old man, and there could be no offense. Perhaps he meant it for tenderness.

Later in the day I sent a despatch to Ruby saying that she must start homeward next morning for important reasons, but that she might not fear evil, saying also that pleasure was in store for her.

That night Bonner had only his own company in the old home, for I stayed in my room, but he went with me to breakfast and to dinner, for which I paid, and he was no more talkative than he had been yesterday.

When I showed him Ruby's telegram, saying that she would reach Happy Hollow at seven o'clock, he folded the paper, and handing it to me, he said:

"Meet her, Henry. I will be in the parlor at home."

When the train drew into the station at seven o'clock I greeted my dear one and put her in a carriage. No sooner were we seated than she said to me:

"What is it, Henry?"

Before I had a chance to answer her, she said, clasping my hand:

"It is father come back!" and I saw that lovely face flush with joy as I answered:

"Yes, my dear."

She seemed as if she could not speak again, but her

hand tightened upon mine, and I knew that poor little heart was filled with strong emotion.

When we reached our gate she went in first, and made as if she would hurry. Then she turned about, and putting her hand in my arm she said softly:

" Take me to him, dearest."

We went upon the porch and in through the door to the dining-room ; thence to the hall, where through the parlor door I caught a glimpse of Amos Bonner walking to and fro. Leaving me, Ruby ran to him. He took her in his arms, and without even kissing her, he began to sob so violently that I feared for him.

Ruby meets her father.

What instinct was it in the girl that impelled her to restrain her own overcharged feelings, and with cooing tones and soft, tender words to try to comfort him? She was like a mother with a boy who had some wild outburst of sorrow. She stroked his head, and kissed his brow, and led him to the sofa, where he sat with one hand holding hers, and seemed as if he could not subdue the violence of his emotion long enough to command utterance.

I went away and left them there, and after a while I heard her voice and his, and I knew that at last that man who had so long suffered anguish was finding peace with the one he loved the best.

Two long hours they sat there and talked, and then I heard Ruby calling for me:

"Come down, Henry. Father wishes to see you," and I obeyed the summons.

They were sitting upon the sofa, and his arm was about her, while his hand held hers. Her face was bright with smiles, but he looked sober, and his face had that queer, timid expression that I had noted when first I met him. I learned to understand it as the sign and token of suffering silently endured for many years.

Ruby talked for him now.

"I have told dear father of all you did for me in my studies, and that you have asked me to be your wife."

"I knew it, Henry," said Bonner, "when you spoke of Ruby upon the porch. God bless you, my son!"

Then we talked, but Ruby and I chiefly talked, of Colonel and Mrs. Bantam, of Dr. Bulfinch and my school, of Elmira, of Spiker, and then of Julie. Sometimes there was a thing to laugh about a bit, and Ruby and I laughed; but Bonner seemed as if he could not laugh. When we told of Spiker and of Julie, and Ruby had become almost tearful as she said she believed Julie really loved him, and how much she loved Julie, Bonner said:

"I always knew about her. She was worthy to care for my girl. We must stand by her, Henry."

So, far into the night we sat together, and when we said good-night we knew how Bonner, having fled away to Australia to escape his misery, had been anchored there and involved in business there so that he could not return when he would, and how A. J. Pelican had written to him constantly, and Julie had written to him to tell him of Ruby.

The next morning it was agreed that Ruby should take up the housekeeping until Mrs. Bantam should return; so we sent for Spiker, who was at the hotel, and he came to us, and Elmira returned in a few days, and we were once more a household.

Elmira was warm in her congratulations to Ruby and to me, and Spiker wrung my hand and said he was joyful; but he looked mournful, poor man, and could not help exclaiming, " And Julie is gone, Sprat, gone!"

Day after day Amos Bonner went sauntering about, examining the wonderful things that had been done, but manifesting indifferent concern about them. He was closeted much with A. J. Pelican, whose activities increased now that great repairs must be carried forward because of Colonel Bantam's deluge; but in general A. J. Pelican seemed to take little note of the new-comer.

After a while Colonel and Mrs. Bantam came to us again and were much surprised to find Bonner in the old house. The very first day of their arrival I passed the parlor door and heard the Colonel saying something to Bonner about " my grave financial embarrassment," and I heard Bonner quietly, but with a tone that admitted no room for controversy, say " No !" and I knew what the Colonel had drawn the new-comer into the parlor for.

By that time Spiker had arranged that Elmira should conduct the Woman's Department in the *Defender*, and she was doing it in her own way when her father and mother returned.

Mrs. Bantam overflowed with joy when Ruby told her of her engagement with me.

"How perfectly, perfectly sweet and lovely!" she said, as she flew to Ruby and kissed her and then came and kissed me. "It is too delightful for anything, you darling child! And Mr. Sprat is so nice. Now you know, dear Mr. Sprat, from your own lovely experience, that love is the very elixir of bliss. How very, very odd that this dear little drama of the affections should go on beneath my very eyes and I should be blind to it! I could never have imagined such a thing; but, of course, the reason is that I am so completely absorbed by my love for darling Joseph; and, really, seeing you two lovers together makes me feel that I love him more than ever. Where *is* your dear uncle, Ruby, my child?"

The Colonel saw me alone when he congratulated me:

"Professor, I am pleased to welcome learning into a family that has been distinguished for valor. Give me your hand. Your choice is as creditable to your sound judgment as it is to the warmth of your affection. You have an old soldier's blessing; but I take the liberty of an extended friendship, Professor, to indicate to you that, unless all appearances are misleading, the dowry of your bride will have insignificant proportions. Amos, I fear, has returned to us in a condition not far removed from most inconvenient impecuniosity. In fact, you may have to take care of him when you marry."

It was a time of surprises. Mrs. Bantam had not

been home many days when Mrs. Purvis-Hyde called
to see her, and before leaving confided to her the fact
that Mrs. Purvis-Hyde had engaged to marry A. J.
Pelican.

"I know, dear Mrs. Bantam," she said, "that Pelican
is a terrible name, terrible; but I need a refuge, and
Andrew loves me tenderly."

She and Mrs. Bantam were so happy that they had
a good cry together—Mrs. Purvis-Hyde because she
loved Andrew so much, and Mrs. Bantam because she
loved love and lovers more than anything else in this
rolling world.

"And they have made Andrew a vestryman in our
church," continued Mrs. Purvis-Hyde, "and he will go
on the committee on finance, and we shall send him as
a delegate to the next diocesan convention, and I am
sure before long he will be a thoroughly sound church-
man. Dr. Fury is delighted."

Mrs. Bantam also was delighted, because all these
marriage matters pleased her, but she said to me afterward:

"It will involve dear Mrs. Purvis-Hyde in complete
loss of tone. There will be no tone at all when she
becomes Mrs. Pelican; and Mrs. L. Addison Merwyn
cannot stand the name of Pelican. But what need
Mrs. Purvis-Hyde care if she has another heart that
throbs in unison with her own?"

Mr. Spiker was not completely satisfied with Elmira
Bantam's method of editing the Woman's Department.
One day in my room he said to me:

"Elmira Bantam intellectually, Sprat, is all right.
She has brains enough for four people; but she doesn't
quite catch the spirit of the Woman's Department, it

seems to me. Brains are not the very first consideration there, you know. Women want to know about
freckles, and hints for the toilette, and how to serve
lunch for four, and how to make lemon pudding. But
Elmira insists upon urging them to break the shackles,
and that kind of thing. I don't notice that women
have so many shackles, not here in Happy Hollow, do
you, Sprat? There are no perceptible shackles on
Elmira.

"And she puts in things about 'How to Rule Hus-
bands' and the 'Advantages of Remaining Single,'
which give a bad tone to the paper.

"Did you ever know a woman, Sprat, that wanted
to be told that her greatest need is to have her yoke
lifted, or that her high destiny is to be released from
thraldom? Well, but that's the sort of thing Elmira
will preach in the Woman's Department, and it's hurting my circulation in families.

"And then she refuses to take any part of her salary
in bonnets and umbrellas, and says she has no use for
the apple-butter and garden stuff that drift in from the
farmers for subscriptions. Insists on cold cash. Elmira
always had nerve, hadn't she? I hate to see a grasp-
ing spirit in a woman!

"What would you do about it? Discontinue the
Woman's Department, or throw Elmira over and edit
it yourself?

"Only the plague of it is I can't answer half the
women's questions. There's a woman over at Bird-in-
Hand writes to me to-day to ask about the language
of flowers, and what buttercups mean. I don't know
what they mean, do you? And when I've finished an
editorial upon the tariff, I'm too much exhausted to go

to studying up the language of flowers and the symbolism of buttercups."

"Why not marry Elmira," I ventured to suggest, "and start a Legal Department?"

"Do you know, Sprat," said Mr. Spiker, "I've had that in my mind? And maybe she'd run the Woman's Department right if she were a partner.

"A woman wrote me only yesterday from over at Purgatory Springs asking advice about smoothing out wrinkles; and I had almost to quarrel with Elmira to get her to let me cancel an answer in which she said that a woman who cared about wrinkles was only fit to be a serf. She advised this Purgatory Springs woman to drop worrying about her countenance and to study Mill on Liberty! Think of that, Sprat, to a regular subscriber!"

But, while Emerson Spiker was considering the demands of the Woman's Department for a more sympathetic editor, events of serious importance occupied the columns of the journal to such an extent as to reduce to a place of comparative insignificance Miss Bantam's editorial work.

Everybody in Happy Hollow knew, and all the countryside knew, that the freshet for which Colonel Bantam seemed to be in some degree responsible, had done much harm to the enterprises of the Improvement Company. The stockholders could do nothing but await an announcement of some kind respecting the matter from the officers of the company. But the bank was supposed to have, and almost certainly did have, close relations with the Improvement Company, and bank depositors are always ready for prompt and sometimes foolish action.

Nothing had happened to supply any good reason for doubting the solvency of the bank, but when fear begins to spread few men look for reason. It is indeed remarkable with what rapidity fear in such a case is communicated to a community without an apparent agency. It flashes from man to man like a current of electricity, and within a few moments those who feared nothing are filled with senseless panic.

One morning all Happy Hollow and all the rural neighborhoods suddenly acquired a belief that the bank would fail, and soon the depositors began to flock to the building, excited and eager to withdraw their money.

Colonel Bantam, who had no money in the bank, observed the movement with anger and consternation, for he thought he perceived in it a menace to the Improvement Company and his blocks of stock. It occurred to the Colonel that he had a duty to perform, not only as a stockholder in the company, but as the chief magistrate of the town.

He went into his office, and in a large, bold hand he wrote and signed a paper which he then tacked upon the front door of the bank.

" To the public :

" I positively guarantee with my entire fortune every deposit in this bank.

" JOSEPH BANTAM."

The paper was read by the persons in line awaiting their turn at the teller's desk, and the clerks thought their anxiety seemed to deepen. At any rate, in a short time the feeling of uneasiness in the town was intensified so that there was a genuine panic. Every man in Happy Hollow who had money in the bank wanted it, and wanted it at once.

The teller was more deliberate than usual in paying the applicants, but every check was cashed until three o'clock came, when further payments were refused until to-morrow. The unsuccessful applicants were angry and clamorous, and many of the women wept.

Compelled to leave the bank building, every one of them believed his money lost, and upon the pavement an indignation meeting was held at which some rash spirits actually proposed to lynch A. J. Pelican and Colonel Bantam.

The Colonel guarantees the bank.

While I was observing the crowd, and mourning deeply that this

21

trouble had come to the town and the people and to
A. J. Pelican, Amos Bonner touched my arm.

"Come here, Henry," he said.

We entered the bank by the side door, and went
into the president's room. A. J. Pelican was there,
with wretchedness written upon his face. He sat in
his chair, fanning himself with his wig, and looking as
I had seen him do upon the stage on that night long
ago, when A. J. Pelican's Stupendous Star Combination
fell to pieces.

"What are we to do now, Amos?" he asked, as we
came in.

"I have wired for money," said Bonner, "and Henry
here will bring it up on the morning train."

"How much?" asked Pelican.

"A hundred thousand dollars," said Bonner, at
which I was more astonished than I could well express.

The look of forlornness vanished from A. J. Pelican's face. He put on his wig and smiled.

"That saves us, Amos; more than saves us."

"You will go, Henry?" asked Bonner.

"Yes."

"Take a large satchel and have a trusty man with
you. Go armed. Get here sure at 9.37 in the morning."

When I had further instructions and the right cre-
dentials, I found a man who could accompany me, and
we went to the city in the night train.

Amos Bonner's requisition was honored, and I
reached the bank just before ten o'clock next morning.
There was a great throng about the door, and in it
were many whom I knew. I did not hide my errand,

but to two or three I told of the visit to the city, and assured them that I had in the satchel money equal to the entire capital of the bank.

A number of the applicants went away at once. Others were unbelievers, but when the bank opened and the bundles of notes were heaped upon the teller's counter, the pressure relaxed, and in a quarter of an hour was ended. Before noon three-fourths of the persons who had drawn their money out the day before re-deposited it, and the panic was over.

But Amos Bonner had acquired a new kind of interest for me.

Chapter XX

The Colonel Finds Scope

HAPPY HOLLOW

SCHOOL opened in September, and when I walked out to the old Academy building upon the first day of the session I had no thought but that I should carry on my work there all winter, as I had done in the preceding year, and that Happy Hollow and its people would remain about as they had been. But changes in this changeful world are likely to come in groups and unexpectedly; and long before the year was ended I and my friends were living our lives under wholly new conditions.

The school was sparsely attended, and Dr. Bulfinch was deeply grieved as he watched the few boys come into the main room on that first morning. The story told by Simon had left an impression upon the parents, and the Doctor's relationship to that bad man had also been hurtful; and so many of the old pupils had been sent away from the town to school, and others were put into the public school.

The Doctor would not open his heart to me about it, but I could perceive that he sorrowed much because of the hurt to his business, and also because of the injustice of the treatment accorded to him. I, too, had cause for sorrow, for I felt sure he could not afford to pay me fully for my services.

But we began our work with what courage we could find, and for a fortnight went along in the old way· Then the Improvement Company passed its first dividend, and at once fell into such discredit that one of the large contractors, unable to get his money, brought action against it.

The Improvement Company collapsed. Collapse indeed seems to be the fate of such booms as that which was started in Happy Hollow by A. J. Pelican. But I do believe our Improvement Company would have been successful had not the Bantam deluge hurt its property. The repairs to the railroad, the park, and the lake called for much money, and the Aramink Hotel, having missed the whole season, stood for a dead investment, besides the cost of putting it in order after the freshet. And then the horse railroad, in spite of its popularity, never paid expenses ; and so, when one of the largest creditors became impatient and suspicious, the whole mass of the property went into the hands of the sheriff.

All the town was in gloom because of this catastrophe; but the gloomiest man was Colonel Bantam, whose dividends, upon which he had counted so largely, had vanished, and whose blocks of stock were now valueless. The Colonel talked about the urgent creditor who had brought about the collapse as if the human race had contained few members of character so atrocious or greed so reckless.

Mrs. Bantam called upon Mrs. Purvis-Hyde to talk the trouble over, and to have a good cry together.

"Andrew, I fear, dear Mrs. Bantam, will be reduced to beggary," said Mrs. Purvis-Hyde.

"And Joseph has lost his all—literally his all—after jeoparding his life to save an ungrateful country."

But all was not lost, for on the day of the sheriff's sale, Amos Bonner took me with him, and at his command I bought the entire property of the company, which he reorganized on a basis of equity to the stockholders; that is to say, any stockholder could have his proportion of interest if he would pay his proportion of indebtedness; and this was very handsome, when we consider that Bonner could have kept the whole thing for himself.

Before this matter had been fully adjusted the November elections came near, and they had a great surprise for us, for the Democratic candidate for Congress for our district and the Republican candidate were both out of favor with the people who disliked machine domination; and so, at the very last moment, the Reformers held a convention and nominated Colonel Joseph Bantam as their representative. The Colonel was chosen, it was said, because of his "war-record."

The chance that the Colonel would be elected, or that any reform candidate could be elected, seemed very small indeed. Had it been larger, quite likely another man would have received the nomination; but upon the night of the election day Happy Hollow was astonished by the announcement that the

Reformers, by rallying the disaffected from both the parties, had elected Colonel Bantam by a plurality of seven votes.

Colonel Bantam was delirious with joy, and after a sleepless night he went about the town all day receiv-

ing the congratulations of the people, and making promises respecting his career as a member of Congress which were almost reckless in their nature.

The road to glory.

In the evening I sat with him and Mrs. Bantam in the parlor at home. Both of them were perfectly happy. Mrs. Bantam's chair was close to the Colonel's, and, excepting when he made gestures as he talked, she held his hand.

The Colonel's mind was wholly engaged in contemplating his coming career as a statesman, and as his imagination played with the subject there was exuberance of joyfulness in his manner and speech.

"Called," he said, "from the camp to the councils of the nation, I shall devote my trained powers to the government of my country. Although the emoluments of my high office are pitifully disproportionate to the responsibilities of the position, my purpose is to engage a luxurious suite of apartments in one of the most spacious hotels in the national capital, and to entertain my friends and constituents with expansive hospitality.

"I shall make, during the first session, a series of orations upon important topics. I shall speak upon Indians and irrigation, and I shall make four, perhaps five, speeches upon the tariff and upon transportation. Then education, our merchant marine, and the torpedo service will also engage my attention, and I shall pursue a bold and vigorous policy with respect to the currency, the propagation of food-fishes, and the expansion of our foreign commerce. In a carefully prepared oration upon agriculture I have determined to arrange for the introduction of banana-culture to Florida, and I shall scatter seeds about my own district until Blair County blossoms as the rose."

Mrs. Bantam was about to interrupt him, but he put his free hand upon her arm, and said:

"One moment, love! I was about to add that I have thought to insist, in a speech of some length, upon consideration of a national law covering marriage and divorce, and perhaps—"

"Marriage should be made compulsory, Joseph," said Mrs. Bantam. "Be positive about that."

"I fear, Edith, that such an enactment might be regarded as extreme. We must proceed with cautious footsteps in these matters. I have it in my mind to propose some kind of a bounty to encourage matrimony. Say we should offer one hundred acres of land from the national domain, and then a free railroad pass, so that the bride and groom could run out and visit their property during the honeymoon."

"The dear lambs!" exclaimed Mrs. Bantam. "It would be just lovely."

"However," continued the Colonel, "I shall give the whole matter adequate investigation, and, besides, I shall at once prepare a dredging bill, to deepen our little brook clear down to the river and to excavate the river out to the great deep, so as to make Happy Hollow into a seaport and to bring the commerce of the world to our very doors. The time will come, my love, when you will look out from this window upon forests of masts lying right over yonder—masts of East Indiamen and other monarchs of the ocean laden with the rich merchandise of far-distant lands.

"The thought has occurred to me, also, why not re-populate our western plains with herds of bison, and why not adopt coercive legislation for the cultivation of the angora goat and other rare fibre-bearing animals? I shall reflect upon this, and probably provide that it shall be done. I have already sketched out in my mind the outlines of speeches upon our waste lands and our foreign relations My purpose, Professor, is ultimately to have my speeches collected, and after careful revision, bound in several volumes, half calf, and I will frank you a set as soon as they appear."

Mrs. Bantam, beaming upon the Colonel while he spoke, now said:

"The Colonel has always needed scope, and now, for the first time in his life, it is presented to him; adequate scope."

"Yes," said the Colonel, "scope; opportunity. Having saved my country upon the field of war, I shall now engage in the more difficult, but by no means un-alluring, task of directing its mighty destinies"

"You will command both army and navy, Joseph, will you not?" asked Mrs. Bantam.

"No, Edith.   That is still the prerogative of the Executive; but I think it a matter well worthy the serious consideration of the Legislator if the time has not come for recasting the fundamental law so that the functions of the Executive Branch shall be circumscribed.   I will give the subject thought.   There is grave danger, in my judgment, that the Executive Branch, by gradual encroachment upon the Legislative Arm, may usurp its powers, and reduce the representatives of the sovereign people to more or less insignificance. I shall speak upon that theme also."

"You may toss a bouquet to me."

Mrs. Bantam explained that she intended to sit by his side while he thundered his orations, and to hold his hat and his manuscript, so that she could prompt him.

"That will be impossible, my love," replied the Colonel. "Women are not permitted to have access to the floor of the House.   You can sit in the gallery, and if the impulses of your heart prompt it, you may toss a bouquet to me from time to time.   I shall, however, insist upon alteration of the rules of the House so that a member may, if he wish, have the partner of his life close by his side.   I shall bring the matter to the attention of the Speaker; that is, if I do not assume the Speakership myself.   I have had an impulse to do it."

"I am sure, Mr. Sprat," said Mrs. Bantam, "no one deserves it so much as the Colonel does.

"In any case," continued Colonel Bantam, "the public offices at my disposal will be many in number, and I am not the man to forget the sacred obligations of friendship.   Think, Professor, if there is any place you would like to have.   I assure you it is yours.   A consulship, for example, in the sunny climes of the Southern continent, in historic Europe, in the hoary lands of the East, in the perfumed islands of the tropic seas.   Make your choice; I place no restrictions upon you "

While Colonel Bantam thus graciously offered me the earth to choose from, Emerson Spiker entered the room. As he seated himself he said:

"I am sorry to say there is some rather bad news."

It struck me Spiker did not look very sorry, but I may have been mistaken in the expression of his countenance.

"You know," he said, "there was a dispute over the vote in the third ward at Purgatory Springs?"

"Well?" exclaimed the Colonel with impatient eagerness.

"And you know," said Spiker, "that the ballot-box was taken into court for a recount?"

"Yes; well?"

Mr. Spiker hesitated; then he said:

"Well, a despatch came to the *Defender* just as I was leaving the office to the effect that the judge threw out eight fraudulent votes."

"Eight votes; well, what of it?" asked the Colonel.

"That elects Billings to Congress," said Spiker.

Colonel Bantam turned white, and Mrs. Bantam drew her handkerchief from her pocket and put one hand to the back of her head.

"It is impossible, sir!" exclaimed the Colonel angrily. "This is but a nefarious attempt to deprive the people of the representative in Congress who was their first choice. I shall fight it, sir, upon the floor of the House. It is scandalous that such crimes should be possible in a civilized country." But the Colonel had difficulty to keep up his courage, and Mrs. Bantam broke down wholly. The Colonel was so much agitated that he forgot to try to comfort her, but walked up and down the room, furious at the evil fate that had befallen him.

"Are you sure, Mr. Spiker," I asked, "that the report is true?"

"Not sure," said Spiker, "I give it to you just as it reached me."

"Suppose we go to the telegraph office and try to learn the truth?" I suggested; and Spiker and I left the room together.

In half an hour I returned and found the Colonel upon the sofa with his arm around Mrs. Bantam's waist. Her eyes were red, and the Colonel looked as if hope had fled from his soul.

"Well?" he said eagerly, as I entered.

"It was a false report. Your election is certain."

. Mrs. Bantam laughed through her tears, and the Colonel said:

" It is well; I thank you! A more dastardly blow at the very vitals of constitutional government than my exclusion from the office for which the people selected me could hardly be imagined. I shall go to Washington, sir, and when I get there my countrymen shall hear from me."

By the middle of November Dr. Bulfinch was offered a professorship in a small college in the western part of the state, and when he told me of it, and explained that his school was a failure financially, I advised him to accept it, and released him from all obligation to me. So the school was closed, and when Amos Bonner had given half a promise to buy the buildings, and Colonel Bantam had promised that Charley Bulfinch, if he would study hard, should go to the Naval Academy at Annapolis, the Doctor left us, not without tears, and took Charley with him, and Bonner made me, a mere pedagogue, unskilled in business matters, general manager of the Happy Hollow Improvement Company. I had also the promise that I should marry Ruby in January.

Thus peace came again to Happy Hollow, and good fortune upon a sound basis, with A. J. Pelican still president of the bank, and behind him and me that quiet little grey man who strangely, in the days of his exile and affliction, had won a fortune for himself in the countries far away.

" It seemed, Henry," he said to me, " as if I couldn't help making money, though little I cared for it "

And he was not forgetful either of Julie Mortimer, for when he had visited her more than once, she went away to Europe far from poor, and there she gained distinction such as her talents warranted, and we heard not long afterward that she married happily in France.

Bonner had been telling us about it in the parlor one night, when the Colonel and Mrs. Bantam and Spiker and Elmira and Ruby sat with him, a happy circle; and after a while Bonner withdrew and went, I thought, to his room.

When he had gone, and we had talked further about the changes that had come to us, I had all at once a strong, almost overpowering impression of the face I had seen at the window months before, and my mind kept running upon the subsequent adventure in the garden. I could not restrain myself from glancing at the window, and I had such a nervous dread of the appearance of the face again that I could hardly conduct sustained conversation.

I was glad Amos Bonner had left the room, and while this pleased me, I had continual fear that he would return and that he would see the face as I had seen it.

The feeling at last grew so strong upon me that, merely to find relief, I arose and went to the dining-room and opened the door to the·side porch.

I saw at once that persons were there. It was a cold night, with a sharp movement of the wind from the northwest. The stars were out, brilliant and blinking in the blackness of the sky. I shivered as I opened the door, and would have stepped back into the room at once had I seen nobody.

The voice of Amos Bonner said:

"She is dying, Henry"

Then I shut the door and came near. I could see

him sitting upon the edge of the porch floor as I had seen him on the day when first I met him ; and plainly, even through the gloom, the form of a woman, stretched upon the floor, lying upon her side with her head upon his breast, while his arms held her fast.   His head was bent so that his face was over her.

"Kiss me, my husband," I heard her say, in a voice not much more than a whisper, but strangely distinct.

As he leaned further forward and kissed her over and over again, she flung up her right arm and tried to put it about his neck ; but the effort was too great, and she would have fallen from him had he not folded her more closely to him.

"Forgive me, husband," she said faintly.

"Yes, my love, my sweet; perfectly, perfect forgiveness !   My love, my wife !" he said; and then, to me, "She is dying, Henry.   She has come back to me to die.   Do not go away.   Help me here   We cannot take her in.   Guard the door."

"Mary !" and he called her.

She tried again to lift her arm, but she could not, and she just turned her face up toward him.   I could see it plainly, that white face there in the starlight, as if there had been no gloom.

He kissed her tenderly and spoke soft words of endearment to her; and then he was silent, and seemed to listen to find if she were still breathing.

At last her head fell back upon his arm, and a sob came from him as he said :

"Dead, Henry ! dead, dead, dead !   It was sorrowful for her, Henry ; she suffered so much.   Alas, my darling !   My Mary !   My dear !"

Then he put his lips to her cold cheeks and broke into a passion of weeping.

I knew not what to do. I feared for him there in the cold. I took off my coat and flung it around him, and then I tried to lift from his arms the body of the poor woman and to lay it upon the floor.

When I had considered for a few moments, I called to our help a discreet neighbor, to whose house the dead woman was carried to remain while we should arrange for the burial.

As she lay upon the bed in the upper room, with her hair tangled about her pallid temples, I could perceive that she had once been beautiful.

Amos Bonner stood by her and looked long at her. He took her hand in his:

"See how white and thin it is, Henry. How terrible has been her punishment! But, if I can forgive, God will forgive. He is most merciful. We shall meet in that other country. Do you notice how sweet her smile is now? She knows she has been pardoned. She died knowing that, Henry.

"She thought this was Ruby's wedding-day, and she had herself driven here, sick and wretched, so that she might look in at the window and see the child. I found her lying on the porch floor. Perhaps I was to blame for it all. I may have been cold to her. We cannot see each other's hearts; but I loved her dearly always. My love, my life!" and he held the white hand to his lips.

When I had led him away from her and we came home again, neither of us could bear to join the group in the parlor, but both went to our own rooms; and Ruby never knew of that pitiful scene upon the porch, when her father and mother exchanged words and kisses for the last time.

I did tell her, long afterward, that I knew her mother died peacefully in her father's arms; but I withheld a part of the truth and she did not seek to know it all. It brought peace to her own soul to learn that there had been reconciliation and forgiveness.

On the twelfth of January Mrs. Purvis-Hyde and A. J. Pelican were married in the Episcopal Church by Dr. Fury, and Ruby and I observed the ceremony with eager interest, because on the nineteenth of January she and I were to be married in the parlor of our house—her father's house.

She had many presents, among them a very handsome silver-plated tea-set from Emerson Spiker, who confessed to me, but asked me to keep quiet about it, that he had taken it in trade. And on the very day of the wedding he whispered to me:

"I think Elmira and I will follow your example, Sprat. I am lonely; and I really need a helper, a strong helper. Besides, I am now convinced that women ought to be unshackled; they don't have half a chance."

'Lias Guff guarded the door on the day of the wedding, and Amelia Powers Guff, with her vocal propensities held severely in restraint, helped the caterer in the kitchen; and so we were married, and began together that journey of life which love alone can make joyful.

THE END.

Out of the Hurly=Burly.

By MAX ADELER,

Author of "Captain Bluitt, etc., etc.

WITH 400 ILLUSTRATIONS BY A. B. FROST AND OTHERS.

A BOOK WITH A RECORD.

Max Adeler's "Out of the Hurly-Burly" has a notable history. It was first published nearly thirty years ago, and every year since that time there has been a large demand for it. The total sales for the American and English editions probably much exceed one hundred and fifty thousand.

The book contains nearly four hundred of the first drawings made by the now eminent artist A B Frost, and is interesting upon that account.

It has had even larger popularity in Great Britain than in the United States. It has been translated into several languages, and copies of it have gone literally to the ends of the earth. A friend of the author's, shipwrecked upon the coast of Norway a few years ago, got ashore and found refuge in a fisherman's lonely hut. The first thing he saw upon entering the building was a Swedish translation of "Out of the Hurly-Burly" lying on a table, and it made him feel at home at once. Another friend discovered the book in the cabin of a steamer a thousand miles up a river in China Cheering reports have floated in from India respecting it, and innumerable tales have come to the author of the pleasure it has afforded to invalids and to the sorrowing, and of the joy it has given to young people all over the world.

The demand for "Out of the Hurly-Burly" continues. In fact, it is beginning again to increase. Of how many books published in 1874 can this be said?

The new generation is learning, as its predecessors did, that here is a book of hearty fun and genuine sentiment, which contains no word that can give offense, and which contributes liberally to society's stock of cheerfulness

For more than a quarter of a century it has supplied innocent mirth to a world in which kindly humor is by no means an abundant commodity, and the promise is that it will have undiminished benefaction for generations still to come.

12mo, Cloth, extra . . . . . $1.25.

HENRY T. COATES & CO., Publishers,
PHILADELPHIA, PA.

CAPTAIN BLUITT.

By MAX ADELER.

A book of genuine humor is not a mere "funny" book. It deals with both the serious and the amusing sides of human life, and the humor is the natural, easy, unforced outcome of the relation of the various characters to the various situations.

There is much grave matter in Max Adeler's "Captain Bluitt"; and sometimes seriousness deepens into tragedy, as in the chapter "Phœbe Tarsel Goes Home," of which a London journal said, "You can't lay the book down to speak to a friend without a lump in your throat, and you can't read that chapter unmoved unless you are built on a different plan from your fellows"; but there is also a lot of good fun, such as is found in few modern stories. When the final verdict is given upon the quality of American humor, we are sure a first place will be allotted to the stories of Captain Bluitt's experiment with a catapult and of his venture into the mysteries of "haruspication".

The modern American school board did not rank high among the sources of fun until Max Adeler described the School Board of Turley, and so immortalized that body; and if the humor of an American election was ever better developed than in the narrative of Rufus Potter's political campaign, we do not know it.

The truth is that the folks in this story are real people, who lead real lives, and out of them and their movements to and fro the author has contrived to extract plenty of good fun, some lively adventures, a bit of tragedy, and many incidents highly charged with feeling.

Max Adeler's "Out of the Hurly-Burly" has retained its popularity for nearly thirty years. The prediction is ventured that "Captain Bluitt" will have as long a life or longer.

12mo, Cloth, extra, illustrated . . $1.50.

HENRY T. COATES & CO., Publishers,

PHILADELPHIA, PA.

Lightning Source UK Ltd.
Milton Keynes UK
UKHW020629160621
385607UK00005B/248